PUBLIC POLICY

—AND—

COLLEGE
MANAGEMENT

PUBLIC POLICY
——AND——
COLLEGE MANAGEMENT

Title III of the
Higher Education Act

Edward P. St. John

FOREWORD BY

George B. Weathersby

PRAEGER

PRAEGER SPECIAL STUDIES • PRAEGER SCIENTIFIC

Library of Congress Cataloging in Publication Data

St. John, Edward P.
    Public policy and college management.

    Includes bibliographical references and index.
    1. Higher education and state—United States.
2. Universities and colleges—United States—Administra-
tion.   3. Universities and colleges—Law and legislation
—United States.   I. Title.
LC173.S7   379.1′54′0973   81-5204
ISBN 0-03-058454-X   AACR2

Published in 1981 by Praeger Publishers
CBS Educational and Professional Publishing
A Division of CBS, Inc.
521 Fifth Avenue, New York, New York 10175 U.S.A.

© 1981 by Praeger Publishers

123456789   145   987654321

Printed in the United States of America

To My Family,
For Their Creativity and Support

FOREWORD

George B. Weathersby

The study of colleges as organizations capable of improved management is a topic of recent development to which this book is a major contribution. The concentration on the developing institutions program, Title III of the federal Higher Education Act first authorized in 1965, provides an illumination of a wide variety of conditions of college and university development. The original purpose of the Title III program was primarily to provide federal support to historically black colleges in the midst of the great attention afforded the civil rights movement in the mid 1960s. Assuming a role once played by private philanthropy, since 1965 the federal government has provided substantial and ongoing financial support to the slightly more than 100 historically black colleges. Unlike philanthropy, the federal government was not able to limit the eligibility of funds solely to a particular type of institution, nor to provide the funds without some policy guidelines. Therefore, over the past 15 years nearly 1,000 colleges have received significant support. Improved management has been a principal focus of federal policy interest.

The unintended consequence of Title III has been a massive natural experiment of an external group using a competitive grant process to entice or enable colleges to improve their managerial capacities. Scholars of college management are fortunate that Dr. St. John was able to take advantage of this natural experiment and to conduct the study reported on here.

Several previous and subsequent program evaluation studies were funded by what is now the Department of Education, with the purpose of justifying or modifying the operational procedures used to distribute money under the current Title III program. What distinguishes this analysis is that the Title III program is used, like a searchlight in the night, to illuminate the managerial processes as they have evolved over the years. The colleges studied are not rich, not oversubscribed by students, and not without concern for their future. The detailed information supplied by colleges participating in the Title III program, data from other federal sources, and extensive personal interviews and site visits provided Dr. St. John with an extremely rich data base for analysis.

Commission for Higher Education, State of Indiana.

In the last decade a number of important theories in organizational behavior have emerged; these provide a conceptual basis for Dr. St. John's inquiry. Specializing and extending existing research, this study makes an important contribution to the organizational theory of colleges. A key concept articulated and studied by Dr. St. John is the pattern of structural development of college management. Managerial patterns evolve not only in size but also in complexity, in information needed for management, in role differentiation among managers, and in other important aspects. Management consultants and federal bureaucrats often prescribe a preferred organizational structure as optimal for a college to make effective decisions. Dr. St. John's research suggests that a single structure is not optimal in all circumstances, and that one can predict not only the characteristics of a preferred structure at each step of institutional development, but also the organizational consequences of different administrative structures. These findings should be of great utility to college trustees and administrators, as well as to executives in many organizational settings.

To some degree, the form-versus-function debate surfaces in discussions of organizational design. Clearly, individuals of high motivation and goodwill can make any structure work, and a perfectly designed decision structure cannot be guaranteed always to reach perfect decisions. The important questions of organizational design include: Are some administrative structures more effective in reaching and implementing decisions than are other structures? If so, what are the characteristics of preferred administrative structures? What are the relationships among characteristics of the organization to be managed and the preferred administrative structure chosen to manage it? These questions are addressed by Dr. St. John, and their answers are suggested by his research.

Improving the managerial effectiveness of colleges is desired not only by college trustees and administrators, but also by those who contribute significantly to the financial support of colleges, especially state governments and private philanthropy. Responsible members of both these groups value the autonomy of colleges (including public colleges) achieved usually through some political insulation from direct intrusion in the decision-making process. While outside funders value academic autonomy, they share with college trustees the benefit of increased managerial effectiveness. The use of public-policy instruments, usually funding, to improve the managerial effectiveness of colleges is also analyzed and reported by Dr. St. John.

The 1980s and 1990s will be decades of substantial change in higher education. Declining student demand, raging inflation, limitations on funding, the rigidities of tenure, and many other issues will greatly increase stress on college and university leaders. Since World

War II, college and university quantitative growth has been almost inevitable. This expansionary climate provided many opportunities for imaginative leaders of education to improve the quality of their services. For the rest of this century, quantitative growth in higher education is unlikely for most institutions. However, qualitative development of many colleges and universities is the preeminent challenge of current educational leaders.

While public policy and institutional experience both reinforce quantitative growth, research on qualitative development of service organizations in general, and colleges and universities in particular, has provided little assistance to college leaders. A special contribution of Dr. St. John's research is its focus on the qualitative development of colleges and universities. This book provides information, examples, and a conceptual framework for educational leaders to develop a greater sensitivity and competence in managing for qualitative improvement.

In sum, this book is a major contribution to our knowledge and understanding of the development of colleges and universities. It is of potential benefit to a wide variety of educational leaders. I commend it to all individuals responsible for leading and managing higher education.

PREFACE

Management development in higher education, particularly improvements in the capacity of institutions to generate viable future plans and to manage scarce resources, has become an increasingly important agenda item to administrators and policymakers during the past decade. In recent years there have been numerous public and private grant programs that have experimented with new approaches to management improvement at colleges and universities. The 1980s will doubtlessly witness an increased emphasis on improvements in management as the financial condition of most colleges worsens, as enrollment drops overall, and the competition for public dollars becomes more severe. While improvements in institutional management will not change the environmental factors influencing higher education, they can enhance the prospects of institutional survival in this new condition, if not provide mechanisms for colleges to improve qualitatively in the face of these dire prospects.

This book will attempt to develop frameworks for improving management and information-system interventions. The study has a five-year history. In 1975 a research team at Harvard University initiated a study of the Title III program, a federal program designed to improve the condition of developing colleges and universities. The director of the project, George B. Weathersby, recognized that new concepts were needed to replace the growth model in the higher education policy arena. As part of that study, a conceptual paper was developed that proposed alternative frameworks for evaluating the effects of external intervention programs. While the original study did not have access to the types of data required to test these frameworks, a subsequent pilot study was funded by the U. S. Office of Education to test this approach. As a result of this study of exemplary Title III institutions in summer 1977 and of the follow-up study in 1980, intervention frameworks for management and information systems were proposed and tested. These frameworks are applicable to the administration of intervention programs such as Title III, as well as to campus-based, management-improvement efforts.

Chapter 1 describes the model used for the study and compares this approach to predominant concepts of how college management can be improved. There has been a tendency in recent years to encourage the development of sophisticated management techniques at colleges and universities. Proponents of this approach usually argue that the absence of these systems is a source of institutional stress. This book argues that intervention programs should take a more differentiated approach than they have in the past, that sophisticated systems are not always necessary, and that these systems can be a burden to small institutions.

The context and conceptual basis for the study are detailed in Chapters 2 through 4. Chapter 2 provides a background on the Title III program and on the concepts of college development that were evident in the policy arena during the period when the program was created. Chapter 3 describes the management-development model and the rationale for the structural approach used in this study. Chapter 4 provides a background on the study, including the selection of the exemplary institutions and the case-study methodology.

The next four chapters develop a general intervention model for college and university management and information-system interventions. Chapter 5 examines the historical development of the case-study institutions in order to verify the general model of structural development. Chapter 6 explores the relationship between the management-improvement activities at the case-study institutions and the general model. The management-intervention framework, developed in Chapter 7, used data from the restudy to elaborate on the implications of the general model for management-improvement efforts. The restudy results also are used in Chapter 8 to explore the implications of the management information system (MIS) intervention framework. Both frameworks detail the types of interventions that appear appropriate for different institutional settings.

The final two chapters consider the implications of the study. Chapter 9 explores the implications of the general model for colleges and universities; it proposes intervention strategies and considers the consequences of the research for organizational redesign. Chapter 10 discusses the implications of the research for public policy, particularly for the design of management-improvement programs.

ACKNOWLEDGMENTS

Several people have provided the intellectual stimulus for the ideas developed in this work. In particular, George Weathersby, my faculty advisor at Harvard Graduate School of Education, has been supportive of the concepts found in this book. Some of the ideas were originally developed with George during an earlier study of the Title III program. He was also instrumental in securing the funds necessary to conduct this study. Frederic Jacobs, another faculty advisor and friend, was also instrumental. Six years ago we collaborated on a study of nontraditional postsecondary programs that generated some of the concepts developed in this book. Jerome Murphy, a third doctoral advisor at Harvard, gave many insightful comments that helped to make explicit the implications of the research for public policy. Other faculty and mentors who have been helpful with the formation of these ideas are John Rockart of the Sloan School at MIT, William Torbert, formerly a faculty member at HGSE, and Mary C. Regan, James H. Meyer, and Orville E. Thompson, advisors and friends at the University of California, Davis.

Without financial support from the United States Office of Education (Grant #41-676-704-2), this study would not have been possible. Individuals in the Office of Education who were particularly helpful were Salvatore Corrallo and Peter Kuch in the office of planning, budgeting, and evaluation, and Robert Suggs in the developing institutions division. In addition, people on the various campuses used as case studies helped by arranging site visits and interviews, providing documents, and completing questionnaires.

James M. Garnes, Title III coordinator at Lincoln University of Missouri, deserves a special thanks for his assistance with the restudy. A questionnaire on the impact of Title III, used as one of the instruments for the restudy, was authored by Mr. Garnes and tested in this study. The data collected with this instrument provided rich detail about the management interventions at the case-study institutions.

Family and friends have been essential in this venture. Teala Sipes, Joy Casada, Careyleah MacLead, Mary Sanderson, and Connie Tuton provided clerical support for the two studies. John Williams and Nancy London provided helpful comments on an earlier draft of this manuscript. Helen Roland helped with details for travel and communications. Finally, I want to thank my family—my parents, Wesley and Gladys, and siblings, Wesley and Maureen—for their freely given emotional support.

CONTENTS

LIST OF TABLES AND FIGURES

PUBLIC POLICY

—— AND ——

COLLEGE
MANAGEMENT

1

INTRODUCTION

Higher education is in trouble. After three centuries of growth and stability, colleges and universities, already affected by financial and political crises, now face the prospect of declining enrollment (Carnegie Council, 1980). Many institutions have cut back on programs and faculty, merged with other institutions, or closed their doors. These crises appear to be permanent, even for the most prestigious institutions (Balderston, 1974; Cheit, 1973; Glenny, 1974-75). Not surprisingly, one result has been a growing concern about better management (Balderston, 1974; Cheit, 1973; Mayhew, 1974).

Unfortunately for these institutions, management development in higher education is only an emerging field, and there is an absence of viable frameworks for interventions in this area. While there has been a recent increase in leadership training for college administrators, there was always a significant shortage of management- and leadership-training programs for higher education administrators (Mayhew, 1974; Webster and Shorthouse, 1976). Studies of management interventions in higher education have not yet revealed the types of management developments that are needed in different settings (Baldridge, 1980; Baldridge and Tierney, 1979). There is also a lack of comprehensive models for management development in higher education institutions (Balderston, 1974; Bergquist and Shoemaker, 1976).

THE MODEL

This study proposes and explores a management-development model for colleges and universities. Based on the work of other researchers, five phases of structural development are proposed with

1

correspondingly appropriate management systems. The model is important because it provides a framework for planning interventions designed to improve college and university management. The model has direct implications for institution-based change efforts, as well as for state and federal programs designed to improve college management.

The model is derived from theories of industrial organization and management, particularly the work of Chandler (1962), Greiner (1972), and Weathersby (1975). Traditional management theory has included both formal organization structure and the general process of management (Massie, 1965). Some theorists argue that changes in the formal organization structure and changes in the appropriateness of different management practices are closely tied, and that the formal structure, to a large degree, determines the types of practices that should be implemented at a given time (Chandler, 1962; Greiner, 1972). This approach is particularly relevant to the study of college and university management (Balderston, 1974; Weathersby, 1975). Balderston (1974), for example, argues:

> The mechanisms and structures of the university—its physical facilities and organization—are ways to make the process operate. Both the physical structure and the organizational mechanisms are largely given at any particular point in the history of the institution. Their sizes, shapes, and conditions are endowments of capability and also barriers to easy and rapid change. Change is costly and requires both design and investment (p. 3).

According to this view, management is a process that is closely tied to structure. There is, however, a great diversity in the sizes, structures, and purposes of colleges and universities (Carnegie Commission, 1973; Baldridge et al. , 1973). Most management-intervention models seem more appropriate for some types of institutions than for others. Balderston (1974) suggests management strategies for large universities and multicampus systems. Bergquist and Shoemaker (1976), in contrast, propose a comprehensive institution-development model that is most applicable to small colleges. The model developed in this study differentiates between the types of management systems that are appropriate for institutions with certain structural characteristics. This model is most applicable to small- and medium-sized colleges and universities, since the institutions used as case studies fall into these categories. However, attempts are made to speculate on the implications of the model for large university and college systems.

Three interrelated concepts were used to develop the general model described in this book. The first, structural development, refers to the size of colleges and universities and to the complexity of their formal organizational structures. Size is usually measured in numbers of individuals—students, faculty, or administrators—in the institution. Complexity refers to the differentiation within the organization, and is usually measured by the numbers of departments, courses, schools, colleges, and administrative units. Size and complexity are highly correlated in statistical studies in higher education institutions (Baldridge et al. , 1973; Platt and Parsons, 1970). These studies also have shown that increased size and complexity are closely related to increased faculty autonomy (Baldridge et al. , 1973) and increased faculty involvement in departmental decision making (Platt and Parsons, 1970). In a national study of higher education institutions, Hodgkinson found that size and complexity had an enormous influence on the prospects for institutional change, as well as on many other college characteristics (Hodgkinson, 1971a, p. 77). This suggests that institutional-management needs are likely to change as institutions develop structurally.

Management effectiveness is the second concept used in the model. It is argued here that management procedures and practices vary in their complexity and sophistication, and that there is a link between an institution's state of structural development and the sophistication of its management needs. According to this view, a college is most likely to be effectively managed if it implements management systems that address local management needs.

The third concept is external intervention. The major concern here is how an external agency can improve management systems at colleges and universities. It appears that interventions are likely to be most successful when their design takes into account the types of management practices and procedures most appropriate for institutions in different phases of structural development. The model proposed here provides a framework for distinguishing between institutions with different management needs.

To explore the model, five exemplary institutions funded in the Advanced Institutional Development Program (AIDP) of Title III of the Higher Education Act of 1965 (P. L. 89-329) were studied. The purpose of Title III was to strengthen "developing" institutions: colleges and universities considered to be out of the mainstream of academic life. This program was used because it is a large program with a relatively long history that is designed in part to improve management systems.

Exemplary institutions were used because they provide the best possible examples for exploring the relationship between structural development and management effectiveness. If it can be assumed that the selected institutions do have effective management systems, a problem discussed later, then it is possible to examine the relationship between structural characteristics and the appropriateness of different management practices. These case studies will show how the formal structure, and the types of management practices, policies, and procedures that have been implemented. Additionally, a follow-up study of the case institutions was used to evaluate the long-term impact of these interventions. The analysis of the case-study institutions also considers the relationship between formal structure and other organizational subsystems—mission, instructional technologies, sociopolitical setting, and groups and individuals—in order to ground this model with broader concepts of organization (Baldridge and Deal, 1975; Udy, 1965).

TITLE III

In 1973 the Advanced Institutional Development Program was formed to give large, multiyear grants to institutions that had shown progress with basic funding. Title III is currently the largest direct institutional-aid program in the federal budget, with a $120 million appropriation in funding year 1979. Slightly over half these funds ($68 million) were reserved for AIDP; the remainder was reserved for the Basic Institutional Development Program (BIDP). In 1979, the two programs were combined into a single program, the Strengthening Developing Institutions Program (SDIP), which marked the end of AIDP as a separate program. Eligibility criteria for both programs were vague; they were given as ranges on several quantitative criteria (numbers of students, faculty, library volumes, and so on) based on the funding decisions of the prior year (Jacobs and Tingley, 1977). Institutions funded in the program do not differ by as much as a standard deviation from other colleges and universities on most of these quantitative criteria (St. John, Tingley, and Gallos, 1977).

Title III-funded institutions undertake new activities or improve existing activities in three general areas: curriculum development, student services, and administrative development. AIDP gave relatively large grants, usually of $1 million to $3 million, to institutions to undertake developments in each of these areas. The model developed in this study is most applicable to the administrative area. Federal regulations for funding in these areas are not well defined. One United States Office of Education (USOE) document offers the following rationale for the institutions to implement planning, management, and evaluation (PME) systems:

> To ensure that in the future the colleges will have the information and capabilities that they require for long-term planning and management and to meet the Title III program

reporting requirements of the Office of Education, colleges will be expected to set aside a small portion of the
grant for implementation of systems and procedures appropriate for modern management, planning, and evaluation. *

In addition to requiring institutions to implement some form of a PME
system, AIDP encourages them to implement management information
systems (MIS), which refers to the information system used by the PME
system, and transactional information systems (TIS), which refers to
the computerization of college records. The AIDP application and other
USOE documents do not define the nature of these systems in much
detail for institutions applying for Title III funds. In theory, funded
institutions can implement any type of PME and information system
they consider appropriate. However, these systems must conform
with USOE reporting requirements. In practice, funded programs
have had to include a standard set of management developments.
    While the USOE documents have not explained in great detail the
concepts of PME, MIS, and TIS, there have been attempts to explain
these concepts by those who administer the programs. Nwagbaraocha
(1979) describes the PME concept as follows:

> USOE defines a PME system as an established set of pro-
> cedures for producing a host of primary facts about the
> activities, costs, and revenues of an institution. A PME
> system is designed to focus the attention of top-level ad-
> ministrators on elementary policy questions, analysis of
> their long-range planning and budgeting implications, and
> resolution of the various issues involved (inclusive of de-
> veloping priorities of resource allocation). Thus a PME
> system entails satisfying the information needs of top ad-
> ministrators and the decision-making processes requisite
> to planning, managing, evaluating and modifying institu-
> tional policies and their associated activities and major
> operations. Institutional data bases and computer configu-
> rations are not parts of the PME system, but support it
> by providing the necessary information (p. 36).

Nwagbaraocha considers TIS and MIS as integral to the development

---

*United States Office of Education. "A Planning, Management
and Evaluation Capability in Developing Institutions." Undated paper
of 8 pages, p. 1.

of effective PME systems: "A PME system requires systematic gathering, processing, and retrieving of data to produce the primary information (that is, facts about activities, costs, and institutional revenues) for institutional decision making. Two systems, TIS and MIS, are utilized to support the PME" (p. 37). He describes the TIS and MIS concepts as follows:

> Transactional Information System (TIS). A transactional information system is concerned with those operating procedures that permit a college to carry out its day-to-day affairs—student registration, financial record keeping, admissions, counseling and testing, and so forth. A college has several separate and distinct TISs, and they are generally operated manually. Each area TIS consists of forms, record books, and files, and the procedures for using them. The generic term TIS may include every individual TIS existing in a college setting (p. 38).

> Management Information System (MIS). A management information system involves the kinds and types of data and information college managers need to make decisions. It is concerned with management information to assist decision makers in carrying out their policy and management roles.

> Inputs are taken in the form of requests for information. These requests direct the processing of the MIS modules, which query the IDB to extract data for analysis and summarization (pp. 38-39).

In spite of an evolving definition of PME, MIS, and TIS, the USOE—Title III AIDP program did not, at least when the institutions studied in this book were funded, require specific types of systems to be implemented. By examining how these interventions have developed over time in a small group of exemplary Title III-funded institutions, this study has attempted to examine the interactions between the institution-development process and the role of a federal intervention program designed to improve college management. The conceptual and research frameworks are explained in detail in subsequent chapters.

A NEW APPROACH

A new approach to the study and practice of management-systems development in higher education institutions is inherent in the model developed in this book. While the field of management is still young, there have already been two generations of predominant intervention strategy. The first was laissez-faire: funds were given by public agencies or foundations to colleges for the purpose of improving management without predetermined constraints on the types of management techniques that were to be implemented. In the early and mid 1960s, when Title III was started, the laissez-faire approach predominated. While there was considerable evidence at the time that improved management was necessary in higher education, most college and university administrators and public-agency staff did not have the experience with college-management systems to determine the techniques that would work best. College enrollment and expenditures were expanding; consequently, sophisticated or fiscally sound management was not as high a priority as improving the capacity of institutions to plan for and develop new programs. Most of the literature on colleges and universities during the period emphasized the importance of curricular change and the improvement or modification of governance systems to accommodate larger numbers of participants or to respond to the stressful conditions of growth (Corson, 1960; Hefferlin, 1967; McConnel and Mortimer, 1970; Smelser, 1974).

As more institutions gained experience with sophisticated management techniques in the late 1960s and early 1970s (Balderston, 1974), and as the fiscal difficulties of colleges were documented (Cheit, 1971, 1973), the emphasis on sophisticated management systems became the rule rather than the exception in external intervention programs. Currently, the literature on college and university management often emphasizes the implementation of specific management techniques, such as systematic academic program planning (Kieft, Armijo, and Bucklew, 1978) or management by objectives (MBO) or MIS (Baldridge and Tierney, 1979).

While the sophisticated systems approach represents an improvement over the laissez-faire approach, it nonetheless has shortcomings. A major limitation is that advanced MIS and other sophisticated management systems are not always necessary, especially for small colleges. Implementation of sophisticated systems can be too expensive to maintain after external funding ceases; their maintenance, in many instances, can lead to complicated procedures that impede the collegial dialogue that is essential to the governance and change processes in small colleges. Unfortunately, most studies that have examined the implementation of sophisticated management at small colleges have not adequately questioned the assumption that sophisticated management techniques are necessary or appropriate.

The management-intervention model proposed here suggests a new approach to the design of management interventions, one that stresses the assessment of actual management needs rather than the benefits of sophisticated approaches. While researchers have proposed new approaches to management-system development (St. John and Weathersby, 1977; Weathersby, 1975) and to information-systems development (Basset, 1979; Weathersby, 1975), which gauge the sophistication of systems design to the needs evident in the local setting, these schema have not been the subject of the basic research that is necessary to develop these concepts adequately. Research is necessary to make these models useful and applicable to the management-intervention process.

The long-term involvement of the case-study institutions in the Title III AIDP program provided an excellent context to develop and test these new concepts. The study reported here has a five-year history. Starting in 1975 as part of a major study of the effects of Title III, a conceptual framework for evaluating the effects of intervention programs on college development was proposed (St. John and Weathersby, 1977). While the national data bases used to study the effects of Title III were not adequate to test this model, subsequent funding was provided by USOE for a pilot study using this approach. When the case studies of the exemplary Title III institutions were conducted, the Title III program appeared to be in transition from a laissez-faire, management-intervention approach to a less flexible approach that encouraged the implementation of sophisticated systems, particularly MBO and MIS. Institutions included in the initial year of AIDP were not required to include these developments. For these institutions, sophisticated systems were often encouraged by Title III program staff as part of the monitoring and review process. Institutions funded in subsequent years tended to include these developments in their proposals. The struggle of the exemplary institutions with the sophisticated management and information systems encouraged (or required) by SUOE and the AIDP assisting agencies, provided an opportunity to assess the limitations of the sophisticated systems approach and to substantiate the applicability of a new approach: the differentiated approach.

The basic assumptions of the sophisticated systems and differentiated systems approaches to management development are compared in Table 1.1. The sophisticated systems approach assumes that technologically advanced management techniques are appropriate, perhaps necessary, for most colleges. Baldridge and Tierney (1979), in their study of the EXXON management-improvement program, concluded: "Overall, it is our impression that management information systems and management by objectives programs are worth their costs" (p. 13). In this discussion, the Higher Education Research Institute's study of the EXXON RAMP (Resource Allocation and Management Programs), conducted by Baldridge and Tierney, is used to illustrate the characteristics and assumptions of the sophisticated

TABLE 1.1

Management-Intervention Concepts: Sophisticated Systems Approach versus Differentiated Systems Approach

	Sophisticated Systems Approach	Differentiated Systems Approach
Management concept	Management viewed as a sophisticated process not common in higher education; innovations are needed to introduce sophisticated processes; sophisticated techniques needed in most settings	Management viewed as basic to the academic enterprise; management development should emphasize formalization of existing processes; new systems should be appropriate for local setting
Intervention designs	Modern sophisticated information systems and management techniques assumed appropriate for all institutions; interventions designed to implement these systems, and to improve efficiency of planning and management	New techniques and systems used to formalize and supplement existing management and academic planning processes; sophistication of new systems related to internal management need and to formal organization structures
Measures of successful intervention	Success of intervention measured by successful implementation of sophisticated techniques; assumed successful implementation leads to efficient management and reduced costs	Success of intervention measured by appropriateness of new system for meeting local needs; effectiveness of management measured by overall financial health and stability

systems approach. Baldridge and Tierney evaluated the effects of implementing sophisticated management and information systems in
small- and medium-sized colleges. In the following discussion the
approach used by the EXXON project is compared to the approach to
management development proposed and explored in this study. It
should be noted that the HEMI study represents one of the most detailed and useful evaluation studies of a management-development
program for higher education institutions. The purpose of the research discussed in this book was to explore a new model rather than
to evaluate the effects of an intervention program.

Another assumption of the sophisticated systems approach is
that since sophisticated systems are appropriate for most settings,
the failure to implement these techniques successfully is viewed as a
problem with local administration. Baldridge described the purpose
of this research on management development as follows: "We wanted
to discover the patterns of behavior that supported managerial improvement efforts, and by contrast, the behavior that undercut those
improvements" (Baldridge, 1980, p. 117). Unfortunately, this approach does not allow the researcher to address basic questions about
whether these innovations are necessary. For example, is information-
systems automation always the most appropriate solution to local information needs? Or, perhaps more importantly, is failure to implement these techniques due to behavioral limitations or to problems
with the system being implemented? By not asking these questions,
the researcher cannot determine the situations in which sophisticated
management techniques are not necessary. It is possible that failure
to implement sophisticated systems may be a sign that local administrators exercised effective analytic techniques when deciding not to
proceed with original plans.

The differentiated approach to management development starts
with a different set of assumptions about the academic-management
process. Instead of assuming that sophisticated techniques are appropriate for most settings, the differentiated approach assumes management is already a basic component to the academic enterprise, and
that development of sophisticated techniques is not always necessary.
This approach suggests that new techniques, such as MBO and automated MIS, are more appropriate for medium and large institutions,
while less sophisticated techniques are more appropriate for smaller
institutions. Research using this approach can explain why automated
MIS and other sophisticated techniques may fail in a local setting, even
when the institutions implementing these techniques appear to be effectively managed.

The probable impacts of the two management-development approaches are compared in Table 1.2. Because the sophisticated systems approach argues that management is new to education, it is less

TABLE 1.2

Management Intervention Impacts: Sophisticated Systems Approach versus Differentiated Systems Approach

	Sophisticated Systems Approach	Differentiated Systems Approach
Relation to academic system	Little relationship between management interventions and formal academic system; major limitation of approach is linkage structure between formal management systems and academic planning processes	High relationship between management interventions and formal academic system; academic management considered integral to management-development process
Role of funding agency	Requires implementation of standardized systems; routine compliance reports considered necessary; adaptation of management processes to fit new techniques considered appropriate	Funds different types of management interventions; encourages institutions to design systems to meet local needs; new systems adaptation to meet local needs encouraged
Long-term impact	Long-term impact uncertain, especially after funding ceases; continued use of modern systems may be too expensive for local resources; continued maintenance of new systems may require external funds or limiting other activities	Systems developments likely to remain after funding ceases; new systems often in local interests to maintain if funding ceases; new developments likely to result from successful implementation

likely to have a direct impact on the academic-management or governance process. According to the sophisticated systems view, management interventions actually compete with other innovations: "Managerial innovations do not come in a vacuum. Every new program has to contend with old programs for support, finances, and administrative attention" (Baldridge and Tierney, 1979, p. 172). The differentiated approach is based on a different assumption: it is based on the concept that management development is essential to the entire academic enterprise. Accordingly, improved managerial practices enhance rather than compete with academic innovations. This perspective is expressed well by Nwagbaraocha: "Perhaps the most serious obstacle to overcome is the misconception that PME is a nonacademic administrative tool. If PME is to succeed in any institution, it is imperative that curricular experts and faculty understand this mode of thinking and participate actively in systems design and implementation" (1979, p. 31). Instead of emphasizing the linkage between budgeting and information, which is the direction advocated by sophisticated systems advocates, the differentiated approach emphasizes the linkage between improved management techniques and academic innovations. Indeed, academic innovation may be the most critical element of higher education management, especially in an era of scarce resources.

The role of the funding agency varies considerably for the two approaches. Funding agencies emphasizing the sophisticated systems approach will tend to make decisions and implement procedures that will maximize this outcome. They will fund only those proposals that include necessary managerial techniques and require a predetermined implementation schedule. The problem with this approach is that it can lead to implementation of unnecessary systems. As Baldridge concluded: "The prepackaged management information systems were usually developed at large institutions with thousands of students and faculty and complex administrative arrangements. When small colleges bought the prepackaged programs . . . they quickly found that systems designed for large institutions were not easily adapted" (Baldridge and Tierney, 1979, p. 37). The differentiated approach does not ignore the importance of the linkage between information systems and budgeting; instead, it emphasizes the importance of improved academic management as a means of achieving quality and efficient education.

There is a movement in the higher education community toward the realization that management interventions need to reflect organizational needs. As one recent NCHEMS (National Center for Higher Education Management Systems) report put it:

> The information-system planner is seldom charged with
> revising basic decision processes, so the task is one of
> observing how well matched the decision system is to the

> organization in question. The schema [a theoretical model
> similar to the one developed here] offers one framework
> for making that set of observations. Knowledge of such
> potential conflicts can help establish reasonable expecta-
> tions of information-system performance, an important
> step in the long-term success of the effort (Bassett, 1979,
> p. 12).

However, if a differentiated approach is to be well enough understood
to be useful to funding agencies, then it is essential to investigate
basic organizational dynamics and the interactions between the organizational structure and formal management and information systems.
The emphasis of funding agencies using the differentiated approach
would shift from requiring standard systems to encouraging a match
between the planned systems and the probable needs of the organization.

The field of management development is still young; it is too
early to determine with certainty the long-term effects of either approach. However, it seems logical that the management intervention
that is most likely to remain after external funding has subsided is
the approach that adequately matches systems-development targets
with local needs. This book proposes such a schema for colleges and
universities. It emphasizes the importance of assessing needs before
implementation, and offers a framework for needs assessment. It is
hoped that this approach will lead to improved management-intervention strategies that avoid the common pitfall described below:

> It seems simple-minded to say that needs assessment
> should precede the innovation. But in all too many situa-
> tions, no serious assessment of institutional problems is
> undertaken. Instead, managerial innovations are picked
> up and used just because they are available, because grant-
> ing agencies provide funds, or because other institutions
> are "doing it" (Baldridge and Tierney, 1979, pp. 166-67).

Baldridge and Tierney identify three factors that typically block
adequate needs assessment: administrators frequently use their own
pet diagnosis of organizational needs; there is a tendency for needs
assessments to be superficial; and the stimulus for management innovations is often the availability of grant money (1979, pp. 167-68).
Underlying each of these factors, and probably the most basic difficulty with doing competent needs assessments, is the absence of a
solid conceptual framework that relates organizational characteristics
to management outcomes. To be useful to the needs-assessment process, a management-development model must include enough specificity to adequately identify organizational characteristics associated with
different management needs.

2

TITLE III IN CONTEXT

Title III of the Higher Education Act (HEA) of 1965 is the largest direct-aid program for higher education institutions in the federal budget. Although its total appropriation ($120 million in FY 1979) is small compared to other federal education programs (such as Title I of the Elementary Secondary Education Act), the HEA Title III program has been able to give relatively large grants to individual institutions and to institutional consortia. It is the only federal program designed to improve the condition of financially troubled colleges and universities. However, the Title III Strengthening Developing Institutions program has become the focus of considerable attention in the politics of higher education policy in Washington, D. C. While the program's rhetoric supports the types of developments needed by many financially troubled colleges and universities, the implementation and management of the program have received severe criticism. A recent report by the General Accounting Office (GAO, 1978b) even recommended that Congress consider whether the program was still needed. This comes at a time when the demands for the program's services are greater than at any other point in its history.

This chapter undertakes a critical examination of the Title III program, including consideration of the history of the program and the results of relevant policy research on Title III. This analysis provides a context for this study of Title III. The issues facing Title III are important in the policy arena precisely because they illustrate some of the most critical problems facing higher education policymakers: the limitations of growth-oriented policies and the need to identify new concepts of college development that can replace the growth model that has dominated higher education policy during the past three decades. Before discussing the Title III program, however, this chapter considers emerging concepts of institutional development.

14

INSTITUTIONAL DEVELOPMENT: A CHANGING CONTEXT

During the past decade a strong concern about the management and even the financial survival of colleges and other postsecondary institutions has become a major issue in the educational public-policy arena (Carnegie Council, 1975b). By the late 1970s, after a quarter century of increasing expenditures on public higher education, state governments were faced with new financial demands from private institutions at a time in which even many public institutions were facing financial difficulties (Henry, 1975). The federal government and private philanthropic organizations also have been attempting to address this issue by supporting programs and organizations dedicated to facilitating institutional development.

In the past, institutional development in higher education has usually referred to growth, to increased number of programs, students, faculty, and administrators at existing institutions, and to the creation of new institutions to meet ever-increasing student demand. Too seldom has development referred to qualitative changes in institutions, their instructional activities, and their management. As the Carnegie Foundation (1975) put it: "Now, for the first time in our nation's history, the prospect is that growth may be both unsteady and uncertain" (p. ix).

From World War II until the early 1970s was a period of rapid growth, a movement toward mass higher education, with enrollment on a constant upswing. The war had a direct influence on enrollment. Some increases were due to training programs during the war, and others were due to the flood of ex-GIs, supported by the GI Bill, entering colleges and universities (Henry, 1975). Not only did higher education experience increase enrollment, but public support also increased. The purposes of education also changed as higher education institutions started to play a more important role in scientific research (Kerr, 1963).

The federal investment in research increased dramatically during the entire period. It started with war-related research during World War II and expanded to other fields, especially the physical, biological, and health sciences. As early as 1963, Clark Kerr warned of the extensive nature of this investment and how it might change the character of the institutions (Kerr, 1963). It is interesting that these investments became the subject of student protests in the late 1960s; the protest themes ranged from the neglect of instruction due to extensive research activities to the demands for the abandonment of war-related research during the Vietnam era. It is perhaps even more interesting that the federal investments did change the structure of many institutions through the development of numerous research institutes.

In addition to changes in size and financing patterns due to increased enrollment and federal expenditures on research, there were many changes in the organization and structure of higher education during the 1960s and early 1970s. One development has been the emergence of state systems of higher education. This educational and organizational concept did not come of age until the 1960s, but by the end of the decade it was firmly established: "At the end of the 1960's, they enrolled more than 900,000 students, some 17 percent of all students in public four-year colleges and universities and 27 percent of those enrolled for advanced degrees" (Lee and Bowen, 1971, pp. 7-8). In the late 1960s and early 1970s, state coordinating agencies in higher education had begun to develop and to become much stronger (Carnegie Foundation, 1976). By the late 1970s states were taking a more active role in the planning and coordination for higher education.

Thus despite the decades of growth and plentiful resources, higher education institutions suddenly found themselves in unexpected difficulties. Earl Cheit, in his study of 41 institutions considered typical of the many higher education institutions in the United States, identified what he labeled "the new depression in higher education." The financial conditions confronting colleges are unusual: "Unlike economic downturns that have affected higher education in the past, the present income squeeze is perverse. The income of colleges had risen but not as fast as educational costs. This is occurring while many economic indicators and all prices (but stock prices) are rising" (Cheit, 1971, p. 7). Unlike the Great Depression in which costs, such as academic salaries, were cut, costs to higher education institutions have risen in spite of the institutional difficulties (Cheit, 1971). In addition, while expenditures on salaries have increased slightly, the value of faculty salaries has fallen since 1970. Cheit found that 29 of the 41 colleges studied, including such prestigious institutions as Stanford and Berkeley, were either already in financial difficulty or headed for it. In a two-year follow-up study of the financial condition of these same institutions, Cheit (1973) found that although the severity of the condition had lessened, due in part to changes within the institutions, the depressed situation remained.

The "new depression" was not the only crisis facing higher education institutions in the late 1960s and early 1970s. In addition, as the Carnegie Commission pointed out in its final report (1973), there was: a political crisis resulting from the activist politics and protests of the 1960s; demographic changes with the deceleration and decline in growth; the adjustment to universal access; the changing nature of the work place and the declining capacity of the economy to provide places for graduates at their level of training; and a confidence crisis, a declining public faith in the role of higher education. These factors led the commission to ask:

> Will higher education, weighted down by these and other
> crises, follow the course of the railroad industry? Both
> have been great sources of national growth—the railroad
> industry in the second half of the nineteenth century, and
> higher education particularly in the middle of the twentieth
> century. The railroad industry, in the face of new compet-
> itors arising out of new technologies and new public tastes,
> and burdened by old mentalities, old practices, old and
> rigid operating rules, an older and aging labor force, and
> restrictive government controls has declined greatly in
> dynamism and influence; it has become a largely spent
> force in terms of additional national growth. The trans-
> portation segment of the economy kept on growing, but the
> railroad industry declined within it (Carnegie Commission,
> 1973, p. 7).

For the Carnegie Commission, the source of the problems was the
fact that "new competitors and new technologies now challenge higher
education, and new tastes and patterns for obtaining tertiary education
likewise are emerging" (p. 8).

The condition of higher education institutions has become the
subject of considerable study during the past five years. The Carnegie
Council for Policy Studies in Higher Education, formed after the conclusion of the Carnegie Commission, has commissioned studies and
produced policy reports on the roles of college presidents (Glenny et
al., 1976), multicampus system (Lee and Bowen, 1975), and state and
federal governments (Carnegie Council, 1975b; 1976) in facing the
present situation. There also have been in-depth studies of state funding capacities (Cherin and McCoy, 1977), institutional closings and
mergers (Millet, 1977), and strategies for developing institutions
(Bergquist and Shoemaker, 1976; Webster and Shorthouse, 1976).
There is an emerging concern among decisionmakers at all levels—
within institutions, state and local governments, and philanthropic
organizations—about the present condition and possible methods of
strengthening institutions.

An Emerging Concern about Management

In many respects, the present condition of higher education in
the United States is unique. Although there are similarities between
this and other periods (especially between the present and the Great
Depression years), there are even more differences. There is more
than ever before a tension between scarce resources and the emerging
necessity to change and to have a future orientation. During the past

decade, the technologies and potentials of education have been changing faster than the existing institutions. New institutional forms have emerged and the severe stress of survival faces new and old institutions (Rockart and Scott Morton, 1975).

The Carnegie Foundation's report, More Than Survival (1975), addresses the overall situation as well as any document currently available. After considering the present predicament, it recommended that institutions adjust to the new condition by developing "an overall strategy for the new condition, one which projects, realistically, several years into the future" (p. 85). Its recommendations for public policy stress the funding of students, increased state support of private institutions, and continued federal support for the university research capacity. Although increased federal institutional support was not included in its recommendations, issues of survival and development have to be dealt with in a comprehensive fashion at the institutional level, and perhaps can be assisted by public and private institutional aid programs.

To describe the present economic condition facing colleges, Balderston (1974) prefers to use the term "stress" than "crisis" because stress adequately describes the lasting nature of the condition, while crisis suggests a peak or death to the condition. Balderston does not give in to the euphoria of the 1960s, the certainty of federal or state government intervention in the present condition. He argues that universities must become more effective at managing existing scarce resources. His view is optimistic, however, as he suggests "universities may be a prototype of postindustrial organization" (p. 3). Balderston considers the types of management strategies—the use of cost analysis, policy analysis, market indicators, budgeting processes, and information systems—that can be used by universities for effective management. The introduction of these practices to higher education institutions is seen as critical according to this view. Cheit's restudy (1973) of the 41 case institutions affirms Balderston's emphasis: the severity of the financial situation on these campuses had lessened primarily because of the increased awareness of the problems among the administration and faculty on campus, and, in many instances, the implementation of better management procedures.

In a review of the state of the art of management development and training in colleges and universities, Webster and Shorthouse (1976) identified a significant deficiency in professional training of higher education administrators. Traditionally, colleges and universities have promoted people successful in their academic pursuits, usually with advanced training in a specialized academic field, to positions of leadership—department heads, academic deans, and presidents (Webster and Shorthouse, 1976). Once promoted, these people usually have to rely on their native skills and instincts, as

well as their experienced observations of the functioning of their institutions. These people often are not initially equipped to deal with
the complexities of financial stress now facing colleges. There is a
lack of both in-service and campus-based training programs for higher
education managers (Mayhew, 1974; Webster and Shorthouse, 1976).

Another cause of the current institutional stress in higher education is a widening gap between institutional aspirations and the capacity of institutions to finance their programs. To be comprehensive,
each campus had to administer to all the needs of its clients by providing diverse academic programs and also by providing adequate counseling, housing, health care, and the like. In the 1970s, however, the
growth trends receded but institutional aspirations did not. One result
has been an increase in the portion of institutional costs paid by students (Weathersby and Jacobs, 1977).

One possible outcome of this trend of increasing institutional
aspirations and students costs is an unbundling of the functions postsecondary institutions perform. According to this scenario, the functions of collegiate educational programs—assessment of prior and
direct learning, academic and career advising, instruction, certifica-
tion, and linkages to work—can be performed by different organizations
at a reduced cost to students, who can choose the services they desire
(see Weathersby and Jacobs, 1977, for a discussion of this model and
of the general problem of institutional aspirations and student costs).
Some elements of this diverse service network are already evident.
Assessment organizations, such as the Regents' External Degree Program in New York and the Thomas Alva Edison College in New Jersey,
are actively engaged in the assessment of student comprehension of
academic subjects learned outside of formal education. Both institutions award degrees based on the accumulation of credits from diverse
institutions, rather than residency in any single school. According to
Weathersby and Jacobs (1977), such an unbundling has two impacts:
"it changes the structures and incentives for decisions in an education
institution which offers individual services and it alters the student
cost and benefit calculus for students who are now empowered to purchase the services they find desirable" (p. 24).

The advent of new programs offering some of the services nor-
mally provided by colleges will not alter the problems confronting
most colleges. Faced with competition from new service organizations
offering degrees for accumulated learning, credit for prior experiences, or counseling of an academic or career nature, the problems
of traditional higher education may be increased. The challenges are
to develop services adequate enough to insure survival in an environment in which more colleges are competing for fewer students, and
to avoid overdevelopment that might provide services at a higher cost
than if they were purchased separately.

In the past few years there have been several efforts to think comprehensively about the problems facing higher education institutions. The Ford Foundation's multimillion-dollar funding program for black colleges and the Developing Institutions Program are examples of privately and publicly funded programs designed to aid weak colleges in their development processes. Once initiated, however, an institutional-aid or intervention program is often difficult to evaluate or manage because of a lack of development models. If funds are provided to help institutions become more self-sufficient, or to develop to a state where external assistance is no longer needed, it is nearly impossible to insure that target institutions will not become dependent on these additional funds.

Overview

Higher education in the United States is in a transition period between two vastly different eras. During the movement toward mass higher education (the most recent era), continued growth and the development of comprehensive institutions were major themes. The golden age of education was the culmination of nearly three centuries of relatively constant growth and expectations of continued future growth. The past quarter century was the period of the largest expansion in enrollment and expenditures in history. The relationship between education and external constituencies, especially state and federal governments, was also better than it ever had been and probably ever will be.

The dominant themes of the new era are not yet clear. Notions of what post-high-school education is and can be are expanding: the proprietary sector of education is already larger than traditional higher education (Weathersby and Nash, 1974); there are new client groups to be served by traditional programs (Cross, 1976); and new educational forms are emerging (Gould, 1973). Some suggest there is a golden era ahead, with a much stronger relationship between education and the work place than ever before, and with a much more diverse clientele attending traditional colleges. Other future scenarios are not so helpful, however; the adult market may be more limited than initial forecasters thought. The decline in the size and rate of attendance of the traditional college-going age group adds to possibilities of failure for many traditional institutions. The severe financial stress of the present and recent past suggests possible permanent changes in the financing patterns of colleges.

No matter which direction the future takes, the current period of transition is difficult. Institutions have to adjust their aspirations to changing future prospects. Institutions not only face the challenge of a changing educational marketplace, but they do so in a setting in which both their growth prospects and their ability to obtain outside new money to finance new programs are limited. To cope with the present, institutions need a better understanding of the consequences of lessening expectations.

A new concept of institutional development is emerging out of this confused period. In the past, increased activities have served as the main indicator of institutional development. An institution was considered well developed if it had reached a minimum size, offered diverse programs by a well-educated faculty, and provided the diverse services considered part of college life. In the present context, however, these old notions of development are not enough. Institutions are emphasizing the efficient use of existing resources, the effective organization and management of the current enterprise, and new planning processes that allow for the selective development of institutional weaknesses.

BACKGROUND ON THE TITLE III PROGRAM

The developing institutions program, one of the many Great Society programs enacted during the Johnson administration, is the only federal program aimed at institutional development in higher education. It has funded numerous curriculum, student-development, and administrative interventions in hundreds of colleges during its 15-year history. The legislative history of Title III, until 1977, illustrated the conflicting goals of the program (Jacobs and Tingley, 1977).

On the one hand, many of the arguments used to justify Title III by program staff and institutional representatives have stressed that Title III funds could be used to facilitate a development sequence for higher education institutions, and that Title III-funded institutions would experience an up-and-out phenomenon as they progressed along this sequence toward a developed state. In fact, slightly over seven years ago this argument was used to initiate and secure funding for the Advanced Institutional Development Program, which was designed to give large grants of $1 million to $3 million to institutions to undertake intensive development efforts.

On the other hand, Title III-funding regulations have encouraged institutions to maintain activity levels that insured their eligibility for the program. The eligibility criteria for Title III stressed quantitative growth in such areas as numbers of students, library volumes, faculty with doctorates, and expenditures per student. Over time different criteria were used for four categories of institutions: two-year public, two-year private, four-year public, and four-year private. Initially, these were expressed as minimums and maximums below and above which institutions were ineligible for funds. Later, in response to criticisms that these criteria never produced a set of developed institutions, these criteria were expressed as percentiles representing minimum and maximum ranges. Throughout Title III's history, the same institutions usually have remained eligible for the program's funds. In fact, past funding is the best indicator of future funding levels.

Ironically, the five-year maximum eligibility for AIDP was suspended before any institution had been in the program five years. By 1979 the AIDP and BIDP were abandoned in favor of a single Strengthening Developing Institutions Program, perhaps to insure that all the funded institutions would be allowed to receive Title III funds.

As the eligibility criteria became more specific and the arguments for a developmental sequence more vocal, a set of conflicting expectations emerged: institutions that met the eligibility criteria viewed Title III as an entitlement, yet the providers of funds, particularly Congress, expected Title III to produce a set of developed institutions. These contradictory expectations were a major contributing factor to the General Accounting Office's (1975) overall recommendations for Congress regarding the future of Title III:

> The operating problems and the more basic problem of adequately defining a "developing institution" are so fundamental and pervasive that we believe the program as presently structured is largely unworkable. Therefore, the Congress should first determine whether or not the Title III program should be continued, it needs to clarify the program's intent to show which institutions should be served and the goals these institutions should achieve (pp. iv-v).

The same GAO report outlined numerous problems with the administration of Title III. The eligibility criteria used by the program did not adequately indicate why an individual institution was not developed or what it had to do to become developed. The procedures and criteria used for selecting institutions were not consistently or fairly applied to all applicants. Award amounts often were not consistent with proposal reviewers' recommendations. Assisting agencies actively recruited institutions to participate in their programs, often made excessive profits from their involvement in Title III, and were not held accountable for their uses of Title III funds by the Developing Institutions Division (DID), the part of the U. S. Office of Education that administered the funds. Further, it was reported that USOE-DID did not do an adequate job identifying high risk institutions, and that many funded institutions did not adequately adhere to HEW regulations regarding the expenditures of federal funds.

In spite of these indictments against the administration of the Title III program, there is little disagreement in Washington about the need for a federal program that provides the types of assistance Title III has the potential of providing, and does provide in many instances. Even the GAO (1978a), which recently completed a study of the problems and outlooks of small, private liberal arts colleges, made the following observations about Title III's potential impacts:

> The Strengthening Developing Institutions Program assists developing colleges in strengthening their academic, administrative, and student service activities so that they might participate in the higher education community. Most of the small liberal arts colleges we observed could have benefited from such assistance in their recruiting and administrative programs. Some schools received developing institutions funds which, according to school officials, had a very positive impact on their efforts (p. 61).

At the heart of the conflict over the Title III program are basic questions about the definitions of a developing college, the ways in which external funding can be used to improve the future prospects of a college, and how the federal bureaucracy can be organized to provide these services. The answers to these questions are very complex, but an understanding of how these problems have evolved is essential to gaining the insight necessary to critically reexamine the philosophy and regulations of the Title III program.

Origins of Controversy over Title III

When the Higher Education Act was being debated in Congress in the early 1960s, higher education was in a period of rapid growth. Between 1958 and 1962, just prior to the period when the proposals eventually incorporated into Title III were being presented to Congress, all sectors of higher education were growing, especially public two-year and university-level institutions. The growth between 1962 and 1966, when the HEA went into effect, was just as dramatic. Total enrollment in two-year and university-level institutions more than doubled during this eight-year period. A critical factor in understanding the origins of Title III is that higher education enrollment was increasing, and institutions faced the prospect of continued growth in the foreseeable future because demographic trends favored growth.

A second important factor is that the extent of the large federal investment was suddenly evident in higher education. The institutions also enjoyed widespread political and public support; the few campus-based protests of the early 1960s, starting with the free speech movement of 1964, had not yet influenced public attitudes about higher education.

A few groups of institutions, for very different reasons, were adversely affected by this plentiful condition. Small private colleges located throughout the eastern two-thirds of the United States were starting to feel some of the effects of the rapid growth in the public sector. These small private colleges, usually denominational in origin and of limited appeal due to their lack of curricular diversity and relative isolation, were starting to lose their traditional clients to large public universities, which had high quality and diverse offerings, and to two-year public institutions, which were increasingly available to all clientele. They also lacked strong advocates in Washington and the willingness to build strong coalitions. However, these institutions were not yet hard hit by enrollment difficulties, since there appeared to be plenty of students for all institutions.

Two-year institutions did slightly more lobbying in Washington. These institutions were expanding rapidly, but did not enjoy a large federal investment since they were not research institutions. Their sources of support were (and are) primarily state and local. Advocates for community colleges were able to provide a strong voice in Washington during the initial debates, and were included specifically in final legislation: 24 percent of Title III's funds were set aside for two-year institutions (Jacobs and Tingley, 1977, pp. 22-28).

The historically black institutions, however, were most deeply affected by both trends. Black students were increasingly attending other institutions. These institutions also had articulate spokespeople in Washington. Earl J. McGrath, long-time advocate of liberal arts education in the United States, completed a study of predominately black colleges in 1964 that became a blueprint for Title III. His testimony before the Senate in advocacy of a program to strengthen the predominately black colleges and universities emphasized the following:

1. Maintain and strengthen most existing institutions—None of the predominately Negro colleges should be allowed to die until their present and prospective students can be fully assured of better educational opportunities elsewhere. Even the limited and inefficient programs of weaker institutions should be maintained while rigorous efforts are being made to strengthen them.

2. Institutional cooperation—Among themselves and with other institutions, the predominantly Negro colleges and universities must find ways for greater sharing of resources, for participation in state and regionwide projects, and (in some cases) for merger or at least a sharing of facilities.

3. Long-range planning—A center should be established in at least one of the great universities to assist these colleges in forecasting their own potential roles and to plan their services in terms of their own resources and the services available elsewhere. Outside help is needed in making long-range plans for organizing and enriching their curriculums, for recruiting and utilizing their faculties, for making maximum use of space and facilities, for designing and erecting new buildings, and for long-range campus and financial development.

4. Strengthening administrative leadership—Foundations should provide the means to permit individuals now in presidential and deanship posts, and promising faculty members as well, to take leave for periods of continuing education and professional training.

5. Faculty development—These institutions must attach a high priority to the continuing development of their teaching effectiveness, and, as appropriate, outside financial personnel resources need to be made available to assist them. Urgent attention must be devoted to increasing faculty salaries, as well as to provisions for advanced study, leave, relief from nonacademic burdens, and professional contacts.

6. Curriculum—A most pressing need is for the strengthening of instruction in the liberal arts disciplines, better to prepare graduates for graduate and professional opportunities. Many presently taught vocational subjects should be dropped, and others need to be added that lead to opening careers in business, industry and government. The social and natural sciences are particularly appropriate for further development at this time (U. S. Senate, 1965, pp. 392-93).

Regarding the financing of these proposals, McGrath concluded that "an effort to provide the financial means for expanding educational opportunities, since it will run into the hundreds of millions of dollars, is beyond the means of States and private donors alone. The Federal Government, therefore, must assume a major and inescapable role in strengthening the predominantly Negro colleges and universities" (U. S. Senate, 1965, p. 393). During the years since McGrath's testimony, the federal government has spent hundreds of millions of dollars in efforts to improve the condition of black colleges.

The meaning of the term "developing institution" was not specifically defined in the testimony for Title III, in the legislation, or in subsequent program regulations (Jacobs and Tingley, 1977). Generally, it was argued that some institutions, perhaps due to their history or past discrimination, were less well off. They lacked financial resources, had less qualified faculty, and slim course offerings; because of these deficiencies they were not able to attract students. Throughout the testimony it was argued that these institutions would be needed to accommodate student demand. As Francis Keppel put it in his House testimony: "it is unrealistic to think of getting rid of smaller, weaker colleges at a time when the number of young people of college age is reaching record heights" (U. S. House, 1965, p. 79).

Title III, as enacted by Congress, provided the commissioner and the advisory council "with broad discretionary authority to define objectives and establish priorities" for Title III (Jacobs and Tingley, 1977, p. 37). In the absence of any clear definition of what was meant by "developing institution," and in the face of a prospect for increased demand, the eligibility criteria for Title III emphasized growth. The statistical profiles of funded developing institutions, presented in congressional hearings and in Title III documents, emphasized the need for increased enrollment and expenditures, decreased student-faculty ratios, increased percentages of faculty with doctorates, and so forth. By the mid 1970s, however, higher education had experienced its first overall enrollment decline in a quarter century (Golladay, 1976).

A New Condition

By the mid-1970s the condition of higher education had undergone a drastic change. Instead of facing a prospect of continued growth, it faced the prospect of an overall enrollment decline; nor did higher education in the 1970s enjoy the public confidence and federal support it did during the prior two decades. Public policy has been slow to adjust to this new condition. In many instances it creates incentives for institutions to increase their aspirations, or even to plan for expansions, when there are not adequate prospects for new resources and students. Title III has been trapped in this quandary. Its eligibility criteria clearly identify growth as the key factor in measuring success, and institutions have often had to stress program growth in order to secure funds.

During the past two years, the Office of Education initiated an effort to modify the eligibility criteria for Title III. The proposed criteria were partly an attempt to respond to this new financial condition. However, it was also an attempt to avert growing criticism from the General Accounting Office, from a Congress that had expected Title III to produce a set of developed institutions, and from a succession of policy research reports that had been unable to assess the impact of the program. The problem with proposing a new set of eligibility criteria was compounded by the increasing demands for Title III's services by a larger and more diverse set of institutions.

Although the eligibility criteria for Title III have never emphasized the racial composition of the applicant institutions, this is the
one variable that clearly differentiated funded from nonfunded applicant institutions (GAO, 1975; St. John, Tingley, and Gallos, 1977).
This silent relationship between Title III and the traditionally black
institutions worked relatively well during the early years of the developing institutions program, when financial and enrollment conditions
were better for most colleges. There are now several special-interest
groups, such as the Council for the Advancement of Small Colleges
(CASC), and national associations, such as the American Council on
Education, that have strong interests in Title III. Unlike the political
environment of the mid 1960s, when most colleges and universities
did not have a strong presence in Washington, by the late 1970s there
were a number of strong interest groups concerned about the future
of Title III.

The Title III eligibility criteria proposed by USOE during fall
1978 were an attempt to move away from the growth-oriented criteria
that were largely unworkable in the new condition, and to formalize
and preserve the largely informal relationship between USOE-DID and
the historically black institutions. This was done because it was assumed these institutions had higher percentages of low income and
minority enrollments than some of the more recent recipients of Title
III funds. The criteria were explained in one USOE document as follows:

> The proposed regulations for the Title III Developing Insti-
> tutions require that an institution receive a minimum score
> of 175 from a scoring system based on its average Basic
> Educational Opportunity Grant (BEOG) per full time equiva-
> lent (FTE) student, and on its average educational and gen-
> eral (E & G) expenditure levels an institution's final score
> is the sum of its BEOG and expenditure points (Fernko,
> 1979, p. 1).

The proposed eligibility criteria emphasized two variables: E
& G expenditures per student and BEOG award per student. In the abstract, the two criteria do a better job of identifying weaker or less
advantaged institutions than the program's historic criteria. E & G
would identify institutions that expend fewer resources per student,
thus identifying those less well-off financially or more cost efficient.
BEOG would identify institutions that enroll large percentages of low
income students. There were some significant problems with the way
these were used to create the proposed scoring system. One problem
was that the proposed regulations overemphasized BEOG per student.
The scoring system weighed this variable twice as heavily as E & G
expenditures per student. A second problem was that a maximum

range of eligibility was identified. The combined effect of these two problems was that many of the currently funded institutions, especially the nonminority institutions that tend to have lower BEOG per student, were suddenly excluded from Title III eligibility.

The proposed modifications in Title III eligibility criteria were met with strong resistance by higher education lobby groups and became a prominent subject in many higher education newsletters. When faced with this opposition, HEW Secretary Joseph Califano announced the delay of implementation of the new criteria for at least another year. The decision was claimed as a victory by these special-interest groups. Although these initial attempts to change the Title III-funding regulations have been delayed, the critical problems facing the future of Title III are not diminished. The GAO has criticized the proposed regulations because "it is not clear that these revisions will be more adequate than the regulations in effect when GAO made its review in assuring that those institutions intended to benefit by the law receive Title III support" (GAO, 1978b, p. iv).

Unfortunately, the intent of Title III has never been made explicit. In the face of new competitors for Title III, black college administrators have often argued that Title III funds should be restricted to black colleges. For example, the National Advisory Committee on Black Higher Education and Black Colleges and Universities (1979) has recommended:

> Given the present framework of Title III, it alone cannot successfully bring minority institutions into the mainstream, counteract years of discriminatory funding, and target institutions with a primary commitment to the education of Black students. Measures must be undertaken to restrict the ever widening pool of recipients to the set of minority institutions for which the original legislation was intended—the institutions which have historically and presently undertaken a unique responsibility and task which other institutions either could not or would not undertake.
>
> Black institutions represent the few positive outgrowths of institutionalized racism in this country. Their experiences and development have been unique. They, therefore, warrant unique solutions. It is recommended that,
>
> 9. 0 Title III of the Higher Education Act be made explicitly for the benefit of Black colleges and universities.
>
> Concomitant with this effort should be the development of a broad funding base for these institutions. Presently, many

Black institutions are stymied in their efforts to garner wider sources of support due to the absence of a strong and focused mission acknowledging their primacy in a given field. Due to limited resources, it is difficult for them to compete for funds and grants with the mainstream institutions. Hence, it is recommended that,

10. 0 Title III funds should be used to help institutions plan for and develop programs to further a well defined mission and purpose. In so doing, institutions could begin to impact the appropriate funding sources concordant with this focus.

Initiatives such as these will help Black institutions compete more successfully for a wider range of Federal and private sources of funds including R and D grants (pp. 63-64).

In spite of these recommendations, the intent of Title III legislation is not well defined, partly because of the drastic change in the condition of higher education since the enactment of the Higher Education Act. In 1965 Title III was designed to strengthen weaker colleges that could provide essential educational services to an increasing student population. Fifteen years later, numerous colleges can potentially benefit from the services provided by Title III because many more colleges are suffering from financial stress and enrollment losses. In this new context, more basic information is needed about the process and prospects of college development, especially development other than growth.

POLICY RESEARCH ON TITLE III

Policy research on the effects of Title III on funded colleges and universities has been hampered by vague program definitions and criteria, as well as by a limited social science theory base to guide research. Because of this, it has not been a potent force in the political debates over Title III. This research has not generated a set of findings that either proponents or opponents of the program could use to support their arguments about Title III's future. A review of the few major attempts to assess the effects of Title III helps explain the political difficulties the program has encountered. The difficulties arise because of the symbiotic relationship between the lack of clarity in the intent, design, and administration of the Title III program, and the probing and inquisitive nature of social science research. The lack of specific Title III program objectives created a difficult situation for the researchers evaluating the program. As a consequence, their findings seldom proved useful in the political process.

With the absence of a specific program design or legislative intent, policy researchers assessing the effects of Title III have turned to social science theory to find a basis for assessment. Unlike the hard sciences, where there is a significant theory base or at least commonly accepted paradigms on which to base research (Kuhn, 1962), the social sciences lack a common theory base. In many instances there are competing theories or paradigms. For example, during the period when Title III was being planned and implemented (from the early 1960s through the present), organization theory, the field from which models to assess the effects of Title III are most likely to be drawn, went through fundamental changes. Prior to the early 1960s, theories of organization as applied to colleges and universities were dominated by two schools of thought: one argued that the university was and always had been a "community of scholars" (see, for example, Goodman, 1962); the competing theory was that the university was a formal bureaucratic organization with defined centers of authority (see, for example, Corson, 1960). Neither theory was informative about the process of change in higher education that was evident throughout the 1960s.

The field of organizational behavior and development (Argyris, 1962, 1965; Bennis, 1966; McGregor, 1960), which argues the importance of considering individuals and interpersonal factors in the process of organizational change, may have had the potential for reconciling the differences between these dominant and competing views of university organizations, but the events of the mid and late 1960s rapidly diffused this potential. Instead, as a result of years of campus turmoil and protest, a political view of the university change process began to dominate the thinking of experts in this field (Baldridge, 1971, 1972). Currently, the limits of the political model in explaining the continued situation of stress in higher education are being explored by researchers who advocate improved management systems (Balderston, 1974), improvements in management and leadership training (Higher Education Management Institute, 1976; Webster and Shorthouse, 1976), and integrated models of college and university organization and decision making (Bassett, 1979; Helsabeck, 1975; Weathersby, 1975).

The rapid progression of organization theory, as it applies to the university as a social organization, has left few consistent conceptual threads for the successive studies of Title III. An examination of major studies shows how research on Title III can potentially inform policymakers about the effects of public policy on the development and change processes in colleges and universities. This is an arena in which well-designed research can inform and improve policy.

While the growing need for intervention programs designed to improve the condition of colleges is evident, there are few conceptual models that can guide these efforts.

Major Studies of Title III

There have been four major studies of the Title III program. A comparison of these evaluations provides an interesting example of the different methods of evaluating college development, and of the difficulties researchers have had in evaluating the impact of Title III. Each study took a different evaluation approach. Howard (1967) evaluated the effectiveness of the selection criteria using quantitative measures of academic quality. Miller et al. (1970) measured the attitudes of administrators and faculty as a means of evaluating program effectiveness. Hodgkinson and Schenkel (1974) used a combination of financial, structural, and process measures to develop a phased model for developing institutions. Finally, Weathersby et al. (1977) used existing quantitative data bases to evaluate the impact of Title III. The results of the four studies varied according to the research method and measures of development used.

Lawrence Howard (1967) worked with quantitative measures to evaluate the selection criteria the Title III program staff used during the first year of operation. His study was based on the assumption that "as Title III is now administered, and indeed as many of the public and private programs are operated, quantitative measures are used to make qualitative judgments" (p. 82). Howard attempted to generate a ranking system for institutional quality. He first tested the reliability of different variables, then computed what he considered the five most useful ratios for ranking institutions: "faculty/student, students to Ph. D. 's, library volumes to enrollment, income to enrollment, and first time enrollment to bachelor degrees awarded" (p. 92). He concluded that these five variables "represent the beginnings of criterion indicators which relate quantitative data to institutional quality" (p. 92). His institutional quality rankings did not prove to be consistent with the actual selection criteria used in the operation of the Title III program. As Howard noted in his report: "In short, the neat distinction between established and developing colleges, which seemed so logical when the empirical listing was used, literally comes apart when ratios, weighting, and multidimensional analysis are applied" (p. 97).

Even though the official criteria used to determine minimum and maximum institutional eligibility (age of institution, enrollment, and so on) were quantitative, the actual funding decisions made by the Title III staff, as Howard's findings indicated, were not based entirely on these criteria. Howard concluded that the statistical approach he used "to distinguish developing institutions could be useful for the administration of Title III, in spite of the many hurdles which have not yet been surmounted" (p. 101).

Miller et al. (1970) emphasized program development and evaluation as an important aspect of judging institutional development. They studied the effectiveness of Title III-funded programs at selected funded institutions. Rather than selecting institutions on a random basis, they selected institutions with programs that were either exemplary or unique. Acknowleding that Title III allocations relate not only to the question of what programs to support, but also to which institutions to fund, the authors compared the questionnaire responses of faculty and administrators at each institution to the institution's quality ranking. Variables included in their quality rating were "student-faculty ratio, percentage of faculty with doctorates, education and general expense per student, number of library volumes per student, and average test scores (CEEB or ACT) of entering freshmen" (p. 62). They developed five quality categories with equal numbers of institutions, based on responses from individuals at 37 institutions. Their findings showed little relationship between institutional quality, as ranked by the quantitative measures, and faculty and administrators' attitudes about program success.

They were cautious about using their quality rankings either to make quality judgments about the institutions they grouped or to make judgments about which institutions to fund. In evaluating which institutions should receive funds, they suggested that there might be a reverse relationship between institutional quality and program success, since the low quality institutions had the greatest need, and consequently their Title III programs were sometimes seen as more important.

Hodgkinson and Schenkel (1974) used a staged model of institutional development in their evaluation of the impact of Title III. The stages of institutional development they proposed are analogous to the initial stages of growth in national economies proposed by Rostow (1960): traditional society, preconditions for take-off, drive to maturity, and maturity. Hodgkinson and Schenkel suggest that the first three stages are most applicable to the study of the Title III program since a mature institution, using this scheme, would not be eligible for Title III.

Their evaluation used both a survey of institutions receiving Title III funds between 1965 and 1974 (325 respondents out of 638 institutions) and institutional case studies (for 41 institutions). The case studies were initiated only after the survey failed to reveal anything conclusive about Title III. They then proposed the developmental model. The case-study institutions were broken into three groups that

corresponded with the three stages outlined above: "high range institutions, those which . . . are well on their way to becoming self-
sustaining and effective institutions; medium range, those which are
developing more gradually and somewhat unevenly and whose future
is somewhat less certain; and low range, those . . . hampered by
very basic problems in their daily operations" (p. 191). The purpose
of the analysis was to suggest the institutional characteristics of colleges and universities at each of the three stages. The measures of
viability used to compare the campuses were: leadership dynamism
and efficiency; financial stability; range of programs and activities
offered students; cost-effectiveness; sense of role and long-range
direction; student demand for involvement, and/or outreach efforts
by school to uninvolved students; faculty-administration relations;
and community relations (pp. 196-97).

In the opinion of the Title III program staff, the Hodgkinson
study may have been subject to biases resulting from the historical
trends of the late 1960s; it also failed to address a variety of questions
about the actual Title III programs. Yet the same staff report that
criticizes the Hodgkinson study for its limitations suggests that it
"does tell us some things about the movement of institutions along
the line of general and total institutional development," and that it is
in this area that the Hodgkinson study was the most productive. While
the Hodgkinson study illustrated the importance of something other
than a growth-oriented development model, it did not propose a model
that identified the types of developments that are likely to be most
appropriate for different groups of institutions, which limited its applicability in the policy arena.

The most recently completed study of Title III, the one by
Weathersby et al. (1977), also suggested that a developmental approach
is needed for the evaluation of Title III. It considered four possible
approaches to the evaluation of federal aid programs:

> (1) the structural development of colleges and universi-
> ties; (2) the levels of various collegiate activities such
> as the number of students, faculty, library volumes, or
> terminal degree recipients on the faculty; (3) the relative
> efficiency with which colleges and universities provide in-
> struction and, where appropriate, public service and re-
> search; and (4) the determinants of student demand with a
> special focus on those institutional actions which affect
> individual's college going choices (p. 1).

The first two areas have the most direct implications for this
discussion. While the last two areas of investigation had interesting
findings—that institutions with similar levels of services have wide

variations in the efficiency of their resource use, and that student aid has a greater impact on student attendance than do college character-istics, especially activity indicators—they had the fewest direct im-plications for Title III. Regarding structural development, Weathersby concluded that although alternative sequences of development could be proposed, and that this type of intervention makes the most sense for public policy, existing data sources did not permit the testing of devel-opmental concepts (see Weathersby et al., 1977; also St. John and Weathersby, 1977). Regarding activity indicators, it was found that although these measures may be a useful means of measuring program impact, they do not distinguish well between funded and nonfunded ap-plicant institutions, except for institutions funded in the advanced pro-gram. Even when differences can be identified, funded institutions do not appear to change faster than nonfunded institutions (St. John, Ting-ley, and Gallos, 1977; Weathersby et al., 1977). One conclusion from this investigation was:

> While we attempted to describe what is discernible from existing quantitative data bearing on the four areas of im-portant concern to the Title III program, it has become increasingly clear to us that the most significant data either have not been collected or, if collected, have not been made available coherently. In the area of patterns of institutional development in particular, the available data do not speak at all to the types of measures we have suggested. We believe the measures we have suggested should be pilot tested and refined for a limited number of institutions. If they prove to effectively identify the vari-ous patterns of institutional development experienced by these pilot institutions, a more substantial effort could be mounted to determine the patterns of institutional de-velopment experienced by institutions in general (Weath-ersby et al., 1977, p. 44).

This incremental approach to generating and testing develop-mental theories, it was argued, would have had the greatest possible benefit to Title III and to institutions in general. However, the design of the Weathersby study did not include site visits to institutions, nor did it include gathering data directly from institutions. The research conducted for the study of Title III reported on here has taken the in-cremental approach to the formation of new concepts of institutional development proposed in the Weathersby study.

IMPLICATIONS AND CONCLUSIONS

After 15 years of operation, the Title III program is faced with a myriad of problems. Demands for the program's services are higher than at any point in its history, with many previously unserviced institutions applying for Title III funds at a time when other government agencies are questioning the need for continuation of the program. The arguments used to justify Title III to Congress have caused a set of conflicting expectations: the providers of funds view Title III as a developmental program that should produce a set of developed (or unfunded) institutions, while the eligible institutions often view Title III as an entitlement, an additional source of revenue they merit because of their condition and history. Evaluators of the program, unable to assess Title III's impact due to both the lack of specificity in the program's definitions and regulations, and to an absence of social science theory and knowledge about how colleges develop, have been forced to examine some of the most basic questions about the process of and prospect for change and development in higher education.

One of the apparent contradictions in the administration of the Title III program has been the tendency to fund a rather limited range of development activities, even though the program's rhetoric and regulations specify no single approach. While the literature on Title III, including the application information, has not specified the types of management developments funded institutions should implement, experience shows that some types of management developments have been more likely to be funded than others. A critical concern to the future of Title III will be the recognition that a differentiated approach to the institution-development process will be required in the 1980s. In the past Title III has encouraged institutions to move down an ill-fated path. It has often funded new programs, services, and management systems that institutions may not be able to support when Title III funds run out. Consequently, they keep reapplying for funds. Funding strategies should reflect the fact that different types of institutions have different developmental needs, and that overfunding institution-development efforts can be as dangerous to the future of the institution, and to its prospects for self-sufficiency, as not securing developmental funds.

A critical examination of evaluative research on the Title III program illustrates some of the most pressing problems facing higher education policy. As policy gradually changes to reflect the new conditions in higher education, especially declining enrollment and continued financial stress, new concepts of institutional development will be essential. In the case of Title III, a shift away from the growth-oriented eligibility and funding criteria is only the first step in the redesign of the program. Changes in program regulations and administration also will be necessary.

At present, social science theory and research cannot inform policymakers about how existing higher education policy can be modified to improve the plight of institutions. While there have been some efforts to make broad policy recommendations about how to improve the quality of institutions in this new condition (Carnegie Foundation, 1975), there has been relatively little research on the effects of declining enrollment on the operations and management of colleges and universities. There have been even fewer attempts to identify or propose new development models that can replace the growth model in the policy area. Yet new concepts of development are essential to the design of sound public policy that will retain and improve the quality of institutions during a period of enrollment decline. Research studies on the effects of Title III are among the few scholarly attempts to identify and document new concepts of development.

The challenge facing researchers who are evaluating the effects of college-development programs, or who are attempting to inform the providers of developmental funds about the potential impact of their programs, is to identify the types of developments most likely to be useful in different situations. While the study reported on here was limited to administrative interventions, the same logic can be applied to curricular or student-services reforms as well. It is increasingly apparent that colleges can afford to provide only a limited range of services if they are to remain financially stable. Certainly small- and medium-sized colleges and universities are less likely to have the resources to be comprehensive, both in their student services and academic programs, without pricing themselves beyond the economic means of their clientele. Policy researchers can play an important role in informing policymakers and philanthropists about the viability and possible impacts of their intervention programs.

3

THE MANAGEMENT-DEVELOPMENT MODEL

The effort to create a viable management–intervention model began with an exploration of alternative theories of organizational development and change. At the time this investigation was initiated, it was obvious that enrollment was likely to decline and many colleges were in trouble in spite of more than two decades of growth in finances and enrollment. It also was evident that a new model was needed to replace the growth model in the public–policy arena, and that an increasing emphasis on management was likely in higher education. However, there was no obvious model for policymakers or researchers to use as a guide for research or policy decisions.

This chapter covers the conceptual background of this study. First, alternate theories of college development were considered. Since none of these provided the necessary basis for the proposed research, three alternate developmental theories from the literature on organizational and economic development were considered as a possible starting point for a study of college–management development efforts. One of these was selected and used as a basis of the study of Title III institutions.

ALTERNATIVE THEORIES OF COLLEGE DEVELOPMENT

Despite a sizable literature on the administration and governance of colleges and universities, there have been few systematic treatments of their development patterns. There have been numerous campus histories (see Beach, 1975, for a bibliography), case studies of the development patterns in single institutions or systems, and even some systematic treatments of different historical periods (Jencks and

Riesman, 1968; Veysey, 1965). However, there have been few attempts to articulate the stages most institutions have passed through in their development. Unfortunately, there have been only several attempts to use general institution-development patterns as a basis for comparative research in higher education (Heron and Friesen, 1973; Hodgkinson and Schenkel, 1974).

Heron and Friesen (1973) derived from the literature on organizations a general stage theory (birth, youth, productive, mature) to study the historical development of community colleges in the province of Alberta, Canada. Their model emphasized the increasing structural complexity of institutions as they age and increase in size. Hodgkinson and Schenkel (1974), in a study of Title III-funded institutions discussed in the previous chapter, used Rostow's stages of economic growth and Maslow's (1954) theory of individual need emergence as the basis of an institutional stage model for developing institutions in the United States. In contrast to the model proposed by Heron and Friesen, this latter model is not age or size related; it emphasizes the necessity for an institution to meet basic survival needs in order to increase management effectiveness. Although neither study examines the relationship between management effectiveness and structural development, they both suggest that the developmental approach is potentially useful in institutional planning and public policy.

This chapter considers three alternative perspectives on institutional development in postsecondary education. Although the developmental perspective on organizational growth and evolution of management practices has a long history dating back to Max Weber in the modern era (Bendix, 1960; Weber, 1948), more recent developments in organization theory suggest that a multilevel perspective on development is important. Taken individually, no existing organization-development theory is broad enough to use as the basis of a general model of institutional development in higher education.

The first perspective emphasizes external influences, or institution-environment interaction. Baldridge (1972) has advanced a political-systems perspective of organization change that moves "from an exclusive emphasis on internal features of the organization to a wider view that takes in the influences of the environment" (p. 9). Kaufman (1975), in his evolutionary perspective on the natural history of human organizations, has suggested that environmental factors are the most important influence on the change process in organizations. For higher education, these views suggest that advances in the education industry—shifts in the technology of educational practice and management—can outdate a campus's academic programs and management practices, and thus make shifts in programs and management necessary for survival in the educational marketplace. This view is supported by Baldridge's (1971) study of the changes implemented at

New York University after the City University of New York, the local public, multicampus university, instituted an open-admissions policy. As a result of this study, Baldridge developed his political-systems perspective (Baldridge, 1972).

Theories about qualitative changes in the interpersonal processes of organizations have a slightly longer history (see, for example, McGregor, 1960; Argyris, 1965, 1972; Bennis, 1966; Likert, 1967). They provide the basis for the second perspective. These theorists believe the internal climate of an organization affects the behavior of organization members and vice versa. They argue that more democratic approaches to management are essential and necessary (Bennis, 1966), that more open organizational climates can enhance productivity (Likert, 1967), and that behavioral interventions can improve the work environment (Argyris, 1972; French and Bell, 1973). In addition, in recent years a developmental or staged approach to qualitative changes in the work environment has been developed as well (Lippet and Schmidt, 1967; Torbert, 1974-75). Concerns about changes in the internal environment are especially important in higher education because, as part of the liberal arts tradition, it has long emphasized individual development.

The study of large-scale changes in the growth and death of formal organizations—the basis of the developmental view of administrative decision structures used here—is the third perspective. Katz and Kahn (1966) argue that studying structural and system-level features, in addition to studying changing individual roles and attitudes, is important to the practice of organizational change. In their book The Social Psychology of Organizations, they suggest one of the first stage theories for the structural development of organizations. They maintain that systems pass through three structural stages in their development: primitive system, stable organization, and elaboration of structure (pp. 77-83). Although more complex structural-development models have been proposed since Katz and Kahn presented their system (see, for example, Greiner, 1972; B. R. Scott, 1971), their macrolevel view of organizations has added an important dimension to the systematic study of the development and change processes in human organizations. This level of analysis is especially applicable to higher education, where rapid increases in attendance in recent decades have created numerous structural changes.

In the following pages, three development theories are compared in Table 3.1 and are applied to aspects of the institution-development process in higher education. They fall into the three perspectives described above. Each provides a possible model of development for an intervention program. Table 3.1 compares each theory: its purposes, the assumptions underlying it, the characteristics researchers observe, and the specific aspects of development or change each author

TABLE 3.1

A Comparison of Three Developmental Models

	(Rostow (1960)	Torbert (1974–75)	Greiner (1972)
Stages designation	Traditional society Preconditions for take-off Take-off Maturity High mass consumption	Shared fantasies, investments, determinations, experiments, predefined productivity, openly chosen structure, foundational community, liberating symbols, and disciplines	Creativity, direction, delegation, coordination, collaboration
Assumptions	Historical sequences of national economic growth Economic growth related to technological advancement in national industries	Analogous to Erickson's theory of individual development Qualitative stages of organizational development not related to size	Analogous stages of individual development Internal organizational history determines future
Characteristics observed	Rise in rate of productive investment Development of substantial manufacturing sector(s) Political, social, and institutional framework that exploits expansion	(Education Program) Derived from author's experience as program administrator Descriptive characteristics of each phase based on observed incidents	(Observation of businesses) Age, size, stages of evolution Stages of revolution Growth rate of industry Organization practices Management focus Organization structure Top management style Control system Management reward system
Implications	Shifts in technology and production Political, social, and institutional change Public investments, policies for national industries	Policies and change strategies for organizational members and interventionists Helps individuals move toward greater self-direction and greater collaboration	

40

addresses. First, Rostow's stages of economic growth provide a framework for considering the technological transformation currently taking place in higher education and its implications for the institution-development process. Second, Torbert's stages of organizational development provide a framework for viewing qualitative developments in interpersonal processes within institutions and programs. Finally, Greiner's phase theory for the growth of business organizations provides a framework for viewing the staged development of college and university decision structures and the types of interventions that can facilitate this development. These theories are used here because they have the broadest application to higher education when compared to other developmental theories in each of the three categories.

Although Greiner's theory is the most applicable to the management problems identified in the previous chapter, all three theories can be used as a basis for suggesting a general model of institutional development. The model developed in this book relies primarily on the view of administrative decision structures described in this chapter. However, the research and analysis undertaken to explore the model are based on a broader concept of organization. The following considers the implications of each of the theories for higher education.

Technological Developments

Rostow's theory offers a context from which to view technological transitions in the higher education industry as a whole, and to consider their implications for institutions. In Rostow's model, the transition of national industries, especially agriculture, is critical to national economic development. In a traditional society the majority of the populace works in agriculture. As a society advances through the various stages, an increasingly smaller percentage of the population is employed in a more productive, technologically advanced agricultural industry, and other manufacturing sectors develop. During the transition period, the preconditions-for-take-off stage, changes are both economic and political, with the political changes often being the decisive feature. During this period, "new types of enterprising men come forward—in the private economy, in government or both—willing to mobilize savings to take risks in pursuit of profit and modernization" (Rostow, 1960, pp. 6-7).

The take-off is a period of industrial revolution characterized by a rise in the rate of productive investment, the development of one or more substantial manufacturing sectors, and the creation of a political, social, and institutional framework that supports growth. The drive to maturity is a lengthy period, lasting roughly 60 years, during which the national economy develops. During the age of high mass consumption, the real income of the population increases, there is a shift in population, and skilled and office jobs increase. Writing in 1960, Rostow was able to offer little speculation about the stage beyond high mass consumption, although he suggested the United States was entering a new stage. The shifts now taking place in the education sector may be a critical part of this transition.

Although Rostow's theory has been used as a basis for developmental models of organizational change (Hodgkinson and Schenkel, 1974; B. R. Scott, 1971), it is more appropriately applied to the role of technological change in education. It can be applied to transformations now taking place in higher education in the United States and other developed countries (especially England and Western Europe). The Carnegie Commission (1972) suggested that higher education is moving through its first technological transformation in modern times, which is a technical revolution in educational practice. Ashby (1974), a member of the commission, has described four major transformations in educational practice. The first three—the shift of educational responsibility from the extended family to the church or synagogue, the adoption of the written word, and the advent of printing—took place before the modern era and before the first industrial take-off described by Rostow.

A new institution in Ashby's own country (Great Britain) was the first national institution that incorporated a totally new design in higher education. In five years (between 1969 and 1974) a new higher education system was developed, the British Open University, with a capacity to reach 75,000 people through the use of television and other technologies, including new course material and teaching methods (Perry, 1975). Although a single advancement of similar magnitude has not yet been created in the United States, there are a number of signs that a transition is occurring in higher education. Recent innovations such as the University of Mid-America, a regional university with a televised curriculum located in the Midwest, and the New York Regents' External Degree Program, a nationwide examination, degree-granting program, are adding new options to an already complex and accessible higher education system.

The new technologies have had a significant impact on the methods used in higher education in the United States, and have been part of a larger transformation that is extending higher education beyond the campus (for example, see Vermilye, 1972, 1975). They have played an important role in transforming campus-based education by facilitating new alternatives to traditional classroom methods, including the use of new technologies—videotapes, television, individualized learning methods, and so on—and have been important in increasing off-campus learning options at home and in industry (Cavert, 1975; Cross and Valley, 1974; Gould, 1973; Houle, 1973). In addition, the use of new technologies is now evident in the management of higher education, especially in the development of information systems that are helpful in the management of colleges and universities (Balderston, 1974; Weathersby, 1975).

The combination of changes in instructional and management activities can potentially contribute to both more technologically advanced and more efficiently organized educational systems. Unfortunately, the limited success of different financial measures in higher education makes the efficiency of new practices difficult to evaluate. Balderston (1974) suggests that there is "no convenient and operational test of financial viability to apply directly to the observable accounting picture of an institution [in higher education]" (p. 180). Howard Bowen has made attempts to evaluate the efficiency of traditional and nontraditional approaches to liberal education (Bowen and Douglas, 1975), and also of external degree programs using heavy initial technological investment (Bowen, 1973). Weathersby and Henault (1976) have attempted to assess the cost-effectiveness of experiential-learning programs. In general, however, studies of the efficiency of new and old methods have been limited.

The past decade has witnessed considerable advancement in the technologies available to higher education and the innovations in the types of delivery systems available to students. New educational technologies are being tested; public broadcasting in this country is already a very diversified system, with the capacity to reach 80 percent of the population (Witherspoon, 1974, 1975). Computer technology also has advanced to the point where it can enhance the learning and research process in higher education (Rockart, 1976; Rockart and Scott Morton, 1975; Suppes and Morningstar, 1969). Although available and in many instances tested, the implementation of new technologies has not proceeded as rapidly as it might. One of the problems, according to Rockart and Scott Morton (1976), is financial. They argue that although many environmental factors support further implementation of new technologies in higher education, there are many internal constraints, especially an aging professoriate already threatened with loss of employment opportunities due to declining enrollment.

Since technological change is a gradual process in the higher-education industry as a whole, it has few implications for institutions per se. Table 3.2 illustrates one conceptualization of stages of technological change that has direct institutional implications. Institutions will seldom undergo a stage transformation—from the traditional to electromedia stage, or from the electromedia stage to the cybernetic stage—in one year, or even ten years. Instead, technological change will come from the creation of new institutions or through the addition of new activities at established institutions. According to this scheme, most institutions are now in the traditional stage; some institutions

TABLE 3. 2

Stages of Technological Development

Stage	Focus	Example of Technology
Traditional	Cognitive and affective	Lecture, books, writing paper
Electromedia	Cognitive	Self-paced learning
		CAI (Computer Aided Instruction)
		Programmed learning— automatic testing
		TV with or without feed-back
Cybernetic	Learning how to learn	Data bases
		Methods of inquiry
		Theory/practice principles

Source: St. John and Weathersby (1977).

have started to transform their activities and are entering the electro-media stage; and a few new institutions have established programs in completely new ways, as institutions in the electromedia stages. Examples of this category of institutions include the British Open University and the University of Mid-America. The cybernetic stage remains a possibility. Long-range government and institutional planning should take into account this gradual transition in institutional activities.

This technological transition is not entirely mechanical, however. Even the implementation of new hardwares, such as television and computers, requires the development of softwares, such as learning packages and course material. Perry (1975), vice-president of the British Open University, suggests that the United States has "spent too much on sophisticated hardware and not nearly enough on sophisticated software, namely on producing high quality teaching material" (p. 15). Echoing these same concerns about educational television, Witherspoon (1975) has observed that "we tend not to pay enough attention to the requirements of the program, the software, which is all too often the hard part and, in every case, the most important part" (p. 286).

In spite of the gap between educational hardwares and new softwares, some diverse delivery systems are emerging. Houle (1973) and Gould (1973) have documented the movement toward the nontraditional in higher education. Many traditional campuses have developed new methods for extending their programs off campus, and many new noncampus-based programs, such as the Regents' External Degree Program, have emerged. Along this line there is a growing literature heralding the movement toward the nontraditional, open learning, and external degree networks as the wave of the future (Benson and Hodgkinson, 1974; Gould, 1973; Houle, 1973; King, Moor, and Mundy, 1975; P. Scott, 1975). In addition, the increased connection between work and education is a particularly evident trend (O'Toole, 1973; Mushkin, 1973).

The evolution of more sophisticated delivery systems in post-secondary education also can be viewed developmentally. Table 3.3 presents one conceptualization of the development of delivery systems from traditional campus-based programs, to extended campuses, and finally to independent learning networks. Prior to the middle and late 1960s, most U.S. higher education institutions were traditional campus-based programs. There were a few exceptions such as Antioch and Goddard, which have had off-campus programs for students for decades. Although the University of London's external degree program, a credit-by-examination, worldwide learning network, was in operation during the nineteenth century, the development of learning networks is a recent phenomenon. Like the stages of technological development, these stages of delivery-system development are not

TABLE 3.3

Stages of Delivery System Development

Stage	Focus	Examples
Traditional campus	Learning in single location	Traditional academic programs, residency requirements, learning about external world
Extended campus	Learning on campus and in community	Cooperative programs, internships, part-time programs, off-campus learning centers
Learning network	Learning in multiple locations	Credit for life experience, examination degree programs, televised credit and degree programs, work-education programs

necessarily sequential stages for a single campus or program, although this is a definite possibility and some institutions, such as the Antioch system, have progressed through them.

Technological trends have diverse implications for institutions. The present context is a highly political one, and change may well come through the political process. States are taking a more active role in higher education policy than in the past (Glenny, 1974-75); faculty unionism is increasingly evident (Garbarino, 1972, 1975); there are internal constraints on change (Rockart and Scott Morton, 1975); and there are increasing pressures on administration in a time of declining enrollment (Carnegie Foundation, 1975; Mayhew, 1974). Most innovations are political in one way or another, however, as the history of the British Open University indicates (Perry, 1977; Tunstull, 1974). The combination of technological developments and political changes creates a complex set of forces facing institutions that may help them to devise a more diverse system.

Interpersonal Processes

Torbert's theory of qualitative stages of organizational development provides a perspective from which to view changes in the interpersonal process within higher education institutions and programs. His stages depict qualitative changes in the work climate (or spirit) of an organization or program; they are not focused on changes that occur as size and age change because "changes in size and age do not necessarily generate changes in quality" (p. 1). According to Torbert, most theories of organization assume bureaucracy is an advanced and rational form of organizing. In contrast, his theory places "bureaucracy as a middle stage of organizational development representing a lower form of rationality than three qualitatively distinct later stages" (p. 2). The predefined productivity stage, most often experienced as bureaucracy, is the predominant organizational form in society. The next stage in his organizational scheme, the openly chosen structure, is possibly the next stage for many organizations. Torbert's predefined productivity stage refers to a mode of structuring behavior within organizations that is commonly described as bureaucracy in the literature on organizations (Torbert, 1975-76; see also Bendix, 1960; Bennis, 1966; Likert, 1967; McGregor, 1960).

The openly chosen structure stage in contrast refers to a different, and according to Torbert (1974-75, 1976), more sophisticated mode of structuring interactions within the organization. It places a greater emphasis on individual growth and collaborative interaction and decision making.

The purpose of Torbert's paper was to introduce "a new vision of what organizational growth can mean" (1974-75, p. 25). In this sense, growth means qualitative change rather than increased size. The latter three stages in this theory—openly chosen structure, foundational community, and liberating disciplines—are relatively uncommon in most institutions. These stages place a much greater emphasis on the impact of decisions on the members of organizational programs than is the case with most other organizational theories. Although most organizations experience the stages required to attain predefined productivity or bureaucracy, few ever advance beyond this stage. The rest of this section, and most of Torbert's paper, speculates about how this difficult transition from predefined productivity to openly chosen structures might occur, and what this new stage might look like.

Concerns about the quality of campus decision making have long been important in higher education. For over half a century, the involvement of faculty in the decision process of their institutions has been considered an important, if not critical, issue in the United States. At present it is the norm rather than the exception for colleges and universities to involve faculty in the decision-making process (Jencks and Riesman, 1968; McConnell and Mortimer, 1970). In the past decade, the involvement of students has become a critical concern, and many institutions are experimenting with alternative methods of involving students in the decision processes (Helsabeck, 1975; Hodgkinson, 1971b; McGrath, 1970; St. John and Regan, 1973). Organization-development techniques also have been introduced to campuses as a method of improving both faculty and student involvement. Keeton (1971) has suggested strategies for improving the quality of the university environment by involving administrators, faculty, and students in mutual decision making and collaborative work arrangements. Others have documented the use of organizational design (McKelvey and Kilman, 1975), change-agent teams (Sikes, Schlesinger, and Seashore, 1973), and individual change agents (Jenks, 1973) in attempts to improve the quality of institutional decisions.

The qualitative factors that distinguish an organization in Torbert's openly chosen structure stage from the predefined productivity stage can be considered measures of viability for institutions and programs (see Table 3.4). Accordingly, institutions that examine their relations with external communities and organizations are more advanced. Although it is not a necessary component in Torbert's theory, institutions that involve faculty and students as well as administrators in policy formulation and implementation decisions also are more advanced in that this process can add to their commitment to the institution. When students and faculty feel committed to new programs because of their involvement in them, the program may have a greater impact than one that has a limited investment on the part of those in-

TABLE 3.4

Characteristics of the Stages of Organizational Development

Predefined Productivity

Focus on doing the predefined task;
Viability of product—single criterion of success;
Standards and structures taken for granted (often formalized, institutionalized);
Roles stabilized, job descriptions written;
Effort to quantify results based on defined standards;
Reality conceived of as dichotomous and competitive: success-failure, leader-follower, legitimate-illegitimate, work-play, reasonable-emotional.

Openly Chosen Structure

Shared continual reflection about larger (wider, deeper, more long-term, more abstract) purposes of the organization;
Development of open interpersonal process, with disclosure, support, and confrontation on value-stylistic-emotional issues;
Evaluation of effects of own behavior on others in organization and formative research on effects of organization on environment ("social accounting"); i.e., determining whether abstract purposes are being realized in practice;
Direct facing and resolution of paradoxes: freedom versus control, expert versus participatory decision making, etc.;
Creative, transconventional solutions to conflicts;
Organizational his-story becomes my-story;
Deliberately chosen structure with commitment to it, over time, the structure unique in the experience of the participants or among "similar" organizations;
Primary emphasis on horizontal rather than vertical role differentiation;
Development of symmetrical rather than subordinate relation with "parent" organization;
Gaining of distinctive public repute based on the quality of collective action within the organization.

Source: Torbert (1974-75, pp. 6-7).

dividuals it is supposed to benefit (Hodgkinson, 1971b; McGrath, 1970; Sikes, Schlesinger, and Seashore, 1973). Unfortunately, there are not many models as to how more open systems can be achieved in higher education.

Another aspect of the openly chosen structure stage of organization is an emphasis on interpersonal relations and the development of the individual. In higher education, researchers have long paid attention to the maturation and intellectual growth of student populations (Feldman and Newcomb, 1969), and many institutions consider these factors in developing programs. Designing an educational program flexible enough to meet the needs of individuals at different ages and stages of development has become a more recent concern (Chickering, 1975). There appears to be increasing concern about these same issues as they apply to faculty (Lindquist and Noonan, 1975) and administrators (Weathersby, 1975). Consideration of the implications of institutional plans for the development of individuals in the institutions—whether through educational programs for students or staff development for faculty and administrators—may be an increasingly important measure of development for institutions and programs in the future.

There have been a few exploratory attempts to evaluate openness in administration (Argyris, 1962, 1965, 1974; Likert, 1967), although not in higher education. The Higher Education Management Institute (1976) is currently adapting Likert's work to higher education, but this is still at an experimental stage. When evaluating a college's plan or proposal, there are no proven methods of evaluating the openness of the administration, the degree of faculty and student commitment to institutional programs, or the contribution of programs to individual development. Judgments by experts in the field and opinion polls are perhaps the best, and definitely the most common, methods of evaluating quality or excellence in higher education.

Decision Structures

Greiner's theory provides a framework for viewing the phased development of college and university decision structures. Greiner suggests a developmental model with five predictable phases through which organizations pass in their development:

Phase 1: Creativity
In the birth stage of an organization, the emphasis is on creating both a product and a market.
Phase 2: Direction
The companies that survive the first phase by installing a capable business manager usually embark on a period of sustained growth under able and directive leadership.

Phase 3: Delegation
The next era evolves from the successful application of a
decentralized organization structure.

Phase 4: Coordination
During this phase, the evolutionary period is characterized
by the use of formal systems for achieving greater coordination and by top executives taking responsibility for the
initiation and administration of their new systems.

Phase 5: Collaboration
The last observable phase in previous studies emphasizes
strong interpersonal collaboration in an attempt to overcome the red-tape crisis. Where Phase 4 managed more
through formal systems and procedures, Phase 5 emphasizes greater spontaneity in management action through
teams and the skillful confrontation of interpersonal differences (pp. 41-44).

According to Greiner, there is a crisis between each evolutionary phase: a leadership crisis between the creativity and direction
phases; an autonomy crisis between direction and delegation; a control crisis between delegation and coordination; and a red-tape crisis
between coordination and collaboration. He also suggests that organizations require a period of evolution (prolonged periods of growth)
when in the midst of any phase, and a revolution (a period of substantial turmoil in organizational life) when passing between phases.

Greiner's theory was derived from the observation of business
organizations, and his suggestions relate primarily to these management and decision structures. It is based in part on a study of industrial organizations conducted by Albert Chandler (1962). Greiner con-
tends "that the future of the organizations may be determined less by
outside forces than it is by the organization's history" (p. 38). His
perspective is derived from the legacies of European psychologists
who suggest "individual behavior is determined primarily by previous
events and experience" (p. 38). His model is based on numerous case
studies in which he observed changes in the following characteristics:
age, size, previous stages of evolution, previous stages of revolution,
and growth rate of the industry.

These characteristics have been the subject of research in higher
education and appear to be interrelated. An institution's age has been
shown to be related to increased structural complexity (Heron and
Friesen, 1973), and is considered to be related to an institution's
ability to adapt to changes in the growth rate (Carnegie Foundation,
1975). Increased size has been shown to be related to increased structural complexity and increased faculty autonomy (Baldridge et al. ,
1973; Platt and Parsons, 1970); to greater program flexibility and the

availability of funds to start new programs (Holdaway et al. , 1975); and to shifts in presidents' images of their role as leaders (Cohen and March, 1974). Institutional case studies have shown that sudden downward shifts in the growth rate can cause an organizational crisis (Baldridge, 1971; Millet, 1976); that institutional conflict can result from sustained periods of growth (Smelser, 1974); and that once rapid structural changes or responses are made to a crisis situation, there appear to be relatively long periods during which the new systems develop and mature (McConnell and Mortimer, 1970). These findings suggest that the variables Greiner considered important in determining evolutionary and revolutionary phases are interrelated factors that change as colleges and universities develop structurally.

In Greiner's view, an organization's history has important implications for its future, especially in the recognition of the limited range of solutions to growth-related crises at different points in an organization's history. A crisis stage can be ended only by certain specific solutions. Weathersby (1975) has elaborated on the implications of Greiner's theory for higher education. Changes in organizational phase may be characterized by transformations in the structure of the decision-making process. He used the institutional decision-making schema shown in Figure 3.1 as a basis to propose and describe the evolution of decision structures that accompany each new phase. The three rectangles shown in Figure 3.1 represent the three decision relevant roles of administration:

> formulation of policy options, actual decisions and implementation. These decision roles can be assumed by one individual, or they can be differentiated in a very complex pattern of delegated authority and responsibility, or they can be shared in a loosely structured, fluid, collegial structure, or they can be reorganized weekly—but these three roles must be included in some manner in the organization (p. 59).

Adapting Greiner's model, Weathersby has described the sequential development of institutional administrative decision structures as follows:

Phase 1 (creative) organizations combine the policy formulation decision and implementation roles and informally share these roles among the small group of colleagues. While individuals may have functional specialties, they are not formally structured. Communication is direct, personal, informal, and frequent. The conception-decision-action-evaluation-reconception process is constant and unstructured, occurring over lunch, in the car on the way to a meeting, in the store-

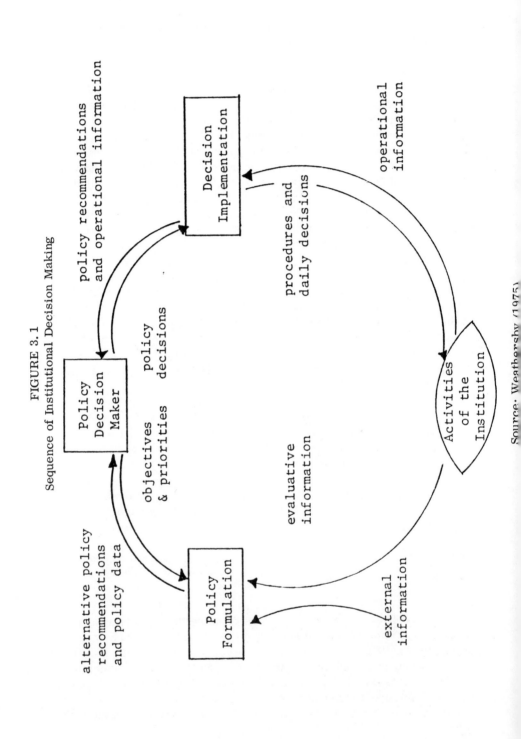

FIGURE 3.1
Sequence of Institutional Decision Making

Policy Decision Maker

Decision Implementation

Policy Formulation

Activities of the Institution

policy recommendations and operational information

objectives & priorities

policy decisions

alternative policy recommendations and policy data

procedures and daily decisions

operational information

evaluative information

external information

Source: Weathersby (1975)

52

FIGURE 3.2

Phase 1 Decision Structure

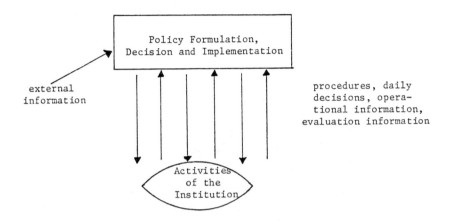

Source: Weathersby (1975).

front, or wherever. For phase I organizations, the decision structure is very simple and is shown in Figure 3.2.

Phase 2 (direction) organizations are functionally organized; communication is formal and structured; authority usually is hierarchial and the decision structure looks like Figure 3.3.

With the operational information filtered through functional managers, top policymakers become increasingly remote and detached from daily activities and increasingly dependent upon implementors for both data and policy recommendations. It is understandable how a crisis of autonomy results from this structure.

Phase 3 (delegation) organizations deal with the autonomy crisis by differentiating the policy-implementation structure both horizontally (more specialists) and vertically (more decentralization of authority and responsibility). The resulting decision structure is shown in Figure 3.4. This graphically visible fragmentation of implementation suggests why the crisis of control usually results from this organizational phase.

Phase 4 (coordination) organizations attempt to cut through the mass of overlapping and conflicting functions, procedures, activities, and policy recommendations by consolidating implementation units (more powerful vice-presidents or provosts) and by establishing a

FIGURE 3.3

Phase 2 Decision Structure

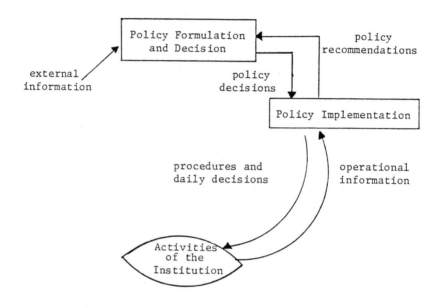

Source: Weathersby (1975).

separate evaluation, planning, and/or analysis function (see Figure 3.5). To be effective, this separate policy-formulation function must obtain evaluative information about the activities of the institution and about external realities, and must interact with the ultimate deciders (president, board of trustees, state legislature, governor, or whomever) to make objectives and priorities explicit (at least in-house) and to propose and evaluate alternatives. This process of evaluation-analysis of alternatives-policy, recommendations-decision, implementation-evaluation becomes increasingly formalized, complex, time-consuming, and expensive. Institutions, and particularly state systems, are becoming large bureaucracies heading almost inexorably toward procedural strangulation: the crisis of red tape.

  Phase 5 (collaboration) organizations merge the policy formulation and implementation roles into one that is shared by teams of multi-functional specialists organized around particular problem foci. Top management is involved primarily in general direction setting, assignment of individuals to multidisciplinary teams, resource acquisition, coordination feedback (see Figure 3.6). (Weathersby, 1975, pp. 59-65—modified slightly from the original.)

In addition, Weathersby suggests there is a relationship between the organizational phase and the most appropriate type of information or inquiring system. An inquiring system refers to data base—personal knowledge, computerized information, and so on—used for management decisions. Table 3.5 relates the most appropriate type of inquiring system for each organizational phase. In phase I organizations, "information is essentially personal, possibly dialectical, but certainly multiple theories and alternative options are freely considered. Meaningful information is both personally collected and synthesized" (p. 68). In the second phase, transactions become more "monitored and classes of data collected to insure some control in functional specialities. Accounting payroll and student records become more important even if ledger entries are done by hand" (p. 68). Phase 3 organizations need to compile more detailed transaction data and "more complicated management accounting and control procedures are used" (p. 70). Organi-

FIGURE 3.4

Phase 3 Decision Structure

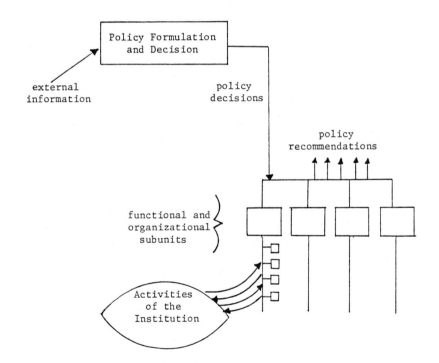

Source: Weathersby (1975).

FIGURE 3.5

Phase 4 Decision Structure

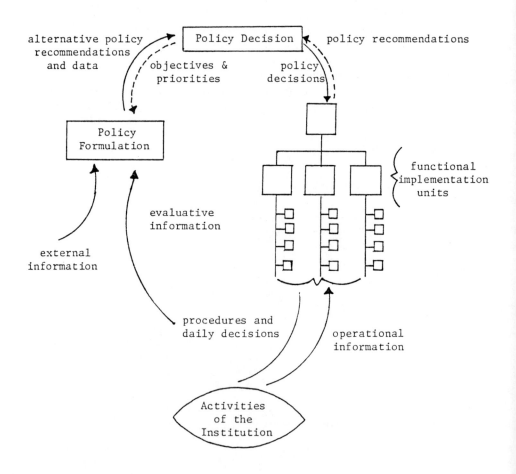

TABLE 3.5

Relationship between Organizational Phase and Type of Inquiring System

Organizational Phase	Types of Data	Type of Inquiring System
Creation	Personal observation, experience direct feedback	Informal, interpersonal, judgmental, synthesis, consensual
Direction	Add: Functional transactions (accounting, student records)	Add: Standard format reports of transactions; functional budgets; annual reports; some computerization
Delegation	Add: More detailed transaction data by operating unit, sources and uses of resources	Add: Unit cost analysis; seeking comparative data on costs, workload, and performance data; computers required
Coordination	Add: Standardized data elements	Add: Objectives expressed as programs, PPBS attempted; simulation models to evaluate alternatives; program cost analysis; regular data exchange; extensive computerization
Collaboration	Add: Personal feedback, process feedback	Add: Flexible output formats

Add: Means the listed characteristics are in addition to the characteristics listed above in the same column.
Source: Adapted from Weathersby (1975).

FIGURE 3. 6

Phase 5 Decision Structure

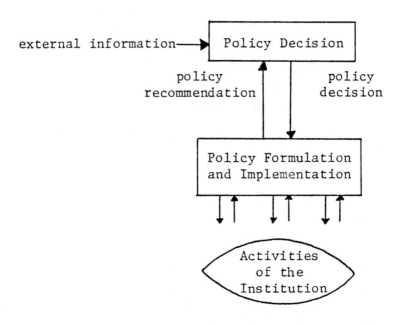

Source: Weathersby (1975).

zations in the fourth phase "need information to examine alternative decisions much more carefully than previous phases and they demand an explicit objective, analysis of consequences of decisions, program budgeting and costing" (p. 70). Weathersby concluded that since there is little evidence of phase 5 organizations in higher education, the type of information system they would require is a matter of speculation.

Measures of Development

The multileveled view of institutional development presented here can be used to suggest ways of implementing existing measures of institutional change to evaluate different aspects of the development process. Table 3. 6 differentiates among the three types of development discussed and suggests the measures that can be used for each.

The first set of measures relates to the technological development of the institution. "Technological" is used in its broadest sense here. It refers to the relative degree of sophistication and efficiency

TABLE 3.6

Measures of Institutional Development in Postsecondary Education

Development	Dimensions	Measures
Technological (institutional characteristics and viability)	Technological characteristics Softwares	Institutional characteristics, capital investment Types of programs and services, proportion of spending on softwares
	Hardwares	Types of technologies, proportions of instruction budget spent on technological aids
	Program efficiency	Labor productivity, cost-effectiveness (efficient surface) Percent of staff in teaching
Interpersonal processes (assessment of openness of the decision process and the impact of the programs on students)	System openness	Decision analysis, qualitative stage determination, degree of participation
	Program impact	Individual change, individual commitment to institution and program, comparison of student and institutional goals
Structural development (developmental phase of institutions based on internal history and observable characteristics)	Organizational phase	Match of organizational pattern and developmental phase, case histories
	Management effectiveness	Complexity measures, differentiation of staff, percent overhead

59

of institutional activities, and includes both traditional and nontraditional teaching, student service, and management activities. The first dimension relates to observable characteristics of the institution. Measures of development at the institutional level will include quantitative measures such as enrollment, number of faculty, faculty with doctorates, faculty salaries, library volumes, and so forth. In light of the discussion of technological change in this section, the technological characteristics have been further broken down into two categories: hardware and software. Software includes development in instructional programs—say, of basic skills programs, individualized instruction programs, work experience programs, and assessment of prior experience. Hardware refers to the use of equipment (such as television, video, and computers) in the instructional delivery process. The second dimension of technological development refers to measures of efficiency for institutions and institutional programs.

The second set of measures relates to the qualitative development of the institution and its programs, and to the openness of the system and its impact on individuals in the institution. Subjective judgments by students and professionals (opinion surveys) and measures of individual change can be used to evaluate program impact, while decision analysis and analysis of the governance process (participation in policy making and implementation) can be used to evaluate openness. Qualitative changes are the most difficult of the three levels of development to suggest objective measures that are useful in evaluation, but they are important nevertheless.

The third set of measures relates to the phase of structural development of the institution and effectiveness of the management system. The first dimension, a determination of phase, can best be assessed either through case histories or by matching organizational patterns with developmental phase. The second dimension is related to the effectiveness of the management system, a phenomenon that is difficult to measure in higher education.

These three perspectives suggest that developmental changes in an institution's technologies, interpersonal systems, and decision structure are interdependent and yet independent. Institutions that are more advanced in their technologies, delivery systems, or interpersonal processes have the same sequences of structural development to contend with as institutions that are correspondingly less advanced. The implementation of new technologies, such as televised or computerized instruction, has an obvious impact on interpersonal processes since the amount of human contact can be changed by their implementation; however, it does not necessarily have to take away from the quality of interpersonal interactions or orientation of an educational system toward the maximum realization of human potentials. At the institutional level, the interrelationships between these factors need to be taken into account when any type of change is being considered. For the public-policy decisions, an intervention model that incorporates all three aspects of development—technological, interpersonal, and structural—is desirable. However, the testing of these theories and their application to higher education probably should progress incrementally.

One of these perspectives, the development of administrative decision structures, has the most possibilities for management interventions. The development of an appropriate management process, information system, and leadership style for a given campus is a necessity for institutional self-sufficiency and for survival in these troubled times. A developmental view of institutional decision structures suggests that no single management process, information system, or top leadership style is most appropriate for all institutions, or for the entire history of any single institution. To be useful to planners, however, the structural-development theory needs further investigation and elaboration.

TOWARD A GENERAL MODEL

Because of the diversity of institutions—in terms of their structures, missions, technologies, students, and management histories—no single management solution will work for all institutions. Of the three theories of institutional development already considered, the structural-development paradigm offers the most possibilities for a model that can distinguish between institutions with different management needs. The remainder of this chapter outlines a general model of structural development and management effectiveness. However, before discussion this general model of institutional development, some of the important cautions about the application of developmental theories in general and of this theory in particular will be mentioned.

First, development theories do not suggest a cookbook approach to solving institutional problems and do not provide specific solutions for each crisis. Instead, most developmental theorists view all organizations as unique in one way or another. These theorists do suggest that there are predictable types of problems facing all organizations as a result of their history. Sarason (1972) addresses this problem when discussing the development of new, creative organizations: "The fact that things develop in a certain way is not synonymous with the statement that things must develop in a certain way, as if nothing can stop or alter the process" (p. 69). For research on the structural development of colleges, this first caution suggests that it is possible to formulate a general sequence that predicts crises of a general nature, although there may be a variety of particular solutions for a given organization at a given point in time.

A second caveat when applying a theory of structural development such as the Greiner-Weathersby model is that most of these theories are growth related. Greiner's theory (1972) does suggest phases of development that are related to organizational growth, and that changes in management practice are tied to structural changes that result from organizational growth. Even though higher education is entering a slow- or no-growth era, this theory is still applicable because institutional management is now a more important issue in higher education than it has been in the past. A theory that actually suggests the general types of management practice that may be appropriate for different institutions is potentially useful. This theory not only can be used to suggest the next predictable crisis, but it also can be used to suggest the appropriate type of management—although not the specific practices—for institutions in a given phase of development. In this application of the Greiner model, future growth is less important than finding ways of attaining congruence between an institution's phase of structural development and its management system.

Third, few structural-development theories are specific to higher education institutions. In the case of Greiner's theory, it is based on the study of business organizations. Although there is some evidence to suggest there are similarities between business organizations and education organizations (Balderston, 1974; Hodgkinson, 1971c; Likert and Likert, 1976), education organizations are subject to different pressures and their characteristics are considerably different. Weathersby's (1975) application of Greiner's theory, discussed in depth in the previous chapter, is used as the conceptual model for this investigation. The general sequence, as applied to higher education, seems to depict accurately the development of colleges described in the historical literature. The model will have to be modified to depict the actual management development needed by higher education institutions. For example, Greiner suggests that a directive management style is required for success in the second phase, a style of management that probably would not work in higher education due to the historical autonomy of faculty. Nevertheless, a new college entering the second phase of development does need an individual with the authority to make key decisions and to speak for the institution in crisis situations.

Finally, most developmental theories use a narrow organizational paradigm. Greiner's theory relates specifically to the structure and management of organizations and does not necessarily take into account the technological and interpersonal factors raised in the other theories discussed in the previous chapter. It also does not directly take into account influences from the external environment. In higher education, the external environment is probably the most pervasive influence facing the development of colleges. When applying a theory of structural development to colleges, it should be done from a broad concept of organization that accounts for these other influences. The research framework outlined in Chapter 4 addresses this issue.

The Model Reconsidered

The basic model used here is an adaptation of the Greiner-Weathersby theory of structural development. The model focuses on the relationship between changes in the structural characteristics of institutions and corresponding changes in management needs. The research framework takes into account other aspects of the institution-development process, such as changes in technologies and interpersonal processes, although its primary focus is on this relationship. The model suggests a dynamic relationship among a college's administrative structure, management system, and predominant managerial crisis. This relationship is illustrated in Table 3.7. Accordingly, the developmental phases can be described as follows.

During the initial information period, a college is planned, the staff is hired, and the student market is developed. A defined administrative structure has not yet emerged and decisions usually are made informally. It is possible for an institution to remain in this phase of development for a long period, especially if it remains relatively small and no external pressures force it to develop a more defined administrative structure and a long-range planning capacity. Most institutions, however, progress beyond this phase rather rapidly.

Is a college is successful in implementing academic programs and securing students, it may become necessary for someone to speak for the organization and to take responsibility for development of new programs and the maintenance of existing programs. Such an organization must install a defined administrative structure with the ability to maintain existing programs and to develop a long-range planning capacity.

For colleges that successfully install formal administrative structures and continue to grow, perhaps through the addition of new programs, a crisis of autonomy will result. During this period, members of the organization will demand more responsibility in their areas of expertise, and the administration will need to develop a system to insure accountability. A more functionally differentiated administrative structure and delegated management system are needed. In a phase III structure, authority for many operational decisions, both academic and administrative, is delegated from a few top administrators to a larger number of individuals in key positions throughout the organization.

TABLE 3.7

Phases of Structural Development and Corresponding Management Systems

Phase	Administrative Structure	Management System	Crisis
I Creation	Formation of new college, small administrative staff and faculty, student market developed	Informal collaborative management system, decisions made informally	Leadership crises: need for more defined authority structure
II Direction	Centralized administrative structure develops for administrative and academic decisions, functional subunits (departments, colleges, etc.) emerge	A few key individuals take responsibility for most systemwide decisions and for initiating new programs	Autonomy crises: members of organizational subunits need more authority
III Delegation	A differentiated organizational structure emerges with delegation of decision authority to numerous functional subunits	Delegated management system emerges, functional subunits responsible for management in particular areas	Control crises: lack of policy and procedure coordination
IV Coordina- tion	A more complex organizational structure, systemwide administrative service units; policy formulation becomes separate function	Systemwide administration becomes more active, policies and procedures more regularized across functional subunits, policy formulation becomes a separate systemwide activity	Red-tape crises: conflict over regulations and procedures
V Collabor- ation	An integrated or matrix structure emerges, integration of systemwide administrative and functional subunits	A more collaborative approach to policy formulation and implementation, systemwide administration and functional subunits representatives work in teams on policy formulation and implementation	Unknown

Sources: Adapted from Greiner (1972) and St. John and Weathersby (1977).

Colleges that continue to grow in the delegated phase, perhaps through the addition of new schools at an existing campus or through adding campuses to a multicampus system, may face a coordination crisis. These institutions need a centralized planning and research capacity to coordinate the various organizational subunits. Many services offered in individual functional subunits also can be handled more efficiently through centralized units for administration and student and academic services.

Institutions that successfully grow in a coordinated phase may face a red-tape or political crisis. In the next phase, which is still largely conjecture in higher education, procedures would be established, perhaps through matrix management or the use of task groups, which would allow members of functional subunits and central administrative units to collaborate on new projects. For example, rather than develop a new statewide external degree program in a particular state, existing institutions might collaborate on a method of accomplishing this objective by using existing personnel and facilities. This would entail less additional financial expenditure than the development of an entirely new system.

When continued growth is likely, most institutions could expect to develop structurally. In a nongrowth era, however, this model is particularly useful in distinguishing between campuses with different management needs. It suggests that an effectively managed institution would have a management system compatible with its phase of structural development.

Potentially, an external intervention program such as Title III could use a model of this nature as a basis for assisting institutions in the development process by helping them attain a balance between their phase of structural development and their management systems. Some campuses will need more sophisticated management systems while others, perhaps those adjusting to declining enrollment and program retrenchment, will need to streamline their existing administrative structures and perhaps simplify their management systems.

The purposes of the institutional case studies are to explore the institution-development model and to consider its relevance for public and institutional policy. There are numerous state, federal, and private (philanthropic, nonprofit, and profit) programs now under way that are designed as interventions to improve campus management. To be relevant to public policy, an institution-development model should consider the types of intervention strategies that are useful for institutions facing particular sets of organizational problems. Management effectiveness and intervention effectiveness are most appropriately considered within the context of the institution, rather than being considered solely from a predefined set of policy objectives. If the objectives of the intervention have no relevance to the institution's management needs, then the intervention is likely to fail.

The general model used in this study assumes an interaction among the formal structure of a college, its management system, and the external environment. Actually, the institution-development process is a dynamic one that is difficult to separate into distinct phases. Nevertheless, a developmental scheme, even a tentative one, is a desirable framework for external interventions. If developed adequately, such a framework can provide a general guide for planning institution-development strategies.

The structural development of colleges can be viewed as a continuum from the undeveloped to the higher developed. When compared with each other, colleges' formal structures will fall in different places along a continuum. The five-phase model described in this chapter provides one conceptual map for distinguishing between colleges with different structures, or for categorizing institutions into different places along this continuum. This model also assumes that as colleges develop structurally and become more complex, their management needs increase. Figure 3.7 presents one scheme for plotting the relationship between management needs and structural development. To be effectively managed, a college must attain a balance between its relative place on the structural-development continuum, or its development phase, and the type of management systems it uses. This schema helps explain why a management system that is effective at one point in the life of an organization is not effective at another point: as an institution develops structurally, its management needs increase.

Environmental factors have a significant influence on the structural development of colleges. Structural development can be viewed as a combination of increasing size and increasing complexity. As an institution grows, it will eventually need to install a more sophisticated organizational structure. External factors can force a college to install a new structure in order to be more efficient; they can also force it to stay the same in spite of a need for change. For public institutions, new structural developments might be the result of actions taken by state legislators; for private institutions, it might be an internal response to increasing financial problems. According to this general model, an institution may experience growth in one phase until it becomes too inefficient or outdated. When this occurs it will have to install a new structure and, therefore, will experience additional management needs.

In practice this relationship is not always clear-cut; there are exceptions, especially where colleges have not faced external pressures to change. Harvard University is an example of an institution that has grown in size during the past several decades but has not faced pressure to install a more complex organizational structure. Harvard enjoys large endowments and high demands for its services,

FIGURE 3. 7

Structural Development and Management Effectiveness

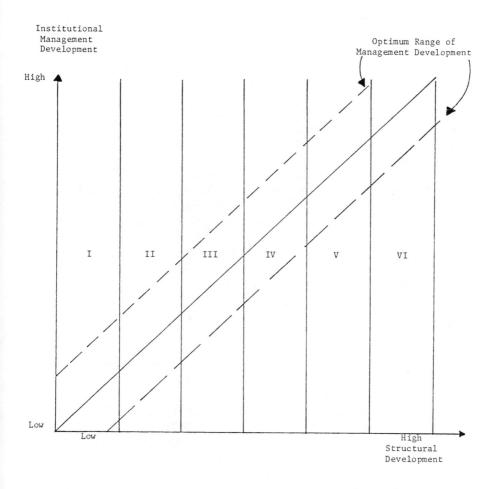

and therefore has not been as subject as most colleges to the few incentives to be efficient. Its structure is in some ways analogous to a dinosaur in the modern era: it is an organization that seems too large to successfully operate with its delegated structure in a time of financial stress. Although Harvard has added new schools and institutes, its organizing philosophy of each tub on its own bottom has not changed. It operates successfully as a highly delegated structure with little coordination among colleges, schools, and institutes. In practice not many colleges enjoy the financial success of Harvard, and therefore most institutions that have become as complex as Harvard have installed more coordinated structures. Baldridge's (1971) study of New York University, another large-complex private institution, documents the transition to a coordinated structure. Two of the colleges used as case studies, North Carolina A & T and Valencia Community College, are responding to the need for increased coordination.

Historically, there have been fewer incentives for colleges to develop effective management systems than there have been for them to develop structurally. Structural innovations—the development of graduate programs, research capacities, multicollege universities, and multicampus systems—have been widely accepted and readily adapted because these allow for increased growth. There have been fewer incentives for institutions to develop management systems that are compatible with the structures that have evolved. As a result, most colleges have operated below their optimum management capacity.

The developmental approach can provide a framework for external interventions designed to improve the effectiveness of college- and university-management systems. Rather than assert one prototype of an effectively managed institution, something that is too often the case due to a poor understanding of institutional dynamics, the developmental approach assumes different plateaus of management effectiveness are appropriate for institutions in different developmental phases. This relationship is illustrated in Figure 3. 8. Plateau X represents the state of the art in management-system development. It is easy to understand why external funding agencies might assume that all institutions should develop to this point. Although it may be true that phase V institutions need the most sophisticated management techniques, these same techniques may be grossly inappropriate for institutions in prior developmental phases. The concomitant to reduced growth is that increased structural development is also less likely. Thus Plateau X is probably far more sophisticated than most institutions will ever need.

A developmental framework for external interventions would set expectations that are relative to the structure and capacity of the institution. Figure 3. 8 illustrates these relationships: Plateau A is more appropriate for phase I organizations, Plateau B for phase II organiza-

FIGURE 3. 8

Model for External Interventions

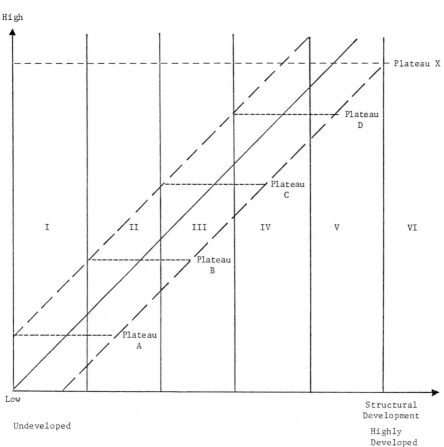

Institutional
Management
Needs

High

Plateau X

Plateau
D

Plateau
C

I   II   III   IV   V   VI

Plateau
B

Plateau
A

Low

Structural
Development

Undeveloped

Highly
Developed

tions, and so forth. If the developmental approach is taken seriously, measures and methods for determining developmental phases and the appropriate types of management systems for institutions in different phases are needed.

A three-level approach is used for the analysis of the case studies. First, institutional profiles are analyzed to determine if a general sequence of structural development can be identified. Second, the relationship between the structural development and management needs and effectiveness is analyzed. Finally, the types of development and intervention strategies that appear most useful for institutions in different developmental phases are considered.

In the analysis of structural development, the primary concerns are whether or not a general sequence of development can be constructed, and if so, whether a set of measures can be used to identify these phases. This relies on the structural histories and descriptions of the current structural development at the case institutions. Generalizations about structural-development patterns take into account variations in other institutional subsystems, including technological developments and interpersonal systems, in addition to variations in structures. Determination of a structural sequence and identification of variables to identify developmental phases are closely related tasks.

The second level of analysis is the consideration of the relationship between structural development and management effectiveness. This involves a comparison of the management systems used by institutions in each developmental phase. Similarities and differences between the management systems of institutions in each phase are used to explore both the nature and impact of structural development on institutional management needs. For instance, based on the proposed model at the start of this chapter, it can be hypothesized that an institution in a phase I–phase II transition would need to develop a long-range planning capacity; an institution in a phase II–phase III transition would need to maintain and improve its planning capacity, and also would need to develop standardized administrative procedures and a method of decentralizing goal setting and program management; and an institution in a phase III–phase IV transition would need to develop a capacity to coordinate a diversified organization structure in addition to the management practices already mentioned. In Chapter 6 these basic relationships are examined by comparing institutions in different developmental phases.

The third level of analysis assesses the impact of management interventions on the case institutions to determine if a systematic approach to management intervention is feasible in higher education. The institutions studied are funded in the advanced program of the developing institutions program, which has a standard set of management practices each funded institution must include in its proposal.

These include a planning, management, evaluation system (PME), management information system (MIS), and transactional information system (TIS). If the developmental model outlined here proves accurate, it might help explain why some practices work better in certain institutions than in others. For example, the planning component of the PME might be most relevant to an institution making a phase I–phase II transition, while the TIS might be most relevant to the needs of a campus making a phase III–phase IV transition. While the former institution would be developing its first long-range planning capacity and thus be able to make use of a formal planning procedure, the latter institution would be able to use a standardized information system in its efforts to develop a more coordinated management system.

One does not have to follow the developmental logic too far to realize that standardized interventions (the development of a particular set of management practices at all institutions) may not be the most appropriate policy for a government- or foundation-funded intervention program designed to improve management effectiveness. Although initially it might make perfect sense to encourage all institutions to develop the most sophisticated management techniques, on closer examination these techniques may not be needed by most campuses and could even be a hindrance to a campus left to support these practices financially after the completion of an intervention program. The most typical problem of this type is the assumption that all institutions need coordinated computerized information systems. These information needs will be greatest at institutions requiring coordinated management. At a smaller campus these practices may not be needed.

Since the early 1960s, the federal government has initiated funding programs designed to facilitate the development and change of social institutions: public schools, cities, and colleges. It is easy to judge these programs, such as model cities or the developing institutions programs, as failures when policy objectives have not been met or when federal funds appear to be poorly used. Intervention programs should take into account the types of changes likely to be successful for institutions with particular characteristics. This is an effort to develop a model that accounts for institutional differences in the design of interventions.

4

THE STUDY OF EXEMPLARY
TITLE III INSTITUTIONS

The study of exemplary Title III institutions started in 1975 with the initial concept development described in the previous chapter and an effort to use existing data bases to assess the effects of Title III. In the early stages of the initial study it became apparent that existing data bases were not adequate to test a new developmental theory. At that time efforts began to identify a conceptual framework to guide a study that could test such a theory. Once this framework developed and funding was secured from the U. S. Office of Education to conduct a pilot study, several institutions were selected for in-depth study. Using standard case-study methodologies, case studies were developed and analyzed to test the developmental model. Finally, in summer 1980 a follow-up study was conducted to assess the long-term impact of AIDP funds on the institution-development efforts at the selected institutions. This chapter describes the study of exemplary Title III institutions. It discusses the conceptual framework used to develop the case studies, the characteristics and selection of the case institutions, and the research methodologies used in this study.

CONCEPTUAL FRAMEWORK

The research design used to test a developmental model was both comparative and historical. The historical dimension was used to view the evolution of each organization, its subsystems, and inter-actions with the external environment. The comparative approach was "based on the empirical study of management activities in two or more firms in an effort to develop guides for predicting what will work reasonably well in comparable situations" (Massie, 1965, p. 415). Some of the most noted studies of management practices in industrial organizations have used a comparative historical approach (see, for example, Chandler, 1962; Dale, 1960).

To test this particular model of institutional development, case studies were developed along five dimensions: the overall state of development of the organization; its structural history; its current phase of structural development; the development of its management system; and the effectiveness of its management. An elaboration of these dimensions follows.

State of Development

The structure and management of an organization should be considered in the context of the state of development of the organization as a whole. The diversity of higher education institutions is considerable, and structural complexity or development is just one continuum along which these organizations and their development vary. To consider the state of development of the system as a whole, a researcher must examine the various components or subsystems of the organization. In this study, the basic organizational model used is illustrated in Figure 4.1. According to this model, each organization can be defined and described in terms of its subsystems: technologies, environment, mission, administrative structure, and groups and individuals. For higher education institutions, these can be defined as follows:

Environment: Colleges are subject to local, state, and national influences. The overall condition of higher education in the

FIGURE 4.1

Organizational Subsystems

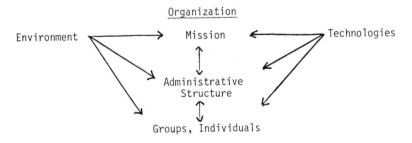

Sources: Adapted from Udy (1965) and Baldridge and Deal (1975).

United States (the subject of Chapter 2) influences all colleges. In addition, other external factors influence colleges: states support public and private higher education in diverse ways; changes in local economies affect colleges; and the growth rate of surrounding communities affects the demand for institutional services.

Technologies: Every organization has a technology for carrying out its work activities. In higher education, instruction, research, and community services are usually the primary activities of the organization. Although most colleges use traditional technologies in their activities, especially in instruction, there have been many innovations in these areas in the past decade. In addition, colleges are subject to shifts in external technologies that can create the need for new or different types of educated personnel.

Mission: The goals or mission of an organization affects its relationship with external constituencies and technologies, as well as its internal activities. Higher education institutions have diverse missions: liberal arts, technical education, professional education, preparatory education, and so on. A campus can define its mission as all, one, or some of these, and the future prospects of a college will vary according to its mission.

Administrative Structure: This is the formal organizational structure of the institution. In higher education organizations this refers to the formal functional differentiation of instruction, research, and service activities into colleges, departments, and institutes as well as to centralized administrative subunits.

Groups, Individuals: In higher education, groups and individuals include students, faculty, administrators, staff trustees, and external constituents. The interactions among and between these groups are the essence of the functioning of a college.

Case studies designed to test the general model of institutional development took these various aspects of the total state of development into account, and therefore did not focus entirely on structure and management. They included the general descriptions of these subsystems, and this total organizational context was considered in subsequent analyses.

Structural History

Documenting the structural history of case institutions is essential to the application and testing of the institution–development model.

The five factors Greiner proposes to identify the developmental phase of industrial organizations are history related: age, size, previous evolutionary periods, previous revolutionary periods, and the growth rate of the industry. It is Greiner's view that "the future of an organization may be less determined by outside forces than by the organization's history" (1972, p. 38). A comparison of previous periods of prolonged, gradual growth, periods of rapid change, and accompanying structural and management changes for several colleges was necessary to identify a general sequence of development.

To the extent possible, the structural history of case institutions was documented. At the very least, this included the milestones in the structural development of the institutions. When possible it also included the addition of new academic programs, colleges, and campuses, as well as the development and reorganization of formal administrative units and functions.

Administrative Structure

The identification of developmental phases requires an in-depth examination of the formal structure of the organization. In addition to a functionally differentiated academic structure there is, on most campuses, an administrative structure that is functionally subdivided into areas such as student services, budget and finance, development, physical plant, and so on. The operation and management of the entire organization is considered in the case studies. The various components of the organizations are described. In the analysis small campuses were compared to subunits of larger organizations to explore further the implications of the model.

Management System

Traditional management theory has "generally included the formal structure of organization and process of general management (Massie, 1965, p. 387). Technically, management can be described as a process of coordinating the various organizational subsystems (technologies, structure, individuals, and so on). In higher education, formal management per se has not received much attention until recently, although the more general process of governance has been the subject of considerable dialogue. Both considerations, formal management and informal governance processes, are important when trying to describe higher education management systems.

Formal management practices include planning, management, and evaluation systems, computerized information systems, and various other budgeting, financing, and costing mechanisms. In the past ten years many colleges that have not previously done so have begun to approach institutional management in a more systematic way. This typically includes the implementation of formal planning and budgeting techniques and the computerization of existing information sources to make them more readily available to decisionmakers. Formal management also includes the implementation of formalized policies and procedures for complex institutions lacking these developments, or the implementation of formalized coordinating mechanisms, such as centralized planning.

The less formal governance processes are an essential part of the management system as well. In higher education, most financial resources are committed to staff, usually faculty. Faculty often have considerable control over what they teach and how they teach it. The amount of control faculty have over their own affairs does vary in higher education. For instance, Platt and Parsons (1970) found "that increasing differentiation enhances departmental autonomy and control over policies directly related to its own operation, although on important policy issues such as educational and particularly financial policy, the administration and trustees play a very influential role" (p. 149). These less formal arrangements within institutions influence operation and management and must be considered when describing a college or university system.

Management Effectiveness

The effectiveness of a campus-management system was considered in the development of institutional case studies. This was necessary for the comparative analysis to determine the types of management that are appropriate for campuses in different developmental phases. Management effectiveness is not easy to measure, however, since criteria that could be used to measure effectiveness have not been uniformly developed. The Hodgkinson and Schenkel study (1974) of the effects of Title III used eight measures of management effectiveness, ranging from leadership dynamism and efficiency to community relations, to test a developmental model for Title III-funded institutions. These criteria were used in an impressionistic fashion by Hodgkinson and Schenkel in their analysis. Cheit's (1972) study of the financial health of colleges matched institutional goals with financial capacity as a measure of financial health. This method, although useful when considering the financial condition of colleges, is of questionable value as a measure of effective management since the reasonableness of institutional aspirations also should be taken into account.

In the absence of standardized criteria for measuring management effectiveness in higher education, management effectiveness was considered along five dimensions in the case studies. These measures were impressionistic and descriptive, but at the time they were the best available. The institutions used as case studies were considered exemplary for their management practices by the Title III staff. As descriptive indicators of management effectiveness, these measures provide a basis for comparing structural development and college-management needs. These indicators are:

Attention Paid to Management Needs: In his study of the financial health of colleges, Cheit (1973) found that improvement in the financial condition of several campuses previously headed for financial difficulty was due not to increased income, but because of a growing awareness that better management was needed. In the past, colleges have not paid attention to, nor set up systems to address, their management deficiencies. In these descriptive case studies, the extent to which institution assessed their management needs was considered.

Implementation of Viable Management Systems: Implementation of viable planning and management practices is not an easy task in higher education. There are now numerous planning and management packages and consulting firms that specialize in different practices or techniques. Selection of appropriate management tools is not always an easy choice nor is the adaption of these standard practices and instruments to an individual campus. A description of this implementation process is included in each of the case studies.

Effective Resource Use and Planning: Colleges need to develop strategies for using existing resources in more efficient ways. In the face of leveling or declining enrollment and increasing costs, colleges have had to cut back on faculty, merge with other institutions, or, in a few cases, close their doors. A descriptive study of management effectiveness should consider the ability of campus-management systems to effectively plan, develop, and utilize financial resources.

Quality and Effectiveness of Constituent Involvement: Effective management in higher education requires the effective development and use of human resources. The degree of involvement of different constituent groups in planning and decision-making processes is an important factor to consider in a study of management effectiveness.

Renewal Capacity: This is the most vague of the criteria proposed here, but perhaps the most important. In a rapidly changing environment—the condition many colleges, even the most traditional, now find themselves in—the capacity of institutions to regenerate, find new directions, and create new alternatives is a key to survival and success. An important indicator of the effectiveness of a management system should be the capacity to facilitate renewal processes.

THE CASE INSTITUTIONS

This study presents case studies of five institutions funded in the Advanced Institutional Development Program: Doane College (Crete, Nebraska); St. Mary's Junior College (Minneapolis, Minnesota); Xavier University of Louisiana (New Orleans, Louisiana); North Carolina A & T State University (Greensboro, North Carolina); and Valencia Community College (Orlando, Florida). The characteristics of the case-study institutions are presented in Table 4.1. Each of these institutions has undergone significant management developments as a means of coping with a new set of organizational problems. A description of the case institutions and the AIDP projects follows.

Doane College is a small liberal arts college located in Crete, Nebraska. Founded in 1872 as an extension of an earlier campus in Fontenelle, Nebraska, Doane is now the oldest independent college in the state. Historically, the college has always been small, its emphasis always on the liberal arts. However, during the past decade it has undergone significant demographic and curricular changes. Although its enrollment declined slightly over the past ten years, the number of Nebraska residents entering the school has increased. There have been subtle curricular changes as well, with a recently modified mission emphasizing a blending of liberal arts and career development.

In 1976 Doane College received a five-year AIDP grant for $1.25 million, after several years of funding with the Basic Institutional Development Program and two previous AIDP applications. The ADVANCE program, as AIDP is called at Doane, is designed to undertake three activities: the integration of the career-development concept into the curriculum; expansion of direct student services; and development of administrative systems and skills. The ADVANCE program appears to be helping Doane make important transitions that were needed to insure its survival during the next several decades.

St. Mary's Junior College (SMJC) is a Roman Catholic, two-year institution specializing exclusively in health, health-related, and human service fields. Located in urban Minneapolis, Minnesota, St. Mary's was founded in 1964 on the site of an old hospital nursing school. Today SMJC is an innovative institution that provides technical education in the allied health and human service fields. It services a diverse clientele of traditional and continuing education students.

SMJC is a small institution with fewer than 1,000 full-time students, and plans to remain small. During its brief history SMJC has experienced remarkable success in its programs and finances.

In 1973 St. Mary's received a five-year AIDP grant for institutional improvements in five areas: the development and implementation of a community service program; improvement of student personnel services; faculty development; curriculum and instruction (which emphasized a systematic approach to individualized instruction); and improvement of management technologies. The original grant was for $703,625. Since the time it was awarded, additional AIDP funds totaling $1.1 million have been received in the form of a supplemental grant, a continuation grant for four areas, and a grant to improve the fund-raising capacity. The college has been considered exemplary by the AIDP staff who have visited the campus.

Founded in 1915 as a high school, Xavier University of Louisiana is the only historically black Catholic college in the United States. Over the decades, many things have changed at Xavier—curriculum, location, enrollment, leadership—but its character and purpose have remained the same. It has played a unique role in the New Orleans area by educating blacks and training black educators. During the past decade, the conditions facing Xavier have changed, as they have for the rest of black higher education. As a result, Xavier has faced some difficult times: financial crisis, racial tension, and conflict over the mission and future of the college. The financial crisis and the resulting need for a sounder management system may have been the most critical test—a test the college appears to have weathered.

In 1974 Xavier received a five-year AIDP grant for $2 million to undertake the following activities:

1. Freshmen Studies
2-A. Curriculum Study
2-B. Curriculum Personnel
2-C. Faculty Development
2-D. Early Childhood
3. Social Science
4. Center for University Studies
5. Student Personnel
6. Transactional Information System
7. Planning, Management, Evaluation

The AIDP grant has helped the college make some needed transitions in its curriculum and management. The attitude toward AIDP at Xavier seems positive. The implementation appears successful, and the college seems better off for having undertaken the development process.

North Carolina Agricultural and Technical State University (A & T)

TABLE 4.1

Characteristics of Case-Study Institutions

Institution	Structural Characteristics	Managerial Crisis	Management & Developments
St. Mary's Junior College (Minneapolis, Minnesota)	A small, technically oriented junior college emphasizing health-related professions. Faculty organized into two divisions. Administrative structure in transition from an informal structure of president and a single vice-president to a more formal structure with three vice-presidents.	After a decade of successful growth, the founding president initiated the first long-range planning process. College decided to limit growth to less than 1,000 students, and to develop formal systems for maintaining college programs.	Management historically oriented toward innovation. Development of formal management systems has proceeded cautiously and with deliberate experimentation. Formal management systems have been implemented in limited ways.
Doane College (Crete, Nebraska)	A small, liberal arts college with less than 1,000 students. Historically a simple administrative structure with a president, dean, and business manager as key decisionmakers. It now has three vice-presidents. Faculty are organized into loosely structured divisions.	In the late 1960s the college projected an enrollment increase to 1,000 students. After a few years of growth, enrollments dropped sharply in the early 1970s by over 100 students in a 3-year period. Faculty were cut back.	Developed a long-range planning process that gave realistic enrollment projections, changed mission to blending of liberal arts and career development, and implemented more formal management processes.
Xavier University of Louisiana (New Orleans, Louisiana)	A medium-sized, historically black university (of almost 2,000 students) with three schools. The largest school, arts and sciences, has several departments. There is also a formal administrative structure	In the early 1960s the university experienced severe enrollment losses (300 students in 5 years) and severe financial problems. Fiscal problems continued into early 1970s, and a large income-expenditure deficit developed.	In the late 1960s and early 1970s the college changed from religious to lay leadership. Management development started with a long-range planning process, then with formalization of management policies and pro-

		cedures, and more recently by implementation of management-by-objectives process in academic departments and administrative units.	In the early 1970s the university established a formal management process with formal administrative policy and procedures; management-by-objectives procedures in departments, schools, and administrative units; and is currently implementing systems for setting universitywide priorities and academic programs that coordinate activities across schools and departments.	After a decade of rapid growth (VCC was founded in 1967), the college is a complex system with diverse management needs. The campuses are developing formal structures and management systems. The central administration is delegating budget formulation and management responsibilities to the campuses and implementing coordinated administrative systems.
North Carolina Agriculture and Technical State University (Greensboro, North Carolina)	An historically black land-grant university with seven schools (over 5,000 students). In addition to an elaborate academic administration with deans and department chairs, the university has a highly developed central administrative structure. The university is also part of a 17-campus university system, which requires compliance with coordinated planning and information reporting.	In the mid 1970s the university had difficulties meeting fiscal objectives in spite of good state support and Title III funds, and experienced operating deficits for two years. External evaluators of AIDP project observed lack of coordination in the management-development effort as a key problem. The impact of the area HEW desegregation regulations is uncertain.		
Valencia Community College (Orlando, Florida)	VCC is a three-campus system (east campus, west campus, and open campus). Each campus has a formal administrative structure. Faculty on the two regular campuses are organized into departments. Open campus uses part-time faculty and regular faculty. There is also a well-developed central administrative structure. (Over 20,000 headcount and 7,000 FTE enrollment.)	In the mid 1970s when the college became a multicampus system, the state's community college system imposed a one-year moratorium on enrollment growth, and the new campus was opened with faculty from the older campus. All new program developments are now implemented in a coordinated fashion when possible.		

was founded in 1891 as the state's land-grant institution for blacks. Originally named A. and M. College for the Colored Race, North Carolina A & T has evolved into a large, complex university. It now is one of the 16 campuses of the University of North Carolina system, has six undergraduate schools and a graduate school, and serves a student population of over 5,000. An historically black institution, A & T now provides varied academic programs to an increasingly diversified student population.

In 1974 A & T received a five-year AIDP grant for $2 million to undertake 17 activities in the following areas: faculty and administrative development; academic development and career options; student affairs; planning, management, and evaluation; and management information systems. In 1975 it received a supplementary AIDP grant for $630,000. Throughout its short history in the AIDP project at A & T, the school has been considered exemplary in its use of AIDP by most people who have visited the campus. A & T received a continuation grant for 1977–78 for $257,000. This allocation allowed A & T to increase its expenditures on the following activities: planning, management, and evaluation; management information systems; accreditation of the teacher education program by NCATE; accreditation of the school of business and economics by AACSB; the cooperative education program; and the urban problems program.

Valencia Community College (VCC) is a young, rapidly developing, public two-year college located in Orlando, Florida. Founded in 1967, Valencia is now a three-campus system with two permanent campuses located on the outskirts of the city and an open campus with administrative offices located in downtown Orlando. The most recent college catalog indicated that over 20,000 residents of the Orlando area are involved in some capacity as students of the college. Valencia reaches a large number of local citizens through linkages it has developed with the community. In 1976 Valencia received an AIDP grant to undertake a development process guided by the following objectives:

Program Component I—Open Door/Open Access
A. Objective One: Personal Assessment and Goal Setting System
B. Objective Two: Student Center Learning Laboratories
C. Objective Three: Active Recruitment Program
Program Component II—Alternative Modes of Instruction
A. Objective Four: Curriculum/Instructional Development Center
Program Component III—Short-Range and Long-Range Institutional Planning and Development
A. Objective Five: Student Records System
B. Objective Six: Follow-up Information Program

C. Objective Seven: Revision of Needs Assessment Model
D. Objective Eight: Identification of Community Resources
E. Objective Nine: Governance Process
F. Objective Ten: Information Dissemination Model
G. Objective Eleven: Management by Objectives System
H. Objective Twelve: Program Planning and Budgeting System
I. Objective Thirteen: Management Information System

Valencia's AIDP grant was for $1.2 million, with a $821,439 matching institutional commitment. The grant period, nearing the end of its first year of operation at the time of this research, will run through 1981.

Selection and Comparability

A careful procedure was used to insure the comparability of the case-study institutions. The criteria used for the selection of schools for case study were:

Exemplary Institutions: Since it was desired to identify a relationship between phases of structural development and the appropriateness, or effectiveness, of campus-management systems, institutions were selected that were considered exemplary in this regard. These institutions were judged exemplary by the AIDP staff for both the effectiveness of their management and their use of Title III funds. The management effectiveness of case institutions is considered in the case studies.

Structural Diversity: Selected institutions were in three of the five phase categories. The eligibility criteria tend to exclude phase I institutions due to age and size restrictions. Phase V institutions are the most advanced institutions in higher education, and therefore would not be funded by Title III. At least one institution in each of the three remaining categories (phases II, III, and IV) was selected. To insure this, institutional data in the program files on the structure and management of candidate institutions were compared with the general phase descriptions.

Geographic Diversity: Institutions in different geographic locations were studied. This would increase the likelihood that all the institutions selected would not be subject to the same external influences.

A fourth criterion—selecting institutions with similar type (two-year, four-year) and control (public, private) coding—was considered. After reviewing the files for 18 institutions selected by the AIDP staff as possible subjects for case study, it was found that it would be difficult to meet the types and control criterion. Private colleges funded in the program did not appear to vary as much in their structural characteristics as the public institutions. It also appeared difficult to find enough either two- or four-year public colleges that met the other criteria, since private four-year schools were the dominant category. After reviewing Title III program files on several schools it was discovered that colleges with different type and control codes seemed to have relatively similar structural characteristics when they appeared to be in the same phase. For instance, the three institutions (in the original 18) that were categorized as making a phase I—phase II transition when they applied for AIDP funds varied in type and control—a two-year public, a two-year private, and a four-year private—but appeared relatively similar in their structural characteristics.

After reassessing this situation, it was decided to choose schools with different types and controls in order to have structurally diverse schools. An examination of the literature on comparative organizational research suggests that the original criteria may have been too narrow. Some of the most noted comparative studies of industrial organizations have included firms with diverse products; in fact, they often compare public utilities and private firms (for example, see Chandler, 1962; Dale, 1960). Also, most comparative studies of higher education organizations are not restricted in this regard. Therefore, institutions selected for the study are of mixed types and controls.

The case-study institutions were compared with other similar Title III-funded institutions on three variables: total education, full-time-equivalent (FTE) students, and general expenditure, and total education and general expenditures per FTE. These variables were chosen because of their comparability to other data bases (such as HEGIS Enrollment and Finance) and because they are relatively good indicators of the level of institutional activities.

In funding year 1973, the year before AIDP started, St. Mary's Junior College did not differ much from other Title III-funded, private two-year institutions. Its total FTE enrollment, total expenditures for education and general, and expenditures for education and general per FTE were slightly larger than the other two-year private institutions, although less than a standard deviation.

Valencia Community College is similar to the two-year public colleges funded in 1973 and 1974. Its total FTE enrollment was slightly less in 1972-73 and slightly greater in 1973-74, although not as much as one standard deviation. Its total expenditures for education and general purposes were less than AIDP-funded institutions in 1973-74 and were slightly more in 1974-75, although not by a standard deviation. Valencia has continued to grow at a rapid pace, however, and may be larger than these same schools today.

Doane College is smaller, in terms of its level of activity, than private four-year institutions funded in 1973 and 1974. In 1973-74 and 1974-75 its FTE enrollment differed by more than a standard deviation. Its total expenditures for education and general purposes were more than a standard deviation less in 1973-74. Its expenditures per FTE were slightly less than comparable institutions, although not a standard deviation.

Xavier University appears near the average in all of its activity indicators. Its total FTE enrollment, expenditures for education and general purposes, and expenditures for education and general purposes per FTE were all within the average range for the two years compared.

North Carolina Agricultural and Technical State University is larger and better funded than other public four-year colleges funded by ADIP. Both years' total FTE enrollments were larger than average, although not by a standard deviation. Its expenditures for education and general purposes, however, are more than two standard deviations above the average for both years. Its expenditures for education and general purposes per FTE were above average for both years, and a standard deviation above average for one year.

In summary, the selected institutions appear to be near average in their activities when compared to other AIDP–Title III–funded institutions and when type and control are taken into account. One of the schools (Doane College) appears smaller than average and another (North Carolina A & T) appears larger. Education and general purpose expenditures per student vary slightly, with one institution (North Carolina A & T) being above average. Overall, there is no reason to consider these schools different as far as their activity levels are concerned, although they do represent a range in this regard. The only major difference that can be attributed to these institutions is the judgment on the part of the AIDP staff that they were doing an exemplary job in their use of Title III funds and in their management effectiveness.

CASE-STUDY METHODOLOGIES

Generally four methodologies are used for case-study research: document studies, observations, interviews, and surveys (Baldridge, 1971; Murphy, 1976). Surveys are most frequently used if information is needed to gain feedback on program delivery (Murphy, 1976), or to gather in-depth information on social and political processes (Baldridge, 1971). Since these were not the purposes of this study, surveys were not used. The other three methodologies were used as appropriate. Extensive use was made of document studies throughout the investigation. Observations were limited by time and travel resources, although one two-day visit was made to each institution. Interviews were the primary activity during the site visits, although tours of facilities also took place.

Document Studies

Document studies were an essential part of the selection of institutions and of the actual development of the case studies. Several sources of documents were available. First, prior studies of the Title III program were reviewed (St. John and Weathersby, 1977). These reviews helped define the conceptual framework for this investigation. Second, during the selection and review processes, the U. S. Office of Education, Developing Institutions Division (USOE-DID) application, monitoring, and award files for AIDP were reviewed. Third, Harvard University libraries were searched for literature relevant to the case-study institutions. Finally, the institutions were asked to supply documents related to their AIDP projects and to their current and past administrative organization and management practices.

During the selection process, USOE-DID files were particularly important. USOE-DID officials supplied a list of 18 institutions they considered exemplary for their use of Title III funds and their management effectiveness. Application and award files were reviewed for each institution. Six institutions were selected for case study based on the criteria of structural diversity and geographic diversity. * The refined applications were particularly helpful in the selection process. These documents, which ranged between 200 and 500 pages, give details about the organizational structure and the state-of-management development at the institutions. The applications included considerable details about the types of planning and management procedures used at the institutions prior to the applications, and those they planned to implement with AIDP funds.

The amount of material available in USOE-DID files varied according to the length of the institution's involvement with AIDP. Those institutions that had been involved for three or four years had considerable material in the files, including external evaluation reports,

---

*A sixth institution, Baptist College at Charleston (South Carolina), was selected in the initial six, but was eventually dropped because a site visit could not be arranged during spring or summer 1977.

consultant reports, and, in a few instances, site-visit reports from USOE-DID staff. Institutions in their first year of funding tended to have only the initial and refined applications in their files. Site-visit reports were particularly helpful when available since they provided an informed outsider's view of the AIDP project. Documents prepared by the institution being studied can be biased, especially those written as part of the application for funds, since these materials are slanted to sell the proposed program (Murphy, 1976). However, these documents were useful during the selection stage since they provided valuable insight into institutional officials' perceptions of their management and organization.

Once the institutions were selected for case study, a second stage of document study was initiated. Howard libraries were searched for materials concerning the case institutions. Although few references were found, information was available that was relevant to the financing of higher education in the various states in which these institutions are located. A second trip to Washington, D. C. was arranged to review USOE files in more depth for the selected institutions. At this stage the selected institutions were contacted and asked for additional documents. Soon after notification, the AIDP coordinator at each institution was contacted by phone regarding other documents the campus could provide and arrangements for site visits.

Prior to the site visit, profiles were written for each institution. These profiles (five to seven pages) were shared with the USOE officials working most closely with the project. Profiles included the author's assessment of the relative phase of development of each institution. Documents were supplied by the case institutions prior to, during, and after site visits. These included monitoring and evaluation reports not available in USOE-DID files, annual budgets, academic and administrative plans, consultant reports, reports by planning and research offices within the institutions, documents detailing plans for a particular program on campus, and correspondence with USOE-DID officials. The documents that proved most useful varied from institution to institution. A list of documents used for each case is included in the Appendix.

Site Observations

Site observations were arranged by the AIDP coordinator at each institution. Before the site visit, the coordinators were informed of the types of individuals the author needed to interview. This included top administrative officers, middle managers involved in implementing the institution-management systems, coordinators of various AIDP activities, and faculty and others who were aware of the history, organization, and management of the campus.

All five institutions were visited during June and July 1977. Visiting during the spring and summer months had advantages and limitations. The principal advantage was that most of those directly involved in the administration of the campus were present and free to spend time with the author. Summer sessions were not large at these campuses, except Valencia Community College. The absence of on-going operations did skew the types of observations the author was able to make. Administrators and faculty were caught at a time when they were reflecting on the year's activities and making plans for the next year. However, the principal disadvantage of the site-visit timing was that the summer months limited the types of people who could be interviewed, especially students. In no instances were students available. Faculty were available at four of the five campuses, since these visits were arranged in June soon after the school year ended. A visit to the fifth campus (St. Mary's Junior College) was delayed until late July due to the unexpected illness of one of the key administrators. The only faculty available to be interviewed here were members of the college's administration.

A diverse group of people was interviewed at each campus. The top administrators were interviewed in all instances; this usually included the president, vice-president(s), dean(s), and head of the academic senate. In the one instance when the president was not interviewed (at Xavier University), the executive vice-president was interviewed for approximately two hours. The two consultants who were most directly involved in the management-development efforts at Xavier University were also interviewed. In addition, at each institution one or more individuals were interviewed who had long-term knowledge of the institution. In several instances these people were thought of as local historians. For the younger institutions (St. Mary's and Valencia) it was possible to locate people who were with the college since it was created, while at the older campuses it was possible to find individuals whose involvement with the campus spanned several decades. At Xavier, a person was interviewed who was writing a history of the campus.

Interview arrangements varied from campus to campus, depending on the local customs and culture and on the complexity of the organization. In each instance individual interviews were conducted with key members of the administration. However, the reliance on group meetings as part of the interview process varied considerably. Two institutions (Valencia and Xavier) exclusively utilized individual or small group interviews of two or three people. At the other three institutions, some combination of group and individual interviews was used. Two of these three were small institutions with collegial administrative environments; the third (North Carolina A & T) was one of the largest.

Interviews

Interviews conducted for this study averaged approximately an hour in length, with time varying between one-half and two hours. Individual and small group interviews were of an unstructured variety (Murphy, 1976). Exploratory interviews were designed to get at the nitty-gritty of operations and management. The author obtained a common set of background information about each interviewee, and then proceeded to ask questions and enter into conversation about the individual's area of expertise.

Interviewees were engaged in conversations about one of the areas of interest to the study: campus history, organization, management, and AIDP activities. Most of the interviews were an interchange: the purposes of the study were explained and interviewees described their perceptions of the activities they were directly involved with. The author took notes while interviewing, and reviewed the notes and made additional observations about the day's investigations each evening.

In addition to individual and small group interviews, occasional group interviews were conducted. The purposes of these meetings were twofold: the author was always trying to find out more about the campus and its programs, while at times it seemed that group interviews (of six to a dozen people) were arranged to familiarize the institutional representatives with the author and his purposes. The author answered all questions in these sessions, and his responses often had an effect on how he would be treated during subsequent interviews.

Case Studies

The case studies were compiled and drafted using information gathered from document studies, site observations, and interviews. When more evidence was needed during the review and writing period, campus representatives were contacted and the information was requested. In one instance, a major reorganization of the institutional administrative structure was planned after the site visit; the reorganization plans were sent to the author by mail.

Each case study was written in a common format utilizing the framework outlined at the start of this chapter. Drafts of the case studies were reviewed for factual accuracy by campus representatives before they were finalized and analyzed. The finalized case studies were used partially in Chapters 5 and 6 and as a basis of the analysis contained in subsequent chapters.

FOLLOW-UP STUDY

In spring 1980 a follow-up study of the exemplary Title III-funded institutions was initiated to assess the long-term impact of Title III funds on these institutions, and to substantiate intermanagement-intervention concepts developed as a result of the original study. Subsequent to the completion of the case studies in 1977, analytic efforts were undertaken to use the general institution-development model to development-intervention frameworks for planning, managerial, evaluation, and inquiring systems (St. John, 1980c), for management-training and institutional change strategies (St. John and Weathersby, 1980), and automated management-information systems (St. John, 1980a). In order to better assess the implications and relevance of these frameworks, a follow-up study was designed. Two detailed questionnaires were administered and documents were provided by the institutions. Site visits were not conducted due to financial constraints and because case institutions supplied ample information in the questionnaires and supplemental documents.

The Garnes Questionnaire

An evaluation instrument developed by James Garnes, AIDP coordinator at Lincoln University (a historically black land-grant university in Jefferson City, Missouri) was administered to the case institutions. This 25-page instrument was designed to assess the impact of Title III funds on management and information systems, student services, and academic programs. In addition, the instrument has several questions about the change methodology used, the access of the Title III coordinator to other key administrators, and the involvement of other groups and individuals in the institution-development effort.

The responses gained on this instrument were extremely helpful in the restudy. Major use of the institutions' responses on the impact survey is most evident in Chapter 7 on management-systems interventions; however, detailed responses to the survey also are used in the subsequent three chapters. This instrument was particularly helpful in gaining the perspective of Title III coordinators about the long-term impacts of these funds on their institutions.

MIS Development Questionnaire

During the two years between the initial study and the restudy, the author's research was expanded to include the study of MIS development and automation in higher education. This research was initiated as part of a statewide study of higher education computing in Missouri (St. John, 1980b). One of the five instruments formulated in this study was used to devise an MIS-development framework for colleges and universities that closely paralleled the management-development model derived from the original study (St. John, 1980a).

Responses to the MIS questionnaire were critical to the refinement of Chapter 8 which further refines the MIS-development framework. The data gathered in the original Title III study were not adequate to elaborate on MIS interventions because the original study did not emphasize this area adequately, the institutions had accomplished significant MIS developments during the period between the two studies, and computer and information science technologies had changed enough during this period to modify conclusions reached from the initial study.

Institutional Documents

Several types of documents were supplied by the institutions for the restudy. These included institution-planning documents, Title III evaluations, and reports on various components of the AIDP projects. The documents were important when assessing the long-term impacts of Title III funds. These provided insights into the perceptions of both the evaluators of the Title III projects and the administrators at the case institutions concerning the value and impacts of the Title III programs. These data, combined with the responses to the two questionnaires, provided a detailed picture of the impacts of Title III. Details on documents provided by the case institutions are included in the Appendix.

CONCLUSIONS

A careful study methodology was used for the case studies that were analyzed to develop the management-development model, and also for the follow-up study used to elaborate the intervention frameworks. The original case studies were independent documents. Some of the material from these case studies has been included in Chapters 5 and 6. In Chapter 5, case-study material is used to elaborate on the patterns of structural development; in Chapter 6 the actual implementation of new management practices is used to elaborate on the management model. Data from the follow-up study are used in the last four chapters to elaborate on the intervention frameworks, and to consider their implications for institutions and public policy.

5

STRUCTURAL DEVELOPMENT

The structural development of colleges and universities is a dynamic process. A variety of internal and external factors influence the fate of institutions. In spite of these differences, there appears to be a general pattern of structural development. This chapter focuses on the structural development of the case institutions; it analyzes their developmental patterns and identifies a set of quantitative measures that can predict developmental phases. While these measures are speculative and should be the subject of more investigation, they are a useful starting point for an institution-development framework. In the long term, other methods for identifying the developmental phase of a college or university organization should be developed.

DEVELOPMENTAL ANALYSIS*

Chapter 4 discussed alternative theories of institutional development and suggested one that might be used as a model to improve management practices at colleges and universities. This model describes structural development as a sequential process: a series of structural transitions that have implications for institution-manage-

---

*This section relies on documents and interviews that were cited in the original case studies. The Appendix provides a listing of these documents and interviews. Complete references for documents are not always available for the citations in text since these documents did not always include page numbers or authors.

ment systems. The case studies indicated that transitions of this nature do exist, but that they may not be as clear-cut as the theory suggests. This chapter utilizes data from the original case studies to document a general sequence of structural development; it examines the structure and history of the selected institutions.

Within the case studies there are examples of four of the five phases described by the theory. Examples of phase I institutions include: St. Mary's Junior College and Doane College, both of which have recently transitioned to phase II, and the Open and East Campuses of Valencia Community College. Examples of the direction phase, phase II, include: St. Mary's and Doane, which have recently entered this phase, and Xavier University of Louisiana, which has transitioned to a more complex phase. Phase III institutions include: Xavier University, the West Campus of Valencia Community College, and North Carolina A & T, which is transitioning to phase IV. Examples of phase IV institutions include: North Carolina A & T, which is entering this phase, and Valencia Community College. The following utilizes these examples to piece together a descriptive model. The five case studies were arranged in order from least- to most-complex institution. What follows is a phase-by-phase analysis of institutions according to this model.

Phase I: Creation

Creation-phase organizations are typified by relatively little structural development, a small administrative staff and faculty, and an orientation toward the development of new academic programs as their primary administrative activity. The case studies provide four distinct examples of institutions that are in or have recently passed through this phase.

VCC East Campus

VCC East Campus is the youngest of the institutions represented in this developmental phase. At the time of the site visit, it had a three-year history dating back to the appointment of Dr. Evans as provost in 1974. Prior to that time, he had been a teacher and associate director for academic affairs, dean of academic affairs, and vice-president for academic affairs. He used a modified PERT system to plan the details about the campus, which provided a schedule for what had to be accomplished and when it had to be accomplished. In addition, with the support of the college, he initiated a process of brainstorming about what the new campus should do. Experts were brought in to explore what was new, different, and feasible for a new community college. In addition, Evans took trips to other campuses, such as Oakland Community College, which were attempting to do something different.

During the planning year when the facilities were being built, budget difficulties were encountered that changed the plans to hire a new faculty. The Florida state legislature and the community college system came into conflict in 1975-76 over the amount of state support provided per FTE. The community colleges are funded by a combination of state support (given at a per FTE rate) and student tuition, both of which are controlled by the legislature. Per student costs had risen throughout the system while support per student had remained constant. Although this situation was resolved the next year by an increase in tuition and in state support, the financial condition was stressed in 1975-76 when the campus was opened. One of the ways Valencia dealt with the financial problem was to put a freeze on hiring new faculty. As a result, the new campus took faculty from the old campus to get started.

Rubye Beal, dean for academic and student affairs for East Campus, was involved in starting the new campus. Hired before the new campus opened, she worked with Evans in the early development period. As a result of the financial problems, the college asked for volunteers from the old campus. When volunteers were not available, people were drafted. As Beal put it: "We had to move people from the other campus here—some didn't want to come. "

In its second year of operation (1976-77), the new campus was already in many ways a success. Although the total size of the East Campus faculty was smaller than West Campus, it had a larger number of faculty involved in the curriculum and instructional development (CID) center during the first year; this was considered a significant accomplishment by most people interviewed. The predisposition of those involved in the East Campus during this early period was toward innovation. As Beal described it: "the curriculum future as a blend of traditional and individualized institution. " The atmosphere of the new campus is comfortable and open. All the people interviewed seemed to be hopeful about its future.

The formal administrative structure at East Campus is simple and unencumbered. It has one dean for both academic and student affairs. In 1976-77 the campus had 27 faculty members. In 1977-78 it planned to have 35. Initially, the campus tried to avoid a departmental structure. For the first two years, faculty were divided into two groups of equal size with a mixture of disciplines in each campus; faculty in the same discipline were in different groups and division chairpersons were elected. By 1977-78, however, the two faculty divisions were headed by chairpersons who had administrative appointments. The new divisions were divided according to disciplines. In addition to the formal administrative organization, there is a faculty association on campus. Each year the faculty association elects a convenor. The faculty association is concerned both about actual policies and the policy-formulation process on campus.

The academic structure at East Campus remains relatively unencumbered by departments and divisions. The administrators and faculty maintain an image of East Campus as an innovative institution, and have resisted the creation of a structured environment. However, there has been a gradual movement toward more formalization in the academic structure. The increased formalization was symbolized by the move to appoint chairpersons for the discipline-oriented divisions. Due to the growth and the increased administrative responsibilities of the chairpeople of these divisions, some initial formalization was necessary.

VCC Open Campus

The Open Campus of VCC also had a three-year history in 1977, although many of its programs were of earlier origins. The Open Campus was formed in 1974 when VCC became multicampus. The continuing, recurrent, and community education programs run by the college were reorganized into a separate, autonomous organization. Formerly headed by a single director, these programs had been housed within the existing campus structure and coordinated by the faculty in the various departments of the campus. The fact that many of the activities under the jurisdiction of the Open Campus were in operation prior to its formation added to the sophistication and complexity of this young campus. Its current thrust—which combines in-service training, community education programs, and avocational programs—is the product of several years of developmental work. President Gollattscheck has always been supportive of community-based programs and has encouraged their development. The formation of the Open Campus was not so much an effort to create a new program as it was an effort to give some added emphasis and structure to a program that already existed.

Since its inception, the orientation in the Open Campus has been toward growth through the creation of new programs. In 1976-77 it had 50 full-time and 8 half-time employees. In addition to this permanent staff, there are numerous casual staff and faculty involved in the implementation of various in-service and community education programs. The primary objective of the campus staff is to develop new programs.

The Open Campus differed in its administrative structure when compared to the two other VCC campuses. In 1976-77 there was a provost and three director-level positions. In 1977-78 this structure was modified slightly: the director was upgraded to a dean and another director-level position was added. In 1976-77 the Open Campus offered courses in 80 different locations. The recently upgraded dean is responsible for coordinating these services. In addition, the Open Campus has encountered student-service needs in the past few years, especially in the area of counseling.

Although the full-time staff of the Open Campus has remained small, the campus has a diverse range of activities. It reached nearly 15,000 individuals in its third year of operation. All the students and most of the employees are part time. They are either involved in short, intensive workshops of one to three weeks, or in one or more courses or programs that run for varying lengths of time.

St. Mary's Junior College (Historical Example)

St. Mary's Junior College is an example of an institution that has recently transitioned out of the creation phase. However, during its first decade (until 1973) the college was in this phase. It is still creative, but its formal structure has changed. It was administered by a president and a vice-president who oversaw the day-to-day operations. Innovations in curriculum were encouraged by both administrators, and most faculty took advantage of this situation, often applying for outside grants for curricular innovations.

St. Mary's Junior College is a young institution that has not experienced excessive growth. It experienced rapid growth in 1964 and 1965 and a subsequent plateau, 1965 through 1969, followed by the relatively fast climb to 838 students in 1973, which was the college's maximum enrollment at the time of the study. Although there has not been a history written about SMJC, it is an interesting institution that has experienced one major structural transition.

Prior to the receipt of the AIDP grant, SMJC had undergone little systematic development in its formal administrative structure or its planning and management capacities. The president and founder, Sister Anne Joachim Moore, had managed in a creative fashion. Regarding the planning capacity of the institution, the final AIDP proposal made the following observation:

> During the first decade of the college's existence, the question of long range planning was not a priority. Rather, planning and developing for the immediate and near future were major concerns. Planning was an integral aspect of the ongoing activities, since all available energies had to be devoted to building a viable institution, developing curricula, refining and revising all aspects of the institution, and achieving the necessary program and institution accreditation (St. Mary's Junior College, 1974, p. 59).

As a young college, St. Mary's was highly successful at developing new programs. Once the programs were developed, a new set of management issues began to emerge that revolved around program maintenance. Ordinarily this might be an easy transition for a college, especially if it wanted to resemble other institutions and continue to grow. SMJC has tried to maintain its creative atmosphere, limit growth, and continue as an innovative institution, while trying to maintain existing programs. The college has been successful in obtaining these goals, but it has not found it easy to develop a structure compatible with them. It has approached the task of developing a new structure with the same experimental attitude that governs most of its activities.

To understand St. Mary's Junior College, one has to begin prior to its founding. Its history goes back to the founding of the Sisters of St. Joseph in 1650 as a teaching order. In the early 1800s the order came to the United States, where it established hospitals, secondary schools, and a few colleges. Prior to the founding of St. Mary's Junior College, there had been a three-year nursing program at St. Mary's Hospital. In 1958 Sister Anne Joachim became the head of the independent diploma nursing program. When she assumed this position, she began to make basic changes in the old-fashioned program. There were national reactions to the changes, both positive and negative. In 1962-63 she began to involve many of the staff from nursing programs in a new planning process. They wrote a proposal for a new junior college to train technical-level workers in the allied-health fields. The board of the order gave its approval to the proposal as long as the new school did not compete with the other colleges it supported. Unfortunately, the order could not give financial assistance to the new college. Sister Anne Joachim announced the new junior college in spring 1963, and soon received an $18,000 grant from the Hill Family Foundation for the faculty to plan the college.

Sister Anne Joachim described the early years as "really exciting." The college had to be self-supporting. At first she hoped tuition would support the college. When it did not, and when she discovered that the costs of starting a college were more expensive than could be supported by student's fees, she went after necessary external funds. When the college needed help, she turned to the order. As Sister Anne Joachim put it: "About the second year, I realized you can't run a college on tuition. We had run out of money before school was out and the order gave us a no-interest loan."

In 1964 she hired Tom Scheller, who was finishing his doctorate in clinical psychology at the time, as a part-time student counselor. In 1965 he became assistant to the president, and later became the first vice-president. For several years Sister Anne Joachim and Dr. Scheller ran a creative enterprise that was committed to innovation and was capable of raising funds when needed. Both were committed to change, and the pace of change was rapid. As Scheller described it: "Historically, the rate of change is more rapid than most institutions I know about." When Scheller hired new people, he told them not to take the job descriptions "too seriously," as they would "have to handle fairly quickly some radically different roles." Faculty and administration worked closely on all grant proposals. They were highly successful during this early period at bringing in funds for academic innovations. The college created a board with a majority of layperson trustees in 1967.

In 1973 the college began its first long-range planning effort. The planning committee was headed by Dr. Carol Peterson, who described SMJC's planning prior to the committee as "very curricular and very program oriented." The development of a long-range plan was not easy. As Peterson said in an interview, "as an institution we didn't have a conceptualization of what long-range institutional planning was." Sister Anne Joachim had appointed the committee because she felt that after a decade the college needed to examine itself and its future. The purpose of the committee, as Sister Anne Joachim described it, was to "make plans for what we wanted, then find funds to do what we wanted to do." The plan was completed and was being circulated prior to the formal announcement that AIDP would be a new component of the Title III program.

SMJC had not received Title III funds prior to applying for AIDP. However, when the administrative staff saw the circulars for AIDP, they found the institutional characteristics described in the pamphlets depicted St. Mary's. The college incorporated its 1973 long-range plan into its AIDP application. The emphases on technical education, curricular reform, and limited growth were clearly defined in the proposal. SMJC was one of the first institutions to receive AIDP grants in 1973. The AIDP grant has brought many more changes to the institution, including improvements in its structure and management system. These changes have been part of St. Mary's transition to a more complex organizational phase.

The academic structure of SMJC was also relatively unencumbered during this period. The college stressed a balance between technical and general education. The faculty were divided into two divisions, one each for technical and general education, with an associate dean for each area. The college was formed in 1963 and the associate deans appointed in 1966. There has been a faculty committee system since the founding of the college. Initially, the faculty played a strong role in governance, but their role subsided when they became primarily concerned about curriculum development.

Doane College (Historical Example)

Doane College, prior to its reorganization in the late 1960s and early 1970s, provides another example of a creation-phase organization. Founded in 1872, Doane lasted nearly an entire century as a phase I organization. It has always been administered by a president, academic dean, and budget officer. The budget officer and president have been the primary administrative decisionmakers; the dean, in consultation with the president and faculty, was the primary academic decisionmaker.

Although Doane offered a diversity of liberal arts programs, its faculty and student body remained small. Many disciplines have not had more than one faculty member. From decade to decade, the primary emphasis of the college shifted from religion to politics to music, but the academic side of the enterprise remained loosely structured. In the 1960s Doane was organized into five divisions, each headed by an appointed chairperson who volunteered administrative services to the institution.

Historically, Doane College has been small; its emphasis was always in the liberal arts. Its early curriculum favored Greek and Latin. Practical subjects such as political economy, law, and education were added in the 1880s. One gets an initial sense at Doane that nothing much ever changes; the people, curriculum, and buildings come and go, but the college remains the same. This attitude about continuity was apparent in many of the interviews. An interview with David Osterhout, a 1937 graduate of Doane and currently vice-president for financial affairs and AIDP coordinator, seemed to typify this attitude. It was his opinion that while some things had changed—especially relations with the community and regulations on student life— life at Doane, particularly the atmosphere of the college, was essentially as it always had been. It was his opinion that "this kind of institution is a one-man show. A good board leaves most of the operation up to the president."

In its over 100-year history, Doane has had only nine presidents, including current president Phil Heckman. The long periods of presidency are generally considered the good years at Doane. Prior to the current administration, the president and business officer were the key administrators. The business officer was responsible for the financial operations of the college. While many administrative decisions are still made informally by collaboration between Heckman and Osterhout, many of these informal processes have been replaced in recent years by more formal decision-making and planning mechanisms. This is due in large part to adjustments to a changing environment.

When Phil Heckman came to the campus in 1966, the decision-making process was still informal. As a result, there was no formal, long-range planning mechanism. At that time, Doane was in the midst of a growth period. Its enrollment was climbing and it was constructing new buildings. During Heckman's first few years on campus, enrollment continued to climb and buildings continued to be built, including a new field house, library, and communication building. In 1970 Doane adopted a National Association of College and University Business Officers (NACUBO) planning model. Doane administrators learned about the model at a CASC (Council for the Advancement of Small Colleges) meeting in Grand Rapids. At first the college tried to follow the model precisely; the departments gave the planning group estimates of what they wanted. The result, as Osterhout explained, was that "during the early period, we were saying enrollments would go up when they were going down."

In 1970 Doane began to experience financial difficulties, with a budget deficit of $106,118 for 1970-71, the year the long-range planning process was initiated. This situation worsened due to the large gap between projected and actual enrollment. By 1974-75 the projected deficit for the period 1970-75 was $508,890, which included 10 percent depreciation. At the time of the 1974-75 planning process, the trustees instructed the college "to present a balanced budget in the five-year period projected (1974-75 to 1978-79)." The planners tried to accomplish this by decreasing direct services to students, administrative functions, and plant maintenance. Doane faced some difficult years in its transition to a balanced budget, a transition that required the commitment of the entire community.

The actual deficit accumulated during the period was $560,711. The 1973-74 academic year had been more difficult than anticipated with a deficit of $228,371. The board of trustees pledged $463,000 toward the payment of this deficit so the college could have a clean bill of health in its efforts to attain balanced budgets. In 1977 Bob Dobson, the chairman of the board of trustees, described the board's reaction to the situation and reaffirmed commitment to the college in an interview. When the enrollment projections were off for one year, the trustees did not worry since they considered it just a bad year. After three years of significant deficit, the trustees told the administration they wanted "no more red ink." The reason for the board decision to underwrite the deficit was simple, as Dobson put it: "We didn't feel honest to go out and ask for more money from the public for a deficit."

Budgets are not easy to balance even when this commitment has been made. At Doane, budget balancing meant faculty retrenchment in addition to better development efforts and a change in academic emphasis. Retrenchment, or cutting faculty, was the most difficult. The college always had emphasized the liberal arts, but financial contingencies made it impossible to maintain a complete and balanced liberal arts curriculum and develop new emphases to attract students. Total faculty FTE dropped from 52 in 1971-72 to 45 in 1976-76. Faculty cuts came mostly from the humanities division; the languages were the hardest hit. In 1976-77 there was only one language teacher, who taught both German and Spanish. Dismissals were managed within the college policy and AAUP standards. No major difficulties were encountered, probably because the financial difficulties were obvious to the faculty. Largely as a result of the crisis, the administrative structure and management practices of Doane began to change in the mid 1970s.

Phase II: Direction

Direction-phase institutions are characterized by the formalization of the academic and administrative structures, the development of a long-range planning capacity, and the development of a formal management system. The case studies provide three examples of direction-phase organizations: during the past few years Doane College and St. Mary's Junior College appear to have entered the direction phase; during the late 1960s Xavier University exhibited many of the characteristics of direction phase, although it has since transitioned to a more complex phase of development.

St. Mary's College: 1970s

The base year of St. Mary's Junior College's new direction was 1973. At that time, President Sister Anne Joachim appointed a committee to study the college's future. This set in motion a series of changes that resulted in a transition in the formal structure of the college. The long-range planning committee set new program goals for the institution that have resulted in a series of new technical education specializations and a continuing education program. A new division, called new programs and continuing education, was added to house the new programs. Previously there were just two divisions: technical education and general education. This has been accompanied by increased formalization of the administrative structure.

The story of the administrative reorganization begins with the 1973 long-range planning committee. Prior to the formation of this committee, the college had been run as a creative enterprise; faculty and staff were encouraged by the president and vice-president to undertake innovative projects. The planning committee was the first organized effort to look at the maintenance of the college over the long term. When AIDP funds were received, a steering committee was formed that was comprised of many of the same individuals who were on the planning committee. Carol Peterson, a faculty member who chaired the planning committee, became AIDP coordinator.

In 1975 St. Mary's moved from a system composed of a president, vice-president, and two associate deans, to one composed of a president and four vice-presidents. The two associate dean positions for general education and technical education were eliminated. The associate deans' positions had been instituted in 1966 in an effort to keep technical education and general education on an equal footing. The new system had been instituted when the college hired a vice-president to head the new development office. After considering a variety of alternative plans for the development function, it was decided to undertake a major development effort with a vice-president, two directors, and a clerical staff. This effort has not been entirely successful; in 1977 the college decided to reduce the size of this venture.

The other top administrative officers have been more successful under the reorganization. Scheller functions as an executive vice-president who oversees the entire operation with the president; he also retains responsibility for fiscal and student affairs. Scheller's job changed considerably during the mid 1970s. More of his time had to be devoted to the maintenance of existing operations. Although he wrote most of the college's earlier funding proposals, the original AIDP application was the last one he was seriously involved in. Peterson has been the vice-president more directly responsible for maintaining the innovative thrust of the institution. As AIDP coordinator and vice-president for educational development, she has been responsible for the development and evaluation of new programs. AIDP at SMJC, under Peterson's direction, has been successful in keeping the campus bent toward innovation. Peter D'Heilly, vice-president for general education, and Marcia Hanson, director of technical education, served as the major academic administrators between 1975 and 1977. They were responsible for the continued development and maintenance of the school's academic programs.

This initial experience with a formal organization structure proved to the administration that a more structured organization was needed at SMJC. The first reorganization was the result of the hiring of the vice-president for development. At that time it was decided to upgrade one existing position and to create a new position for educational development. Prior to the reorganization, Peterson had been serving as AIDP coordinator. Next year the structure will continue to evolve at St. Mary's.

The college planned to operate with a new organizational structure in 1977-78. According to this plan, the president will take greater responsibility for fund raising and will have an assistant in this area. In addition to this assistant and the AIDP coordinator, two vice-president-level positions will report to the president. Underneath the top academic officer there will be three dean-level positions: one each for general education, instructional development in technical education, and new programs and continuing education. The top academic administrator will maintain responsibility for technical education. Titles for these new positions had not yet been assigned at the time of the case studies.

The faculty governance structure has undergone a transition in function during the past few years. By 1977 the faculty was reasserting itself. During the first decade, the major concern of the college was the creation and development of programs. Between 1964 and 1969, the senate educational policies committee was active in approving new programs. Now that most programs are developed, their maintenance and quality, and the autonomy of the faculty, have become critical concerns of the faculty. In some respects, the faculty has been less active in governance since 1969. For the first time the process of approving curricular innovations is taking planning and development time. Faculty committees are appointed by the president. She looks over faculty requests for committee assignments, and then assigns the committee membership based on a balance of individual desire and institutional needs. It is natural that some committees, such as educational policies, are at the top of most people's lists, while others, such as library, are at the top of only a few lists. Although relations between faculty and administration at St. Mary's are reasonably good, some difficulties have been encountered in determining the proper faculty role in educational policy matters. This is symbolized by the fact that on several occasions during this period, President Sister Anne Joachim has been invited by the faculty welfare committee to attend its regular meetings; at other times, this standing invitation has been rescinded.

The college has always been open to student involvement, although student participation has never been extensive. The student government has not been active. Students have access to membership on faculty committees in some important areas, including the disciplinary review, educational policies, library, and student life committees. However, their involvement in these committees does not appear to be an important issue to students, faculty, or administrators.

Doane College: 1970s

Doane College's transition to the direction phase was more gradual. The initial signs of the change were evident in the early 1970s, although the transition was still taking place in 1977. In 1970 the college developed its first long-range, five-year plan; in 1972 it moved to a system with three vice-presidents. It took Doane several years to develop a viable planning process, one that projected realistically into the future. While the first few years of this may have been harmful to the immediate future of the college, since it resulted in inaccurate enrollment projections, it helped to establish the rudiments of a new, more formal management system. The new structure with three vice-presidents did not make a big difference initially. For almost 100 years the college had functioned with the president and budget officer as the key administrative decisionmakers. The creation of three new vice-president-level positions—for the budget officer, director of development, and academic dean—did not change this pattern overnight.

The real transition began in 1974, when the spirit of the campus started to regenerate. Enrollment hit its lowest point (595) and the development efforts were successful. As Bill Grosz, vice-president for development, put it: "Beginning 1974-75, a super development year, the mood changed and a new spirit appeared." In 1974-75 the campus had a successful $100,000 campaign in the Lincoln area. Total income from private sources for the year was $372,811, up almost $80,000 from the previous year. Development efforts for the two subsequent years were below the 1974-75 total, although considerable staff attention was given to debt retirement and internal fiscal management during this period. The college also initiated more diverse fund-raising efforts, which included the securing of federal funds from cooperative education and AIDP. By the late 1970s, income from federal sources had increased considerably, even if AIDP is excluded from the calculations. Fund-raising plans included the funding of endowed chairs and more diverse giving programs.

Another aspect of the transition of the institutional spirit and attitude at Doane has been the new emphasis on career development. As a result of a 1972 trustee-faculty-administration planning session sponsored by the Danforth Foundation, the trustees mandated that the administrators and faculty at Doane emphasize the career relevance of the liberal arts program. The retreat had come at an important time; the college was in the midst of its enrollment decline and some kind of institutional renewal was badly needed. In December 1973 Heckman developed a working paper on career education. The paper outlined the elements of a new program: a program director, associate director, faculty internships, faculty improvement, counselor workshops, career library, faculty workshops, and the use of consultants. The paper also outlined strategies for attaining the program's objectives. The campus hired a director of career development in 1974 before federal funding was secured.

Doane has been successful with its career-development emphasis. When AIDP funds were not initially available, the college secured other funds, especially cooperative education funds, and used professional consulting advice to develop the new concept. The college is fortunate to have Dr. Ralph Tyler, a nationally known curriculum expert, as a 1921 graduate of the school. Between 1973 and 1977, Tyler consulted with the school to help it develop its career emphasis and undergo the necessary curricular change. In interviews, many of the administrators and faculty described his input as essential to the transition now taking place.

Doane applied to AIDP on three occasions. Its first request was for $512,000 over a three-year period to undertake the career education program. When this did not succeed, the career emphasis was initiated at the campus anyway. In subsequent years, Doane's sophistication in applying for AIDP increased. In 1976 it received a $1.25 million five-year grant to undertake a comprehensive development program.

The formal organizational structure of Doane College is relatively simple. The three vice-presidents, the director of career development, and director of admissions report directly to the president. The registrar, director of teaching and learning center, director of student affairs, and director of student activities report to the vice-president of academic affairs; the directors of public and alumni relations report to the vice-president for development; the chief accountant reports to the vice-president of financial affairs; and the assistant directors and counselors report to the directors of career development and admissions. In addition, a new office of institutional research has been added as a result of the ADVANCE project, and the staffs of the admissions, student affairs, and career development offices were expanded.

The academic structure of Doane College is also fairly simple. The five divisions—education, fine arts, humanities, natural sciences, and social sciences—are relatively equal in size, ranging from eight to ten FTE. Department sizes range from five FTE for physical education and music to one part-time person in speech. With Project ADVANCE funds, new faculty were added in business administration, early childhood, communication media, and computer science. Faculty interviewed in the departments of business and education, the largest majors on campus, expressed relief about the addition of faculty in these areas. The media person will work closely with the education division since the television operation's function is in education, and the computer science person will add to the capacity of the business curriculum.

In addition to being involved in the board of trustees and the administrative planning process, faculty are also members of a faculty organization. The faculty meets at least once a month to consider academic matters. The chairpersonship of the faculty is the responsibility of the president; however, it can be and usually is delegated to the vice-president for academic affairs. Faculty committees include: steering, faculty affairs, academic affairs, admissions, teacher education, and library. Don Ziegler, vice-president for academic affairs, thinks that faculty "in general feel pretty involved." However, he cautions that "the ADVANCE program may have lessened faculty sense of involvement," perhaps due to the emphasis on administrative decision making. In conversations with Doane faculty, their sense of involvement seemed apparent; their attitude toward ADVANCE was either excited or cautiously optimistic.

Doane College appears to be a nurturing environment for students. Bob Thomas, dean of students, feels that Doane students are relatively honest, basically conservative, generally positive, and have expectations of individual attention. Faculty seem concerned about students, about their learning and personal growth. Even with the addition of a part-time counselor through Project ADVANCE, the dean of students' office is relatively understaffed; as a result, faculty often are involved in counseling students, as well as giving them academic advice.

Doane students have many opportunities to be involved in campus affairs and decision making. Bob Thomas expressed some concern about the quality of student involvement. He suggests that "there is a willingness on the part of some students to become involved," although "in many cases, their preparation for the work is usually inadequate." These sentiments were expressed by others in the administration and on the faculty. They were concerned about the facilitation of high quality student involvement and input. Unfortunately, the author was unable to talk with any current students, although his impression of student access to decision making was favorable.

Doane is an excellent example of an institution catapulted into a more complex organizational phase because of environmental changes. In the early 1970s, the college experienced enrollment decline because of downward shifts in the number of traditional college-age students attending higher education institutions. The college also faced severe economic problems due to enrollment decline and the shaky economy. One of the ways Doane College dealt with this situation was to make some of the administrative changes described above. Another was to reorient the mission of the college toward a blending of the liberal arts with career education. This new emphasis has led to several changes in the college's academic structure, including the addition of a career-development program and reorientation of the basic liberal arts curriculum.

Xavier University (Historical Example)

Xavier University was in the direction phase during the late 1960s; some signs of this phase were exhibited earlier. The three-college structure of the university had emerged soon after the university was created, but during the first several decades the pharmacy school and the graduate school were both small and operated as if they were departments in the college of arts and sciences. In the late 1950s and early 1960s, the college began to formalize its administrative functions; the dean of students, the development office, and business office evolved. In the late 1960s, another series of events occurred: a new president was appointed who commissioned a study of the governance structure as one of his first acts; the college administrative structure was reorganized; and the college began to develop its long-range planning capacity in earnest. Since that time the university has experienced growth, increasing in size by nearly two-thirds. It also has strengthened its existing academic programs, undertaken new curriculum developments, and continued to formalize its administrative structure. These more recent changes have led Xavier into a new developmental phase.

Members of the Xavier University community have always seen Xavier as a distinctive institution. The opening description of the college in the document, A Description of the Planning Process at Xavier University of Louisiana, communicates this image:

> Of the approximately 100 existing American institutions of higher education which were created to serve Negroes, Xavier University in New Orleans is the only one affiliated with the Catholic Church. It was opened in 1925 by the Sisters of the Blessed Sacrament, a Catholic order of nuns founded by Mother M. Katherine Drexel, and dedicated to the education of American minorities.
>
> For the first 35 years of its existence, Xavier's claim to distinction was based on several features. It was, first of all, a Negro Catholic college. It was also something of an athletic powerhouse, and it had a pharmacy college, and a teacher education department which supplied a majority of the Negro teachers and administrators in the schools in New Orleans. Xavier's students were all black, and a majority of them were young women; many of its teachers, and virtually all of its administrators, were white women, members of the religious order of SBS.

A period of major and rapid structural change was experienced in the late 1960s. Having developed the first formal administrative structure and new relationships with external funding agencies, the institution had a capacity to handle more growth. Although enrollment declined in the early 1960s, the late 1960s saw a period of rapid growth. As one document puts it:

But however different Xavier was from the rest of the South's black colleges, it also had many characteristics in common with them, and at the beginning of the 1960's it was, like most of the rest of them, in need of revitalization. It was an isolated island in a sea of segregation and racial discrimination. It was small—about 800 students—and at least relatively poor. Its administration tended to be maternalistic and autocratic. It had been forced for financial reasons to give up intercollegiate athletics, and one result of that change was a drop in male enrollment and a subsequent dip in student morale.

The awakening brought about by the civil rights movement and other social concerns affected Xavier, and the Sisters of the Blessed Sacrament sought to respond. Particularly since 1965, the pace of change has been rapid. In that period, Xavier's enrollment has nearly doubled, to more than 1,400 students. The faculty has also doubled, and the ratio of nuns to lay professors has widened from 1:3 to 1:4. The top dozen administrators included about twice as many nuns as laymen in 1965; now the reverse is true. And the University's Board of Trustees, all of whom were nuns then, is now made up of six members of the religious order and three men—and by next year, a new board of up to 27 members will include as many as 18 persons who do not belong to the SBS (Description of Planning Process).

The administrative changes of the late 1960s were the most significant in the history of the institution. In 1968 Norman Francis became the fourth president of Xavier. He was the first layman, the first black, and the first alumnus to hold this position. He quickly became a symbol and instrument for change. Soon after taking office, he commissioned a governance study that has resulted in a new administrative structure and management system.

In spite of the growth, the transition to a more complex structure run by laypeople was not easy. There were more administrators who were drawing salaries for the first time. Prior to 1968, the school had always managed to show a surplus. For the next three years, the college operated at a loss. Enrollment was sporadic in the early 1970s. Enrollment fluctuation coupled with financial difficulties led to shifts in the newly developing planning process, and to an increased emphasis on sound fiscal management. This general situation led Hodgkinson and Schenkel to make the following observation: "Xavier is an instance of a college that would sink if not supported by Title III funds. The desired independence and entrepreneurial spirit has not developed to the fullest at the college" (1974, pp. 348–49).

Phase III: Delegation

Delegation-phase organizations are characterized by functionally differentiated organization structures with delegation of administrative responsibility to organizational subunits. The case studies
provide three examples of delegation-phase organizations: Xavier
University, which appears to be entering this phase, West Campus
of VCC, and North Carolina A & T, which is showing signs of moving
into an even more complex organizational phase.

Xavier University: 1970s

Xavier University of Louisiana has developed a more sophisticated organizational structure and management system during the
past five years. In 1969 a new planning office undertook the first long-
range plan; it later reviewed this plan before undertaking the administration of the AIDP program in 1974. The AIDP program has added to
the university's institutional research capacity, which is coordinated
by the planning office. A new ongoing planning effort touching most
subunits of the organization was initiated in 1977. The older administrative units also are going through a period of formalization: the development office is implementing a structure with several formal subunits; the budget office has had a high turnover rate during the past
two years as the functions of this office have formalized; the computer
center has experienced greater demands from the rest of the university; and the personnel office is playing a more active role in defining
administrative staff positions.

Xavier University operates as a system with a president and
executive vice-president as the key administrative officers. The new
organizational structure separates operations from planning and development. The planning and development officers report directly to
the president, while the operational units of the college—fiscal affairs,
academic affairs, and student services—report to the executive vice-
president. The executive vice-president is responsible for the day-to-
day management of the institution. The planning officer is also AIDP
coordinator for the institution.

The academic structure is more complex than many liberal arts
colleges of similar size because of the three-college structure. In
1977 the college of arts and sciences had a dean, 22 departments, and
39 majors. The academic department is the strong unit in the college
of arts and sciences. The college of pharmacy has a dean and one
major, pharmacy. Although the pharmacy school is almost as old as
arts and sciences, it has not been as large and, as a result, has at
times been looked upon as the equivalent of an arts and sciences department. In recent years, however, the college of pharmacy has
grown—from 156 students in 1970 to 227 in 1976—and now has a new,

separate building that adds to its autonomy. Of the three schools, the graduate school is the smallest, with a dean, three full-time faculty, a few faculty who also teach in undergraduate programs, and a few part-time faculty who have jobs off campus.

VCC West Campus

In 1977 the West Campus of VCC was experiencing a period of increasing formalization. Between 1975 and 1977 the academic departments were delegated more administrative responsibilities, and department chairmanships were officially recognized as administrative positions. Although the administration of the college is going through more formalization, the central administration moved off campus in 1974 and is no longer considered part of the campus administration. The student affairs organization, the largest administrative unit left on campus, was also going through a period of increased formalization. The dean of student affairs had increased the responsibilities of the directors of the various student affairs programs and was trying to get administrative appointments for the directors. When the case study was completed, West Campus had two deans, one each for student affairs and academic affairs. In addition to the provost, they are the chief administrators on campus. West Campus faculty are organized into 12 departments.

West Campus experienced problems with the transition to the multicampus system. According to James Richburg, dean for academic affairs at West Campus, the campus has "gone through the pains of transition." Richburg came to Valencia soon after the formation of the Open Campus and found West Campus in a situation where it "had to solve the problem of losing continuing education." Continuing education had been part of West Campus activities, and when an independent organization was formed to house these activities, the faculty experienced a lack of freedom and flexibility. West Campus tried to solve these frustrations through formalization of the department structure and delegation of responsibility to departments. During the 1976-77 year, department chairpersons were given status as administrators, which increased their pay and administrative responsibilities, while generally decreasing their teaching responsibilities.

When administration was centralized, new arrangements had to be made at the campus level. Most of the administrative services and financial management were moved to the central office. As already mentioned, the student affairs organization became the major administrative service unit on the campus. Due to continued growth, this administrative suborganization is experiencing increasing formalization as well. The dean of students now administers several subunits with more than one employee. For example, the counseling center has a staff of eight counselors and four educational advisors, and the special services program has a director and two counselors. In spite of the dean of students' efforts to delegate responsibility to program directors, this transition has not been fully successful. In 1977-78 Jerry Odom, West Campus dean of students, was trying to get his program directors administrative appointments.

North Carolina A & T (Historical Example)

North Carolina Agricultural and Technical State University is another example of a delegation-phase organization, although in the late 1970s it showed signs of transitioning to a more complex phase. Over the past two decades, the university has evolved into a highly delegated and differentiated organizational structure. Both the academic and administrative structures at A & T are highly differentiated. The university also has an elaborate governance system that provides for constituent involvement in many policy decisions. The administrative structure has been in fluctuation during the past few years, with several minor reorganizations having taken place. At the time of the site visit, a desk study was being conducted to evaluate the structure and work flow. During these transitions, however, the basic organizational structure with a chancellor and four vice-chancellors has remained intact. In addition to the vice-chancellors, the director of institutional research, dean of administration, assistant to the chancellor, administrative assistant, and director of planning report directly to the chancellor.

Each of the vice-chancellors has major administrative responsibilities. The directors of alumni affairs, athletics, and information and cooperative education report to the vice-chancellor for development and university relations. The directors of accounting, auxiliary services, contracts, personnel, physical plant, and purchasing, the bursar-director of student accounts, and budget officer report to the vice-chancellor for fiscal affairs. The academic affairs and student affairs organizations are even more complex, and have been part of the AIDP development project.

The student affairs organization is in transition from a loosely structured set of services reporting to the vice-chancellor for student affairs to a formally structured organization with an assistant to the vice-chancellor, three deans, and two directors (for registration and records and admission) reporting directly to the vice-chancellor. The actual titles for the deans' positions were still unsettled at the time of the original study; however, they were moving from a system with a dean of men and a dean of women to a system with three deans responsible for student-service areas. One dean is responsible for housing, the university center, and student organizations and activities. A second is responsible for counseling services, career planning and placement, career education, financial aid, and the health center.

The third is responsible for human resources and foreign students, veteran and handicapped student affairs, and religious activities. The directors for each of these services report to a dean. As part of the reorganization, the director of academic advising, an activity supported by AIDP, moved from student affairs to academic affairs.

The administrative structure of the academic affairs organization is the most complex area. The vice-chancellor for academic affairs, Glenn F. Rankin, has several deans and directors who report directly to him. The assistant vice-chancellor for academic affairs, Willie Ellis, who also is AIDP coordinator, reports directly to the vice-chancellor. Each of the schools is composed of several departments with chairpersons who hold administrative appointments.

In addition to the formal administrative and academic structure, A & T has developed an elaborate governance system for faculty and student participation. A & T has a university senate composed of faculty, students, and administrators. Faculty and student members are elected from departments. All academic administrators, from department chairmen to deans, are members of the senate. A & T also has a university council for policy in the student affairs area. The senate is responsible for all things related to the instructional phase of the institution. All recommendations that pass the senate are voted on by the faculty as a whole. The senate appears quite effective; as Senate Chairman A. Bell describes it: "I don't know of any recommendation from the senate to the faculty forum being rejected."

One of the unique features of A & T's senate is that it involves students, a practice started as a result of student unrest in the 1960s. Faculty and students are on committees, and although student attendance at committee meetings often is poor, their attendance at monthly senate meetings is good. Senate Chairperson Bell described participation as "very good for the student." Although some faculty expressed concern about the lack of student participation on committees, the attitude toward student involvement in the senate was very positive on the part of most faculty interviewed. Dr. Prince, chairman of the education department, described the senate structure as "a very good system of checks and balances." It is her view that "any student or faculty can start a curriculum change."

Phase IV: Coordination

During the coordination phase, central administrative services are developed as a means of coordinating the diverse activities within the delegated structure. Coordinated development allows for maximum utilization of resources in a complex institution and can minimize unneeded duplication. The case studies provide two examples of coordination-phase organizations: North Carolina A & T is currently exhibiting some signs of entering this phase, and Valencia Community College already has implemented a coordinated structure.

North Carolina A & T

North Carolina A & T's academic structure shows more signs of a coordination-phase organization than its administrative structure. In particular, two activities implemented under AIDP—academic advising and cooperative education—illustrate the types of development that take place in the coordination phase. Prior to AIDP, responsibility for academic advising was delegated through the administrative structure to schools and departments. The quality of academic advising varied considerably. Under the new system, one office coordinates the advising by developing universitywide information and procedures and by identifying individuals in departments who are responsible for advising. Cooperative education coordinates the experiential-learning options throughout the university. Formerly, these were the responsibility of the individual departments that had developed programs. As a result, there were several inconsistencies in the program and the way credit was awarded by different departments. Some of these inconsistencies, which have been identified by external evaluators for the AIDP project, can be resolved by this coordinated approach.

The administrative structure of A & T also shows increasing signs of coordination. It is part of the multicampus University of North Carolina and has to coordinate its activities with the systemwide administration. The planning office, which currently coordinates the planning activities of all organization subunits, is trying to develop strategies for setting universitywide objectives and priorities. In 1971 North Carolina Agricultural and Technical University became a campus of the University of North Carolina system. The basic organizational structure of the board, president, and vice-presidents remained the same, although the titles changed with the president becoming a campus chancellor. This absorption of A & T by the state has influenced some changes in the governance and management of the institution. A new level of administration has been created, with a systemwide administration and trustees; in many instances approval on this level is needed before program changes at the campus level can occur. In addition, the campus management and financing procedures have to comply with systemwide requirements. The university had to develop the capacity to function in the interinstitutional decision arena. In the opinion of many of those interviewed, the university has done exceedingly well in the statewide arena. The university also is beginning to need a more coordinated management system, which is discussed in the next chapter.

Valencia Community College

Valencia Community College moved full force into the coordination phase when it became a multicampus system in 1974. Prior to that time, all the college's activities had operated on one campus. Both the campus-based and continuing education activities had been housed in the campus-based academic departments. When the college became multicampus, the central administration moved off campus, the Open Campus was formed, and planning began for the East Campus. The movement by the college toward the coordination phase has not excluded the possibility that the three campuses, the major organizational subunits, might remain in a prior developmental phase, as the discussion earlier in this chapter illustrates.

VCC's collegewide administration provides the best example of a coordinated organizational structure. The administrative functions for all the campuses have been centralized. The only major exception to this is student affairs, which is still housed on the campuses. However, even registration, which usually is housed under student affairs, is part of the central administrative services. Whenever possible, academic and administrative decisions are made and implemented on a collegewide basis, especially if they will prevent unneeded duplication.

During the past decade the college has experienced several transitions. First, there was an initial creation period when the college, a junior college at the time, was housed in temporary facilities. Once they moved to a new campus in 1970, there was another period of growth during which the college, as a community college with its own board and representing two counties, began to develop as a community-based institution.

Throughout this early period, President Gollattscheck maintained an "open door" to encourage faculty and administrators to bring him their problems. In an interview, Gollattscheck described his role during the middle years when the college was continually adding new programs as "an act of the man who spins plates, trying to keep them going." As the college grew, it became less possible to maintain an open door. With respect to these changes, he observed: "A big problem we have is that the people in our college have a hard time understanding this growth and transition." Most of the administrators and faculty interviewed were aware of aspects of this transition. Charles Sample, provost of the Open Campus, put it simply: "I used to tell him a lot of things I do—now I write them down on paper."

At present, the college appears to be entering a new era of structural complexity. The older West Campus is maturing, the Open Campus is now organized and in full operation, and the new East Campus is in a creative developmental phase. The college is experiencing a few problems in its transition to a multicampus system and is using the AIDP project to aid this change. The major management task during the mid 1970s was to decentralize; the president has delegated responsibilities to each of the provosts who organized their campuses independently of the central administration.

One problem in the transition has been the faculty need to participate in systemwide policy decisions. During the past year, the administration has worked with the faculty on the development of a collegewide faculty organization. Two years ago faculty were discontented with expansion. This discontent was added to by the state shortfall in income. There was talk on campus of unionizing. Much of this discontent was resolved by the formation of the collegewide faculty governance structure at joint administration and faculty initiative. The faculty now have a mechanism for reviewing administrative decisions and are consulted on anything related to academic policy.

A second sign of difficulty is the relations between campuses. Although generally positive, there are potential difficulties. The East Campus has started under austere conditions. The role of the Open Campus has not been made clear. Some faculty fear that the Open Campus is supported by the revenues from the permanent campuses when, in fact, the Open Campus is self-supporting. Finally, there is a definite movement toward a more centralized administrative organization structure and management system. This potentially competes with the movement toward increasing delegation of authority to the campuses.

Administratively, Valencia Community College is complex. The college administration has tried to develop a structure capable of managing the multicampus system. As a result, it has developed a collegewide administration to coordinate the activities of the campuses. In addition, each of the campuses has developed a structure to manage its activities. The campus administrative structures vary in their complexity. The college has four vice-presidents: one each for administration, business affairs, development and facilities planning, and collegewide instructional services. Prior to the move to the multicampus system, the college had a vice-president for academic affairs—and fewer vice-presidents. The vice-presidents for business affairs and collegewide instructional services were created in 1976. The new structure also makes the three provosts the top academic administrators. In addition to the provosts and vice-presidents, the director of community relations reports directly to the president.

The college is developing its administrative services on a collegewide, rather than a campus-by-campus, basis. An example of a collegewide service is the department of resource development, which is housed administratively under the vice-president for development and facilities planning. This office has two professionals who act as catalysts for individuals and groups in the central administration and at the various campuses. These individuals review all federal requests for funding proposals (RFPs) and other funding sources to see if requests relate to some aspect of the college's activities. If they do, they will alert these people and consult with them on the development of proposals.

Another example of a concerted effort to develop collegewide services is AIDP. Valencia Community College applied to AIDP as one organization. While AIDP regulations make campuses and not systems eligible for funding, VCC made the argument that it should be considered as a single institution because it was attempting to develop as a coordinated system. All AIDP activities are being implemented in a coordinated fashion by collegewide committees. The one component that needs to be housed at a campus, the CID center, is rotating between the East and West Campuses every other year so that it will not be identified with one campus.

The implementation of a coordinated structure received mixed reviews. The two new vice-presidents—Gloria Raines, vice-president for instructional services, and Lee Young, vice-president for business affairs—view the new structure with great optimism. As Raines put it, "People are going to have to learn to rely more on a formalized structure." Young thinks that although the movement toward a multicampus has created problems, it was necessary.

One aspect of the problem has been the skyrocketing number of meetings. In 1975 the size of the administration staff was small. By 1977, with the vice-presidents and provosts, the number of people reporting directly to the president increased markedly. When the deans of the various campuses are included in staff meetings, as is often the case, the size gets unmanageable. Administrators' views on the problem vary: those who have been there for awhile experienced it as a problem, while those who were new thought the committee structures needed to be developed.

In addition to the administrative problems accompanying the development of a collegewide administration, the faculty have felt an increasing distance from the administration. One visible sign of the distance is the movement of the collegewide administration off campus. Instructional services, which remains on West Campus, is the only exception. Another sign is the creation of the collegewide organizational structure. To gain some access to system policy decisions, the faculty have created a collegewide faculty organization. Faculty now have an organization with representatives from each campus that meets with the administration on policy matters and sends policy decisions to campus facilities for review. For practical purposes, the faculty organization represents the East Campus and West Campus since there are few full-time faculty with the Open Campus.

General Model

Based on these examples, it is possible to review the general model of structural development suggested earlier. Table 5.1 refines the descriptions of structural development proposed in the model outlined in Chapter 3. It suggests a focus and general developmental characteristics for each phase.

TABLE 5.1

Phases of Structural Development for Colleges and Universities

Phase	Focus	Structural Developments
I	Creation of new programs	Little administrative development, usually two or three key administrators, small faculty and student body
II	Direction (long range) of institution defined	Administrative structure becomes more formal, multiple academic programs may develop
III	Delegation of authority to functional subunits	Differentiation of administrative structure, administrative responsibilities delegated to subunits
IV	Coordination of subunit activities	Central administration develops, policies and procedures coordinated across subunits, coordinated program development

The model suggests that as institutions develop structurally, they also become more complex. Structural development is associated with, although not synonymous with, increased size. During each phase, a distinctively different organizational form emerges, building on the characteristics of the prior phase. During the initial phase, the structure is simple: the faculty and student body are small, the college usually is run by one or two key administrators, and the developmental focus is on creating academic programs. As the institution enters the direction phase, the administration becomes more formalized, some differentiation of administrative and academic functions occurs, and the focus of the organization shifts to program maintenance and to defining the long-range direction of the organization. During the delegation phase, existing functions, perhaps added

during the direction phase, are formalized into organizational subunits; new functional subunits—schools, colleges, or campuses—may
be added to the organization. The coordination phase is the last phase
for which evidence is available in the case studies. During this phase,
the developmental focus shifts to centralized programmatic development and centralized administrative services to coordinate the activities of diverse functional subunits. The basic outlines of the model
remain consistent with the hypothesized model.

DEVELOPMENTAL MEASURES

The analysis of the case institutions shows that a developmental
sequence can be discerned by examining institutions' structures, histories, and management. In spite of considerable variance in the type,
control, and mission of the case institutions, a generalized sequence
of development can be identified. Institutions that have more modern
instructional technologies do not appear to differ considerably in their
structural characteristics from more traditional institutions. The
task of developing a set of measures to predict developmental phase
is more difficult, but is attempted in this chapter nonetheless.

The structural history of a college, its evolution and development over time, is the key factor in determining the developmental
phase. The structure of an organization is a product of its history:
the addition of new administrative or academic subunits is the result
of past internal decisions and external forces. Yet these structural
developments, along with the individuals that comprise the institutions,
create both the basis and constraints for future developments. Although
the specific characteristics of institutions seem to vary, the actual
sequence appears consistent. An institution must pass through each
successive phase; a new school cannot be created as a coordinated
institution. However, some institutions may reach more complex
phases sooner than others.

In spite of the importance of history, age is a poor predictor of
structural-development phase. Greiner (1972) uses both age and rate
of growth as measures of development in his phased model for business organizations. Figure 5.1 illustrates the importance of the rate
of growth to the structural development of colleges. In this illustration, College A takes over 50 years to enter phase I, while College
B takes less than 10 years to progress through the first three phases
and enter phase IV. A more recent institution is likelier to enter a
more complex developmental phase than an older institution that has
not experienced structural change in a long time. Doane College and
Valencia Community College illustrate this situation: Doane lasted
nearly a century as a phase I institution, while Valencia entered a
coordinated phase in less than ten years.

FIGURE 5.1

Rate of Structural Development

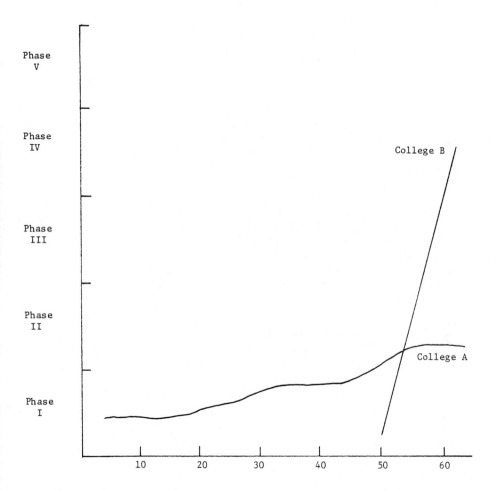

Although there are no examples of movement from a more complex to a less complex phase in the case studies, this can occur. The general theory does not exclude this possibility, and if one examines the condition of many contemporary institutions, one might see how such a move is possible. If, for example, a university with three colleges—an undergraduate school of arts and sciences, a school of education, and a small graduate school that offers a master's degree in education and arts and sciences—experiences a decrease in enrollment in education, a major reorganization into a single college structure might be necessary. To increase efficiency, the administrative structure might be simplified as well. Although decreasing in size and complexity undoubtedly is more difficult than the reverse, it is a reality some institutions might have to face.

To define a specific set of variables to predict developmental phases is not easy. One must examine the history of an institution and its structure and management to be certain where it falls in the developmental sequence. In addition, the developmental phases and categories are descriptive; they are not found within precise places on a table or graph that can be plotted or categorized easily. Instead, the most that quantitative measures can provide is an indication of where an institution might fall on the general sequence, just as an individual's age, within five or ten years, might give an indication of the types of life crises that person might be facing. Age alone is not a definite predictor of developmental phase of the individual adult, and no set of variables can provide definite predictors of developmental phases for organizations. To the extent that it is possible to generate a few measures to predict development, quantitative measures will be useful as indicators for funding and research. However, the more that is known about the history, structure, and management of a college, the easier it should be to determine the types of innovations and developments that would help it.

The most that can be hoped for from this analysis is that a general range can be suggested for a few variables that might be useful in predicting developmental phases. Table 5.2 compares the institutions used as examples in the earlier discussion on selected variables: enrollment and numbers of faculty, chief administrators, departments or divisions, schools or colleges, campuses, and major administrative decisions. Enrollment and numbers of faculty and chief administrators are measures of institutional size, while the rest are complexity measures. A discussion of each of the variables and its usefulness as a measure of structural development follows.

Enrollments: FTE enrollment is the full-time equivalent students enrolled in a given institution. Except for Valencia Community College and its three campuses, the FTE enrollment totals are the

TABLE 5.2

Comparison of Case Institutions on Selected Characteristics, 1976–77

	VCC East Campus	VCC Open Campus	Doane College	St. Mary's Junior College	Xavier Univ.	VCC West Campus	North Carolina A&T State U.	Valencia Community College
Enrollment (FTE)[a]	2,000	650	625	788	1,889	5,000	5,515	7,650
Faculty[b]	27	n/a	32 (F) 4 (P)	79	183	332	322	355
Chief administrators[c]	2	1	6	5	12	3	13	14
Departments & divisions[c]	2	3	5	3	23	12	32	15
Schools/colleges[c]	1	1	1	1	3	1	7	1
Campuses[c]	1	1	1	1	1	1	1	3
Major administrative divisions[d]	1	3	3	3	3	2	4	7

[a]FTE enrollment is actual FTE reported by the institutions, except VCC and its campuses, which are based on estimates provided in interviews, since the college did not provide an enrollment breakdown by campus.

[b]These totals came from various sources: interviews for East Campus, faculty handbook for Doane, catalogs for St. Mary's, Xavier, and NCA&T, and estimates based on 1975–76 reported statistics for VCC and VCC West Campus.

[c]Based on count from college and university catalogs.

[d]Based on examination of organizational charts.

actual numbers reported by the institutions. In the case of VCC, these numbers are estimates given in interviews with campus administrators, since the college did not provide a breakdown of its FTE enrollment by campus. With the exception of the East Campus of VCC, enrollment totals increase as the institutions become more complex structurally. This exception of East Campus makes sense conceptually; it is a young campus and its FTE student enrollment has increased faster than its other characteristics.

Faculty: Faculty is the number of teaching faculty. When appropriate, this data should be collected as full-time equivalent faculty but unfortunately these data are difficult to collect, even in Title III applications. An earlier study of institutional change using the Title III application and award data base indicated that even when asked to report faculty as FTE, many institutions may have reported total faculty (St. John, Tingley, and Gallos, 1977). For the totals used here, different sources were used: catalogs, faculty handbooks, the Title III application and award data, and interviews. The totals from catalogs are the most inflated values since these include administrators who usually hold faculty appointments, as well as teaching faculty. The comparison suggests there is an increase in the number of faculty as an institution becomes more complex structurally. As the number of programs and majors a campus offers increases, the number of faculty increases. If these data could be gathered more accurately and consistently, it would be a good measure of structural development.

Chief Administrators: This is a useful measure that is not collected consistently in the Title III data base and is seldom collected consistently by other sources. The Title III application has asked this question differently for different years—it varies between the number of full-time administrators and the number of chief administrative officers. The totals used here are from the college or university catalogs. The total number of chief administrative officers includes heads of major administrative divisions or programs and academic administrators for schools and colleges. Academic department chairpeople, who in the case of VCC are heads of the major academic units, have been excluded. Again, the general pattern is toward an increase in the number of administrators as institutions become more complex.

Academic Departments/Divisions: This is the number of academic departments or divisions on campus. In the smaller, less complex institutions, faculty were organized into divisions instead of departments. According to these figures, the number of academic

departments tends to increase as schools get larger. The exception
is Valencia Community College and its various campuses. At Valencia,
the department or division is the dominant academic subunit, since
the college is not divided into a number of smaller schools. On this
measure there may be a difference between institutions according to
institutional type: two-year schools may be more likely to have academic departments as their major academic unit, while schools or
colleges with different foci may be more dominant in four-year institutions. If this is the case, academic departments would tend to be
larger and to combine more disciplines at two-year institutions.

Schools/Colleges: This is the number of schools and colleges
in the institution. For the three four-year institutions, this number
seems to increase as the institutions develop structurally: Doane has
one, Xavier has three, and North Carolina A & T has seven. Valencia
Community College and St. Mary's Junior College are not divided into
different schools. At both two-year institutions, technical education
and general education programs operate side-by-side within the same
college structure.

Campuses: This is the number of separate autonomous campuses
associated with a college or university. It does not refer to separate
pieces of land owned by the university, extended learning locations,
or extension stations. There is only one example of an institution with
more than one campus, Valencia Community College. This appears
to be an important indicator since an institution with more than two
campuses has a drastically increased need for coordinated management.

Major Administrative Divisions: This is the number of major
administrative divisions within the institution: financial affairs, academic affairs, and so on. In the instance of a multicampus system,
campuses were treated as single administrative divisions. This measure seems to make the least difference of those considered. Although
it could be argued that the two most complex institutions (Valencia
and A & T) have the most administrative divisions, the evidence to
support the assertion that this is an important measure is slim, especially since there are many confounding factors. The campuses of
Valencia Community College, for example, have many of their administrative services handled by collegewide administration; one of the
campuses (West Campus) once housed the central administration.

The potential usefulness of these seven measures as indicators
of structural development varies considerably. Enrollment appears
to be a useful measure since it tends to increase as the institution

develops structurally. But enrollment alone will not be a good predictor since a young institution, such as VCC's East Campus, might
change faster in enrollment than in other characteristics. Chief administrators appear to be a useful measure since they too tend to
increase as institutions develop structurally. This measure also may
indicate the same type of developments as the less reliable measure
of major administrative divisions. There are instances where this is
not reliable, however, such as with the campuses of VCC, where central administrative services have been moved off campus and the number of chief administrators left on campus is small given the complexity of the organization. The number of faculty could be a useful measure and, if it could be collected more consistently, it might prove a
good complement to numbers of students and administrators.

The complexity-related measures tend to vary even more than
size-related measures in their usefulness as indicators of structural
development. The number of schools and colleges appears to be an important indicator for the more complex developmental phases, especially four-year institutions. An institution with several schools and
colleges faces more management problems than an institution with a
single academic focus. The use of the school's and college's criteria
may be less useful for two-year institutions than for four-year institutions, since four-year institutions are more likely to be organized
into these units. The number of campuses is important, especially as
an indicator of the need for coordination, although this is not the only
indicator of this need. When the number of schools and colleges gets
beyond a certain number, the institution may experience the same
types of organizational and management needs. The number of departments and divisions and of major administrative units appears less
useful because of the way colleges and universities are organized.

The number of administrative divisions does not appear to vary
much. There may be a limited number of top-level administrative
divisions that are manageable, beyond which the organization might
get out of control of the top administrators. For departments and divisions, the reverse is the problem: there appears to be too much
variation. In some institutions departments may be strong administrative units and may have professional administrators, while in others there may be many such divisions or departments for the size,
and the chairpeople may be part-time chairpeople who are primarily
faculty.

Based on a consideration of these variables, it is possible to
suggest ranges for a few measures that might predict development
phases. Table 5.3 proposes four possible indicators of structural
development. These are ranges that can be used to predict developmental phases. These ranges are tentative and should be interpreted
with caution. They could provide a basis for other investigations using
this developmental model. According to these ranges one might expect:

TABLE 5.3

Possible Indicators of Structural Development for
Colleges and Universities

Phases	I	II	III	IV
Enrollment (FTE)	$0 \to 600$	$600 \to 1,800$	$1,800 \to 5,000$	$5,000 \to$
Chief administrators	$1 \to 5$	$5 \to 10$	$10 \to 15$	$15 \to$
Colleges/ schools	1	$1 \to 3$	$3 \to 7$	$7 \to$
Campuses	1	1	$1 \to 2$	$3 \to$

Phase I institutions to have fewer than 600 students, fewer than
five chief administrators, one school or college, and/or one
major location (if it is a nontraditional institution, like the Open
Campus of Valencia Community College, it might offer courses
in diverse locations);

Phase II institutions to have between 600 and 1,800 students,
five to ten chief administrators, one to three colleges or schools,
and/or one major location;

Phase III institutions to have from 1,800 to 5,000 students, 10
to 15 chief administrative officers, three to seven schools, and/
or one or two major locations; and

Phase IV institutions to have over 5,000 students, over 15 chief
administrators, over seven colleges or schools, and/or more
than three major locations.

Not all institutions will fall into these ranges. Within the case
studies, there were many exceptions—more than one for each variable.
Any given institution might have two or three of the four characteristics within the predicted range. However, short of developing descriptive histories, these few measures might help the outsider to make an
informed guess about an institution's developmental phase.

Rather than use a set of measures to predict developmental
phase, in the long run it might be more appropriate to develop a set
of questions about the institution's history, structure, and management. This should be the objective of subsequent research in the area.

First, the relationship between structural development and management effectiveness should be considered.

CONCLUSIONS

The analysis of the case studies suggests that a sequence of structural development can be identified for colleges and universities. This sequence closely resembles the developmental phase described in the general theory of Chapter 4. These labels describe the primary developmental foci of the organization. However, institutions in the various phases do have many characteristics in common.

It is possible to develop a set of measures that can be used to predict developmental phases. Since no single measure can adequately predict developmental phases, the ranges for several measures can be more appropriately used as general indicators. Institutions with some of these characteristics—say, two or three of four proposed measures—might be appropriately considered in one or another of the developmental phases. However, to accurately discover an institution's developmental phase, its history, structure, and management system must be examined. Eventually, it might be possible to develop a set of questions that could be used to predict developmental phases more accurately than quantitative measures.

To be useful to institutional planning and management, or to government or foundation interventions designed to improve institutional planning and management, the model has to do more than suggest measures to structural development. It also should examine the relationship between structural development and institutional management, as the next chapter will do.

6

MANAGEMENT DEVELOPMENT

Although the emphasis placed on management effectiveness in higher education has increased considerably during the past decade, there are few viable models for college and university management development that have taken into account structural differences and local needs. A structural-development model was considered in Chapter 4 that distinguishes between diverse institutional characteristics as institutions develop. This chapter explores the basic relationship between structural development and management effectiveness generally by analyzing the relationship between the structural characteristics and management systems at the five selected institutions.

This analysis relies on detailed descriptions of the management systems at these institutions. A discussion of the management-development effort of each of the case institutions is included in this chapter. These examples illustrate the thesis that a college's management needs will change as it develops structurally; and conversely, that new management needs will continue to emerge as new systems are implemented, until a relative balance is attained between the management systems installed and the demands placed on the system by the formal structure and the external environment. First, however, the effectiveness of the management systems at institutions will be considered, based on data from the case studies.

MANAGEMENT EFFECTIVENESS

The five institutions used in this study were considered exemplary by USOE-AIDP staff for their management and overall use of Title III funds. Rather than accept this professional judgment without question, the effectiveness of the management systems at these institutions was analyzed according to five criteria. The following discussion of these criteria examines both the effectiveness of the management at the case institutions and the usefulness of these criteria as measures of management effectiveness.

Attention Paid to Management Needs

The first criterion considers whether or not a college has examined its own management needs. It is an important and relatively well-defined measure of management effectiveness. Each of the case institutions has made considerable progress during the past few years in identifying its management deficiencies. Two of the campuses—St. Mary's Junior College and Valencia Community College—have emphasized the study of their management problems in order to identify management deficiencies and possible systems that could aid in their resolution. Doane College has been involved in a slow, deliberate process of examining its management deficiencies and adapting its present management system to meet these needs better. The remaining campuses—Xavier University and North Carolina A & T—have implemented one set of management changes only to discover that once the most basic management needs were met, others emerged. At all five campuses, management appears to be an important concern, and considerable attention has been paid to institutional management by faculty and administration.

Implementation of a New Management System

The second criterion considers whether the college has followed up its needs assessment with the implementation of a new management system. The following discussion documents how new management systems address unmet management needs. Usually this requires adaptation of standard systems and procedures to the uniqueness of a particular institution. This is an important factor when considering management effectiveness, since the process of implementing a new management system is a difficult, incremental, and adaptive process. Each of the institutions studied adapted existing models to its local setting. Although at the time of the case studies none had reached an equilibrium between identified needs and the development of a formal management system that addresses those needs, each was in the process of implementing new management systems.

Effectiveness of Resource Use and Planning

The third criterion, the effectiveness of resource use and planning, is the most complex and probably the most important of the effectiveness criteria used in this study. Identifying the gap between an institution's aspirations and its ability to finance its plans is an essential part of this criterion and a critical measure of an institution's financial health. Of primary concern here is whether or not the plans are reasonable for the institution. The performance of the case institutions varies on this criterion, although all five are making some progress in this regard. A synopsis of the situation at each institution follows:

> Doane College ran into severe financial problems in the early 1970s when its growth plans were not realized; enrollment declines were experienced when increases were anticipated. Since that time, Doane has made a more conscious effort to close the gap between what it plans to undertake and its ability to finance its goals.

> St. Mary's Junior College has been the most successful of the case institutions at financing its plans. It is the only institution that consciously addressed the institutional aspiration issue before it became a problem: the college intends to remain small and has been remarkably successful at financing its plans, which are usually needed by the institution.

> Xavier University, like Doane College, experienced financial difficulties in the late 1960s and early 1970s. It too has had to adjust its growth aspirations downward. In addition, the university has had to make improvements in its fiscal management, which had become a source of many problems. Increased size would not have been a solution to the fiscal difficulties if the university's income was not well managed.

> North Carolina A & T is a well-financed institution compared to other institutions in this study and to other public four-year colleges funded by Title III. In recent years it has done well finding the funds to meet its plans. However, there are signs that the gap between the university's aspirations and finances may be widening: during the past few years the university has had a slight operating deficit; it has not been able to meet its matching commitments for AIDP; and its enrollment has increased at a faster rate than its income from the state.

> Valencia Community College, like St. Mary's, has been fortunate to have the ability to generate the funds it needs to meet its

aspirations. It has encountered problems with state funding from time to time; on one occasion it was forced to open a new campus under severe financial conditions. However, in times of financial stress it has shown a remarkable capacity to generate funds from external sources.

The case-study institutions appear to be dealing with the problems of aspirations versus financial capacity in different ways. Some have adjusted their aspirations downward, while others have weighed growth plans against available funding possibilities. In spite of these differences, each is starting to look at the relationship between financial possibilities and the planning process.

Quality and Effectiveness of Constituent Involvement

The fourth criterion is the quality and effectiveness of constituent involvement. Colleges and universities have traditionally placed considerable value on the involvement of various constituencies in the governance process. However, the relationship between effective management and constituent involvement has seldom been examined. In fact, it is often hypothesized that constituent involvement is inefficient and therefore competes with the need for more effective management. Each of the institutions studied has placed considerable emphasis on constituent involvement in decision making. The three four-year colleges have done much better than the average American college in establishing mechanisms for faculty and student involvement. The two-year institutions have been less successful at involving students, although Valencia Community College has recognized the importance of student involvement and is trying to establish mechanisms for it. Both the two-year and four-year colleges have experimented with different mechanisms for involving faculty, and appear quite effective at this. In every instance, the involvement of faculty and student goes beyond involvement in traditional academic policy issues and includes some of the most important planning and management issues. It seems, therefore, that constituent involvement may be an important measure of management effectiveness in higher education.

Renewal Capacity

Renewal capacity is the last and vaguest of the criteria considered as a measure of management effectiveness. Nevertheless, the ability of an institution to renew itself may be the most important measure of the long-range effectiveness of any institution-management system. The case institutions all provide interesting examples of institutional renewal. The degree of emphasis placed on renewal varies from its being a major focus of the institution to its being undertaken only in times of severe stress. Xavier and Doane have faced severe financial conditions and instituted major changes to remedy them; North Carolina A & T has examined its organization and governance in the midst of conflict and made modification of its structure as a result; and St. Mary's Junior College and Valencia Community College have made the renewal process an essential part of their institutional mission.

Overview

Although none of the institutions can be considered to be perfectly managed, each appears to be effectively managed according to the general criteria used in this investigation. Each has made important inroads in the development of more effective management systems during the past five years, and each is trying to adapt standard management procedures and systems.

The five criteria were useful indicators of management effectiveness, especially when used together. They provide colorful pictures of the institution-management process. These are not the only indicators of management effectiveness; nor is it certain that they are the most appropriate. After all, these are exceptional institutions, at least when compared to other developing institutions. These institutions are models not because they represent the state of the art in institutional management in higher education, but because they represent different ways institutions can develop effective management systems.

One measure of management effectiveness that was not considered explicitly, but appears to be important in the case studies nonetheless, is the quality of top leadership. Cohen and March (1974), in one of the best studies of college leadership to date, report that the average length of tenure for college presidents is about ten years, and that for financially less-well-off institutions, this length of tenure appears to be shorter. At the five case-study institutions, the president has been the chief administrator for over ten years. In each instance the president appears committed to the institution. Based on interviews with a diverse cross-section of people on each campus, the author concluded that these presidents are popular, trusted, and respected. Presidential leadership may be a hidden factor that is essential for effective college management or it may be an unimportant by-product. If presidents are successful they tend to stay longer. Whether it is a cause or effect, this factor merits consideration in future studies of management in higher education.

For this study, the measures that have been considered seem appropriate. They show a strong indication that the five institutions examined are well on the road toward developing effective management systems, and therefore provide useful models for analysis.

MANAGEMENT DEVELOPMENT*

This section analyzes the management needs identified and changes implemented by each of the case-study institutions. The institutions were categorized into developmental phases in the prior chapter. While the same examples of institutions in each phase are considered here, a detailed description of the implementation process is discussed for each institution.

Phase I Management Systems

Creation-phase institutions usually are managed by a few individuals who consult with other organization members about the development and maintenance of academic programs. Four examples of creation-phase organizations were presented in the case studies and analyzed in the previous chapter; each is a loosely structured organization with a compatible management system.

The East and Open Campuses of VCC are managed by a provost and dean. East Campus has had this arrangement since it was first created, and Open Campus is currently moving toward this system. Both campuses are oriented toward innovation and the creation of new programs. At Open Campus, the dean and three program directors work closely with adjunct faculty and members of the community on the development of new courses and programs. At East Campus the dean works closely with faculty on curriculum development, while the provost takes more responsibility for planning new programs. Neither campus has an elaborate management system. The management needs identified by administrators in interviews included more budgetary control at East Campus and more access to collegewide decisions at Open Campus. Neither set of administrators identified long-range planning or program maintenance as management priorities; instead, they identified program development as their main focus.

---

*Documents and interviews cited in this section are referenced in the Appendix. The documents provided by the campuses and USOE often did not include authors' names or page numbers.

Management practices at the two new VCC campuses are not standardized. Provost Evans and Dean Beal described management as an open-consultation process on their campuses. Dean Beal expressed the need for more administrative control on campus. Faculty at the East Campus appear happy with this open-consultation atmosphere. At the Open Campus, the management process is probably even more individualistic. Provost Sample manages on an old army principle—AAAΘ—Anything, Anytime, Anywhere, Bar Nothing. For his staff this creates a great deal of freedom. As one of the program directors, Robert Milke, described it: "We'd like to bring in the best programs we can at a reasonable cost." Milke also points to some tensions with the central office: "I've noted at Downtown Center we really have little input into the whole operation." The provost, dean, and directors of the Open Campus have staff meetings, which is their means of coordinating their activities.

Doane College functioned for nearly 100 years as a creation-phase organization. Its self-image has been that of a creative organization, considering itself a miniature Harvard of the Midwest, and often taking on the character of a misplaced Black Mountain College. * Its management system had been informal, with the budget officer and president making most administrative decisions, perhaps through collaboration with others on campus or on the board of trustees. Most academic decisions were made by the dean and president in collaboration with the faculty. The involvement of students and faculty in the governance of the college had been a major concern. Although the major emphasis of the curriculum shifted over time from religion to politics to music, its management system remained relatively constant and its student market relatively secure. One of the most liberal institutions in the state of Nebraska, Doane went about its activities in a quiet way. It also maintained an emphasis on remaining small until the mid 1960s, when the Carnegie Commission and other national organizations emphasized the number of 1,000 students as the enrollment needed to survive in the 1970s. At that time, Doane began to emphasize growth; slowly, its structure and management began to change as well.

St. Mary's Junior College was a creation-phase organization until recently. Created by the director and some of the faculty from an older hospital nursing program, the college rapidly evolved a simple structure with a president and vice-president. Again the emphasis

---

*Black Mountain College was a small, innovative college that emphasized the creative arts. It received national recognition in the late 1940s and early 1950s before it folded (see Duberman, 1972).

at the college was on the creation of new programs and on curricular innovations. The president and vice-president worked closely with faculty on the development of new courses and programs and on the securing of outside funds to experiment with new learning options. It was a creative environment, with all organization members sharing an image of the college as a creative and innovative institution.

Management Implementation at St. Mary's

The following detailed description of the St. Mary's implementation process illustrates the complexities of adapting modern management practices in a very small college with a creative emphasis. The PME plans in St. Mary's final AIDP proposal included: a study of operational data systems; analysis of the planning, management, and evaluation needs of the college; and a general plan for strengthening the planning, management, and evaluation system.

USOE staff members who visited SMJC in April 1976 expressed a concern that implementation of the PME was not moving fast enough. In 1975 the college requested a supplementary grant to conduct an intensive study of the organizational structure, roles, curricular renewal processes, program efficiency, and viability of technical education programs. Thus, even after over two years of AIDP support, St. Mary's was still at a stage of trying to implement a viable PME system. Although the college is exemplary in many regards, implementation of its PME system has not proceeded as fast as other AIDP activities.

The development of a viable management system progressed slowly at St. Mary's for a number of reasons. One important factor was that the administrative structure had been in transition. Another was that the college had been quite successful without a formal management system, so the administrators were reluctant to move too rapidly into new practices that may not work as well. Still another factor is the high priority placed on retaining the college's informal decision-making atmosphere. Finally, the AIDP project had concentrated on other activities to give the system enough time to determine which systems or processes would be more appropriate for the campus. In short, the college made a conscious effort to assess its emerging management needs and to establish a management system consonant with those needs.

Administrators at St. Mary's were aware of the college's management problems, but were approaching the development of a management system with the same conscious and experimental attitudes they used to develop other college programs and activities. During summer 1977 the results of the AIDP evaluations were compiled. These included studies of technical and general education, surveys of students and faculty, and internal and external evaluations of the AIDP project. The major conclusions about the PME from these studies were:

    a. We needed to more clearly articulate the ways our institutional goals were changing as the college was engaged in the intense effort of the Advanced Institutional Development Project.

    b. There was a need to update our data on development needs—to meet immediate practical purposes.

    c. There was a need to begin to set priorities for development needs so that our efforts could be channeled more effectively (Peterson, 1977).

St. Mary's had a tendency to take advantage of available resources when planning for management developments. Development of its management-information system illustrates this. St. Mary's has not changed existing systems in those cases in which consultants or other experts have advised them that a computer capacity would not speed the process (such as with classroom assignments, which can be handled more easily by hand for an institution of SMJC's size). In those instances where a computer capacity is needed, Lawrence Demarest, coordinator of AIDP evaluation, has used the University of Minnesota's computer facility. He points out that there is no need for an institution like SMJC, with a commitment to remain small, to develop unneeded computer capacities.

The management of the AIDP project at SMJC exemplifies its commitment to managing an innovative enterprise effectively. As a result of the long-range planning process in 1972-73, St. Mary's defined a planning process it has used in the implementation of AIDP activities. Each subactivity has gone through the process, which is probably the pride of the AIDP effort of the college. The steps in the process, gleaned out of the planning literature at the time of the long-range planning committee, are: descriptive phase—the problem area and the type of program needed are defined; design phase—an intervention or program is planned; pilot phase—the intervention or program is tested; implementation phase—once the problems with the intervention or program are worked out, it is modified and implemented; and integration in the system—during the final step the intervention or program is integrated into and becomes part of the system. Each of the AIDP activities, including the PME, is going through or has been through this process.

According to this model, the PME system is entering the implementation phase. Earlier the administration identified long-range planning as the major management need. When the long-range planning committee had completed its work and the AIDP grant was secured, the administration began to experiment with the planning and development council (PDC), a group composed of administrators and faculty. The president and senior vice-president were not involved. The formation of the PDC was premature, however, since it was not tied effectively to the structure of the institution. At the time, the college had not developed its capacity for goal setting or its ability to attain or modify its objectives.

Implementation of the PME at St. Mary's progressed slowly as a result of a conscious decision. When the grant was received in 1974, Peterson pulled together a group to discuss the PME. At the time it was difficult to identify unmet management needs. The approved AIDP plan did not call for doing anything about the system until the second year. During the second year, the study of technical education was under way, the results of which would have an impact upon college-management needs; so the implementation was delayed for a year. In 1976 the administration and the AIDP steering committee agreed that the PME had been put off long enough. They identified a variety of problem areas and the coordinator of the PME, Marcia Hanson, spent the entire year studying them. The problem areas studied included: overall governance, academic management, personnel management, institutional planning and development, research and institutional studies, allocation of resources, development of institutional image and resource development, and support services. By mid 1977 the college was implementing a PME system that was compatible with the institution and capable of fulfilling unmet management needs.

Phase II Management Systems

Direction-phase organizations become more structured academically and administratively, and their management becomes more formal, emphasizing long-range planning and program maintenance. Three examples of direction-phase organizations were given in the previous chapter.

St. Mary's entered the direction phase not because of crisis, but because of success. After a decade of innovation, the president commissioned a long-range planning committee, the first in the college's history. The college identified long-term goals, including the maintenance of existing programs and the development of new administrative services. The administrative structure of the college began to change and the administrative staff started to take a more intensive look at the college's management needs. Rather than have the primary focus of the top administrators on program development, their emphasis shifted to maintenance of existing programs; new organizational subunits emerged to manage the innovation process. At first the AIDP steering committee was the focus of the innovation process, but more recently the new programs and continuing education segments have been organized into a major academic subunit. In addition, the college is experimenting with different planning, management, and evaluation procedures that will both maintain the organization and allow for continued innovation.

Xavier University entered the second phase before either Doane or St. Mary's. Structurally it began to show signs of increasing formalization in the late 1950s, but the process of management development began in the late 1960s when a new president was appointed. President Francis commissioned a governance study as one of his first acts. The commission's report recommended the reorganization of the formal structure, a change that was adopted, and at the same time it set in motion a management emphasis that remains today. All the university's administrators emphasize good management, and the university is now making progress beyond these initial beginnings. These first steps, however, illustrate the management developments that occur in the direction phase.

Before Francis took over as chief administrative officer for Xavier University, much of the university's management had been laissez-faire, with the religious order controlling many of the important decisions. One of the first developments beyond the informal day-to-day approach that had epitomized the institution during its early decades, was the development of a long-range planning process. Under Francis, the university rapidly developed and refined its long-range planning capacity and secured an AIDP grant during the early 1970s. The university was more complex structurally than either Doane or St. Mary's, and more structure and management development was essential for its long-term survival.

Doane College is entering the direction phase as a stable organization with a long history. In the late 1960s and early 1970s the college began to experience severe financial difficulties: it had built new academic buildings and dormitories requiring large capital investments; it had experienced a surge in enrollment followed by an enrollment decline; its growth plans were unrealized and some space was not fully utilized; and large operating deficits were incurred. The college had reached a point where old operating procedures no longer worked. A more sophisticated management and planning process was needed.

In 1970 the college initiated an annual five-year planning process that involved administrators, faculty, and students. Although at first this process resulted in unreasonable enrollment projections, the process gradually was adapted to meet the needs of the college, and enrollment projections become more realistic. Slowly, other aspects of the college's management system began to change. The college started to emphasize a blending of career education with the liberal arts, which required that the college interact more with outside agencies and constituencies. Since the faculty would remain the same, under AIDP a process was initiated that involved faculty in the redesign of the basic liberal arts curriculum to include more of a career emphasis. The maintenance and refinement of the basic curriculum became a major concern. The development of administrative procedures to insure the long-term survival of the college also became important. Rather than become just a process to develop long-range plans, the planning process at Doane is becoming a means of managing the system, planning for its future, and, at the same time, systematically maintaining the creative development processes with individuals on campus generating new program alternatives.

Management Implementation at Doane

A detailed discussion of the Doane College experience illustrates the nature of the PME-implementation process in a phase II institution. Doane is using its AIDP grant to improve and develop its management system and to institute curricular change. The process used in the curriculum-development component of the ADVANCE program is an integral part of the management system, as well as a systematic change process.

The long-range planning process as originally implemented did not adequately project the campus's future. In spite of early difficulties, the college has maintained a commitment to developing a long-range planning capacity and to the refinement of the National Association for College and University Business Officers' five-year planning model. When it was originally implemented, the NACUBO model was modified to fit the staffing patterns of the college: for example, the model included a planning officer, a position that does not exist at Doane. It also was modified to involve more members of the campus community, particularly students. Students have always been included in decision making at Doane; when a long-range planning process was established, students were included in some of the steps.

The development of viable long-range planning processes that could deal effectively with the external conditions facing the college was not an easy task. Initially, the planning team solicited estimates from academic departments, and then put together the long-range plans based on these estimates. Although this approach led to difficulties, it is not surprising that the planning effort took this approach. Before the enrollment decline, the college had experienced a period of growth, and established a goal of attaining a size of 1,000 students. This was a goal many small campuses adopted as a result of the recommendations by the Carnegie Commission.

When financial difficulties were experienced in the early 1970s, it became obvious that this method of planning did not work. The planning team began to develop its own projections for enrollments and budgets, and had attained a balance between income and expenditures by the time of its final AIDP application. The membership of the two groups differed: the planning team consisted of the top administrative staff, while the analytic studies team, which reviewed the formal plans, was composed of division chairmen, other administrative officers, and student representatives.

Doane College is using the ADVANCE program to improve its planning process and to make it the key to the overall planning, management, and evaluation system. Two consultants worked with the college on the refinement of its management system: Donald Hoyt of Kansas State University and Nancy Reinkiewicz of the National Center for Higher Education Management Systems. One difference between this new plan and the NACUBO model as previously adapted is the use of task forces to undertake planning in special areas. Formerly, the planning process had dealt entirely with numbers, that is, finances and enrollments. The use of task forces will combine the creative process of generating and developing new ideas and programs with the formal planning process.

The career-development concept is an example of an idea that was generated and developed by administrators, but was done completely outside of the formal planning process of the institution. The new procedure for such a proposal would be for a member of the campus community, perhaps a member of the planning team, to come forward with a proposal; then a task force would be appointed to study the idea and, if necessary, explore its feasibility and feed it back into the planning process. Two examples of task forces under way during the site visit were the task force on student attitudes and the task force on faculty development. The former was researching the attitudes of currently enrolled students toward the college, while the latter was considering a comprehensive faculty-development program at the college.

A second refinement of the planning process was the area of developing measurable outcomes that can be used to evaluate institutional progress. Donald Hoyt, a consultant, worked closely with the planning team on the development of criteria that will define specific characteristics that will be affected as a result of campus programs, and on criteria measures that can be used to determine the success of programs. Previously, Doane did not have an evaluation component as part of the planning process.

A primary means of improving the PME systems at Doane is development of a transactional and management information system. Accordingly, "this component of the PME project is 'data centered,' and achievement of these objectives will provide some mechanisms necessary for sound decision-making" (p. 115). A contractual arrangement with the National Center for Higher Education Management Systems will provide necessary information and data systems requirements. To implement the NCHEMS packages, COBOL computer language software was selected. This cooperative arrangement includes: consultation with NCHEMS staff regarding implementation of the new systems; implementation of NCHEMS costing and data-management systems to develop cost studies for the five-year planning sequence; implementation of NCHEMS information exchange system for comparisons to other similar institutions; implementation of NCHEMS resource requirement prediction model to predict consequences of alternatives in institutional planning; assistance in implementing and monitoring a long-range study of student growth and development; and assistance in integration of NCHEMS systems into the NACUBO planning model.

Implementation of the transactional information system and NCHEMS packages is now under way at Doane. Not all aspects of the implementation process have been smooth. During summer 1977 work began on computerization of historical records. However, there was skepticism about the usefulness of automated information systems at Doane. As the first year external evaluation put it:

> There is some healthy skepticism about some parts of the endeavor, particularly the conversion of the transactional records from a manual to a computer mode. It is the judgement of the consultant that this skepticism is well justified in the light of substantial evidence nationwide that computerized information systems have difficulty meeting expectations (Allen et al., 1977).

Delays in computer installation has been one of the primary reasons for the slow progress in the implementation of computerized information systems. While the author was on campus, several administrators expressed concern and skepticism. One of the vice-presidents, for example, expressed his concern that the research component was progressing the slowest. The director of institutional research remained optimistic about this situation in spite of the delays with computer installation.

Some surveys conducted by the office of institutional research, which consisted of the director and a part-time secretary, were very useful. A survey of faculty attitudes toward the career-development concept was mentioned by several individuals during the site visit. Although there seems to be a gap between the collection and tabulation of data in some instances, the types of surveys being conducted are useful to decisionmakers, as evidenced by the often quoted survey of faculty attitudes about career development. A realistic assessment of the usefulness of the various NCHEMS products will have to be undertaken at some point. The ADVANCE project provides the campus an excellent opportunity to experiment with different information packages, but those that are maintained after the project ends should be the ones that prove useful in the decision-making process. To date, the utilization of these information sources by decisionmakers has been limited.

The curriculum-development process can be described as a critical part of the management system at Doane. Although the process cannot be viewed as part of the formal management system, the process of working with faculty to integrate the career concept into the liberal arts curriculum has to be considered at the heart of the academic-management system in Doane. Donald Ziegler, vice-president for academic affairs, described the curriculum-development process as "a systematic review of the curricula in each area." A person from one division is released half-time from teaching responsibilities to work with the faculty on a review of the program and its relevance to career education.

Richard Dudley, chairperson of the education division, was the member of the division who worked half-time in 1976-77 on the curriculum-development process. He thinks "many of the faculty see AIDP as a push to get the school into career development." Regarding the curriculum-development process, he stated: "The strength of our plan is that this will be able to involve faculty." In education he felt they were successful in integrating the career-development concept into the curriculum, although he is quick to point out that "education was easy" because the orientation of the education faculty is favorable to experiential learning. Changing the behavior of the entire faculty, according to Dudley, will not be easy. During the remaining four years of the AIDP grant, the other four academic divisions would go through a similar process to the one education has been through. The test of the career-development program and its integration with the liberal arts may well rest on the outcome of this process.

Phase III Management Systems

Delegation-phase institutions have much more functional differentiation within their organizational structure, more delegation of management responsibilities to organizational subunits, and more defined policies and procedures than phase I and phase II organizations. They do not necessarily lose the creative thrusts that characterize the organizations in earlier phases, but their complex structures necessitate more sophisticated procedures. Three delegation-phase organizations were considered in the previous chapter: Xavier University, which is entering this phase; VCC's West Campus, which is in the middle of this phase; and North Carolina A & T University, which is transitioning to a more complex developmental phase.

The West Campus of VCC is going through a significant management-development process. Since the central administration left the campus when the college became multicampus, many of the administrative functions that were once on campus are no longer there. At the same time, those functional and administrative subunits that remain on campus have placed more emphasis on increased structural formalization and management. The academic department, the major academic unit on campus, is increasingly being delegated responsibility for management. The dean of academic affairs described a formal process of working with the department chairman on goal setting each year, a process that is evaluated at the end of the year before the funding cycle begins again. During summer 1977 the management-by-objectives process was stressed in workshops held to familiarize faculty and administrators with these procedures. The student affairs organization, the major administrative unit left on campus, also is undergoing increasing formalization and management development. The dean of student affairs is trying to delegate more administrative responsibilities to the directors of student affairs programs.

Although it is now showing signs of moving out of the delegation phase, North Carolina A & T has, during the past several years, demonstrated the types of management development that can take place in phase III organizations. In addition to the increasing formalization of all academic and administrative subunits, there is a growing awareness of management concerns at these levels. Between 1975 and 1977, the planning office worked with departments and colleges to set objectives for the programs; administrative units adopted management-by-objectives processes; and a planning and procedures manual was developed to describe the functions of each of the university's administrative units. A & T is more complex structurally than the other institutions in this phase, and new management needs have emerged as these more basic needs have been addressed. It is discussed in depth later.

Xavier University took several significant steps in the development of its management system in the mid 1970s. These developments can be grouped into two general categories: first, more management responsibility and accountability were delegated to functional subunits, colleges, and academic departments; second, administrative policies, procedures, and job descriptions are being better defined. To increase delegation to middle managers, the university is implementing a management-by-objectives approach in the functional subunits, both administrative and academic. On the academic side of the enterprise, the planning office is working with academic departments and colleges to implement sounder management procedures. The administrative sub-units also are making similar adjustments. The university is trying to clarify the stated purpose and objectives of administrative units. Sounder fiscal management and improvement of the development function have been stressed, and a procedures manual for all administrative units is being developed. There also is a higher staff turnover rate within the administration than has been the case previously.

Management Implementation at Xavier

A detailed discussion of the implementation process at Xavier illustrated the complexities of the management-development process at a phase III institution. Xavier University's administration has addressed itself to a complex set of management needs. When the present administration took over, the university faced an uncertain future. The college was in financial trouble because of changes in external funding sources and the salary demands of the new administration. Academically, the college was in need of an overhaul. Although enrollment was increasing, the prospect of future growth was uncertain, as was the ability to finance a larger enterprise. The new administration began to emphasize the development of an effective management system soon after taking office. Before the start of the AIDP grant, the college was on the road to solving some of its management problems. During the past two years, the AIDP grant has aided Xavier in its movement toward a better management system.

Anthony M. Rachal (1973), executive vice-president at Xavier, gave a keynote address on the implementation of the Xavier long-range planning process at Hampton Institute. The planning effort at Xavier began in earnest in 1970. The planning coordinator started in January of that year. The NACUBO planning model, implemented at Xavier, had to be adapted. The results of the first plan were a bit frightening:

> I should mention to you that in that first round of our planning cycle, the projection showed 100% increase in the budget would be necessary to take care of the aspirations of what the departments felt they wanted to do. One hundred percent increase in the five (5) year period, although we had based it on no more than an average 5% increase in faculty salaries. This was shocking, and of course frightening, when we were already facing an accumulated deficit. But the process of the planning cycle made the review of current programs and courses and the proposed new ones for relevance to institutional objectives less mystic, both to

faculty and department chairmen. It also soothed the anxieties over proposed programs and courses on the part
of administrators, because after discussions and recommendations, many of our anxieties were allayed because
of the cooperation and communication which had begun to
take place (Rachal, 1973, p. 8).

One problem with the original plan had been that each department
was concerned about its own needs. As Rachal put it, "Many of us
in small campuses are not sufficiently aware of our own resources,
and we may not be aware of the needs of other departments. Sometimes there are common needs" (p. 17). After the initial planning
efforts, members of the campus community realized the need for a
much tougher look at institutional and department objectives. The
second time the process worked better. The enrollment objective for
the second five-year plan—to maintain the annual university enrollment between 1,100 and 1,400 full-time equivalent students—was
surpassed during this 1973-77 period.

Xavier had not entered a new five-year planning cycle during
the first two years of the AIDP grant. Much of the staff time in the
planning office was spent with the administration and implementation
of the AIDP activities. The planning coordinator also serves as AIDP
coordinator. However, the office has been working on improving the
types of information available to decisionmakers and has been using
a consultant, John Goode, on the improvement of the institution-planning capacity. One of the areas they were working on is the capacity
to develop quantifiable objectives—an approach they hope to implement
into the departmental structure through the curriculum study, an AIDP
activity. A new five-year planning process, that ties objectives to
budgets was under way at Xavier in 1977.

Another management development has been an increasing formalization of the management system. In an interview John Goode,
the main consultant for this area, described this transition as a "shift
from an ad-hoc management structure to a more formal management
structure." Rachal, the senior administrator most concerned with
operations and management, described institutional needs to "determine fiscal responsibility," to "identify and codify" these responsibilities, and "to come up with a manual." The policies and procedures
manual would be a "document saying what you needed to do when."
This manual is being developed at Xavier. The system is so big that
it is no longer possible to pass on knowledge about what needs to be
done in informal ways.

The development of formal policies and procedures has become
a major concern in the administration. Bhagwan Gupta, director of
fiscal services for the past two years, said the primary management

concern for his office was the need to develop policies and procedures. Regarding the sophistication of the fiscal operations, he observed: "Frankly, it's at an initial stage—before I came aboard, the university had employed Haskins and Sells to do a management study." Haskins and Sells, an international private accounting firm, assisted the college in its initial efforts to improve its fiscal management. According to Gupta, part of the problem had been that "many of the grant funds had not been properly classified." The fiscal problems at the college had been severe between 1970 and 1975. Between 1975 and 1977, however, the college did not show a loss; in fact, it reduced the deficit by $42,000 in 1975-76.

Academic management is a third area of concern at Xavier. The curriculum-development component of the AIDP project is an attempt to integrate goal-setting techniques into the academic structures. A description of this activity in arts and sciences is as follows:

> A critical project is being assisted by AIDP funding. Under the direction of Sister Miriam Francis Quinn, the College of Arts and Sciences is engaged in a curriculum study which will result in the following: 1) a clear statement of goals and objectives by each department; 2) a plan for assessing each department's achievement in meeting its objectives; 3) the selection of alternative routes for teaching and learning—which may entail initiating, rearranging, or dropping programs, courses, and other activities; 4) a plan from each department for stimulating and enhancing students' entrance into graduate schools; 5) the listing of careers open to each department's majors; 6) a cost analysis of each academic program; and 7) a final ranking of programs, courses, and activities according to the degree that each fulfills the university's objectives.
>
> This is, of course, a remarkable undertaking. It involves representatives from each academic area being trained in the writing and assessing of objectives. Because such processes are unfamiliar to many faculty and because discussion of new teaching methods and alternative modes of educating is important for any curriculum study, consultants and workshops have also been provided in this activity (Rice, 1977, p. 11).

The process of change in the management of the academic system is slow at Xavier. In an interview Sister Veronica, the university dean, acknowledged "there was some objection to the curriculum-development study when it started." However, "it gradually toned down." The movement toward a system of goal setting within programs appears to be a permanent feature at Xavier. Regarding the management emphasis, Sister Veronica observed: "People that like it at Xavier must become accustomed to thinking in those terms."

The emphasis on increasing the effectiveness of the management system can be seen at all levels of the Xavier administration. The administration of the AIDP project typifies this commitment. Attempting to make the AIDP grant go as far as it can, the AIDP project has changed the emphasis of some activities midstream, and at times has stopped an activity early if it is not contributing to the overall thrust of the institution. Xavier recently submitted a proposal to use some of the existing AIDP funds for development—funds saved from other activities. Again, the management emphasis is clearly important even in this effort. As Clarence Jupiter, director of development, said in an interview: "The most important thing is for Xavier to manage itself well. Otherwise, the people that are rich aren't going to give us much money."

Phase IV Management Systems

Coordination-phase institutions are the most complex institutions for which there are examples contained in the case studies. Phase IV organizations already have developed functional subunits and delegated management systems; in addition, they have systems to coordinate these diverse activities more efficiently.

North Carolina A & T is showing a few signs of increased coordination in the management of both its administrative and academic affairs. Academically, a few new programs are being coordinated across functional subunits: the academic-advising program is trying to centralize some advising services while systematically developing the academic-advising capacity of departments and colleges; the cooperative education program is coordinating existing experiential-learning programs within the academic departments and furthering the development of these endeavors in a coordinated fashion. The institution is experiencing the need for increased coordination of the management process as well. During the past several years, the university has made significant steps toward improving the management process in academic subunits, but has done little universitywide management development. The university now plans to develop a process for setting universitywide objectives and priorities; this deficiency has been identified by external evaluators of the AIDP project at A & T.

Management Implementation at NCA&T

In their AIDP plan, North Carolina A & T proposed changes in three areas as a means of improving "the efficiency and the effectiveness of long-range planning, short-range planning, management and evaluation process" (NCATSU, 1975, p. 274). These areas were:

> Augmenting the overall process by the establishment of a Long-Range Planning Council;
>
> Developing and implementing the Transactional Information System components of the university's Management Information System;
>
> Analysis of the present Planning, Management, Evaluation function and development and implementation of a comprehensive system for accomplishing the PME process (NCATSU, 1975, p. 274).

The proposal described an already developed planning capacity. At the time of the AIDP grant, A & T had a well-developed planning capacity. The planning information was "assembled at the operational levels and channeled upward to the major administrative units" (NCATSU, 1975, p. 41). A newly created office of university planning "receives information pertinent to planning from each of the major administrative units and forms the major institutional committees" (NCATSU, 1975, p. 41). It is the purpose of this office, and of the top executive level of the institution, to coordinate the planning process. The management system proposed in the AIDP grant was to coordinate these diverse institution-planning and management activities.

A & T's planning, management, and evaluation system was designed to coordinate systematically institutional activities: "Because North Carolina A & T State University has shown a growth pattern, and because continued growth is expected, it is imperative that the capability to plan, budget, manage and evaluate be systematically implemented throughout the university" (NCATSU, 1975, p. 276). Implementation of the PME and MIS systems has not progressed rapidly at A & T. The directors of both systems spent their first two years developing a planning, management and evaluation manual (NCATSU, 1976). The manual is a two-and-one-half-inch thick document detailing the operations of the university. The two largest chapters in the nine-chapter document are on the goals and objectives for each subunit of the institution (171 pages), and on the office procedures for the administrative side of the enterprise (76 pages).

This process of goal setting by individual departments is seen as the primary benefit of the PME system thus far. After the workshops a planning task force was developed. The task force, composed of planning office staff and others familiar with management processes, provides technical assistance to departments. The major planned outcome of the task forces and workshops, according to Willie Ellis, AIDP coordinator and assistant vice-chancellor for academic affairs, was that "they have gotten all of the schools to partially complete their objectives." Another outcome was unplanned: "We've had a lot of changes that weren't necessarily designed. I'm sensing a better attitude toward planning as a result of the workshops outside and training on campus."

The two-year external review of the AIDP project at North Carolina A & T was not entirely positive about either PME or MIS. Regarding these two program components, McManis Associates (1977) observed:

> The NCATSU PME system is developing slowly and, in our judgement, with some effectiveness; however, much work needs to be done before the full value of successful implementation is achieved. Some good work has been done in writing University, Program, and department goals and objectives, and some good work has been done in the planning area. At present, however, NCATSU does not have a PME system in place which impacts on the total University in a significant way. Therefore, the full benefits that could accrue have not yet been felt, although some PME benefits have been realized, particularly in the area of better planning and clarification of functions.
>
> In analyzing the development of a PME system, Mc-Manis Associates is pleased to see some increase in the commitment and support of the top management to such a system. No PME system will work without strong support from the Chancellor and his top staff members (p. 23).

At the end of the first two years of the project, the directors of PME and MIS left the university. At present, the placement of two offices in the administrative structure is unsettled. One likely alternative is to have both activities run by the director of university planning. After the first round of PME development on campus, the chancellor and the rest of the administration have a strong commitment to improving the management system and to making it work more effectively.

More universitywide coordination is the next step in the PME-MIS-development process. The need for coordination is well phrased in the recommendations of the most recent McManis (1977) report: "Add to the PME model some University-wide one- and five-year objectives in order to give the colleges, staff, and others some future priorities and direction and a framework within which to set their objectives and directions for the future" (p. 3). The next step in the

PME-development process, according to Edwin Bell, director of university planning, is to establish a universitywide planning process. At present, the office is trying to establish guidelines for the planning process. During the past year Bell has been reviewing different planning models as a means of establishing one for the university. In addition, Bell noted, "We have agreed to establish a budget committee. They will look at new programs and at old programs and make recommendations to the Chancellor." Previously, the university has not had a capacity to prune old programs from the curriculum, even if they were costing the university too much money. A few of the administrators interviewed commented on the need for such a mechanism if the university was going to become more cost-effective.

The implementation of new management practices is not an easy process in higher education, and for those institutions that have faced difficult environmental conditions during their history (as most black institutions have), the acceptance of new practices can be even more difficult. At North Carolina A & T there has been resistance to new management practices on the part of some faculty and administrators. Bell described this resistance in a positive light: "One of the things that I'm coming to grips with is that administrators here have been successful because they have been careful." To accept a new practice, he suggests, "They have to see that it is successful." Gloria Phoenix, an analyst with MIS, observed: "We who are trained in management are saying that we can no longer survive—they say prove it." This slowness to change seems to be a natural part of the institution. Glenn Rankin, vice-chancellor for academic affairs, has been with the university since 1950. In a discussion he commented, "We haven't found any ways of getting anything done fast." A & T has found ways of getting new practices accepted, however, and if a new management system is implemented it is likely to prove useful and successful.

The academic-development activities, the bulk of the AIDP project, are primarily oriented toward the development of individual programs, departments, and schools. They vary in their emphasis from hiring of faculty, to developing curriculum, to preparing for accreditation. These activities consume the majority of the funds for the AIDP project. They are being implemented through the delegated structure of the institution with individual deans, department chairpeople, and faculty being delegated responsibility for their implementation. There are a few academically oriented AIDP activities that relate to the entire academic program at A & T, but these also have to contend with the delegated structure.

One of these is the chancellor's commission on curriculum reform. Its major concerns during its first year were "noncompulsory class attendance, an honors program, class size, individualized instruction, and the need for a data base for decision making" (McManis,

1976). As the work of this task group—composed of 18 members including administrators, faculty representatives, and one student—nears completion, implementation of the recommendations becomes the important issue.

Another example of a development activity that cuts across department lines is cooperative education. This program is designed to coordinate experiential-learning and internship programs on campus. Successful implementation of a coordinated effort of this type, however, is dependent on the flexibility of the delegated structure as well. Regarding this activity, McManis (1977) made the following observations:

> There is some inconsistency in the granting of academic credit for Cooperative Education Program participation. Depending upon the discipline in which the student is enrolled, he or she may or may not receive academic credit for this experience.
>
> The recruiting and career advising undertaken by the staff in the Cooperative Education Program may be an overlap of those functions which are the responsibility of the Office of Admissions and the Office of Placement and Career Planning. Though there may become advantages or rewards to both the University and the student in this kind of overlap, it may prove to be, on a long-range basis, somewhat unsound economically (p. 6).

There is some resistance to coordination in this area. Departments that have developed programs, or that are in the process of developing programs, desire to maintain control over them. If resources are to be utilized more effectively, and if programs are to be developed more consistently across departments and colleges, then some efforts to communicate and coordinate, at least to the extent of having consistent policies, will eventually be necessary.

A third AIDP activity designed to coordinate between academic units is academic advisement. Initially housed administratively in student affairs, and later moved to academic affairs, this activity is designed to coordinate and improve the university's academic-advising system. The quality of academic advising presently varies considerably from school to school and department to department.

Under the new plan, a person in each department will be designated as responsible for advising. In addition to coordinating the activities of these individuals, the person heading this office is undertaking a variety of developmental activities, including: development of a manual for academic advisors; development of a curriculum guide for advisors and students; and evaluation of the academic-advising program by students and faculty. The coordination needs in this area appear great. Regarding the future development of this activity, Mc-Manis (1977) observed:

> To avoid the possibility of becoming overwhelmed by all the things that need to be done in such a short period of time, the objectives should be prioritized. This would also enable the University to direct its limited resources for this activity toward those objectives which are critical to the success of the Academic Advisement Program.

In sum, there are two types of management development taking place at North Carolina A & T, as evidenced in the development of the formal management system and in the academic-management process. The first type is the development of the structure itself and the delegation of responsibility to subunits. The second type is the coordination of the diverse range of activities taking place in the institution. Both sets of management needs appear to exist simultaneously.

In the PME and MIS, emphasis was placed on the development of the PME manual the first two years. By-products of this activity were increased awareness of management practices at middle management levels and improved goal-setting capability at the department and college levels. At the same time, there was a need to develop a system for coordinating among the various university activities. To do this, the institution is establishing processes to develop universitywide objectives and to review the cost-effectiveness of new and existing programs.

In the academic area these developments have taken a slightly different form. The first type of activity has consisted of developing academic programs. The second type is the few efforts to coordinate curriculum reform and program development across departments and schools, such as the commission on academic reform, cooperative education, and academic advising.

Management Implementation at VCC

Valencia Community College provides the clearest example of a coordinated administrative structure and management system. Whenever possible, the college addresses its management needs on a collegewide rather than a campus-by-campus basis. During the past several years, all administrative services have been centralized and physically moved from the West Campus to the downtown center. Rather than replicate services for each of the new campuses, the college has chosen to centralize the administrative services—financial affairs, development, and administrative services including registration—thus providing coordinated services for all campuses.

The management system is both delegated and coordinated. The campus provosts have been delegated major administrative responsibilities for campus affairs. At the same time the central administration, composed of the chief administrative officers from the campuses and from collegewide administration, makes decisions on a collegewide basis whenever possible. The college has a strong need for a better management-information system to aid the coordination between programs by providing information to both the campuses and the central administration. The development of procedures and systems that will allow for this dual management process is the primary objective of the management development taking place at VCC under AIDP. Each component of the AIDP program is being implemented on a collegewide basis. Each uses committees composed of individuals from each of the campuses to oversee and coordinate its implementation.

Valencia Community College is developing a management system that is compatible with its organizational structure. The AIDP project is heavily oriented toward the development of a management system. The planning, management, and evaluation system proposed in the approved AIDP plan is the means of providing more collegewide coordination and coordinating among the AIDP components. Valencia's management system has to be viewed from two vantage points. First, the movement toward a multicampus system creates collegewide management needs. At present, these needs are primarily for a better system to coordinate college activities. In addition, the individual campuses have their own management needs. As the campuses continue to grow and become more complex structurally, their management needs will change.

In an interview, President Gollattscheck commented that he has had "to study governance and look at management theory" in order to do his job effectively. He has served on the board of directors for the National Center for Higher Education Management Systems and teaches courses on higher education for several universities. His work with NCHEMS included serving as chairman of the future committee and vice-chairman of the board. He has used these activities as a way of keeping himself informed on developments in the field. However, he has tried to implement management packages and systems at Valencia only when he has seen a real need. As the college moves toward a multicampus system, he envisions the following as some of the key problem areas: the need to explore new funding mechanisms for the campuses to develop their own budgets; the need to explore new mechanisms for accountability and follow-up; and the need to explore new methods of quality control for VCC Open Campus.

The college is using different strategies for addressing these needs. With respect to the last area, the college is involved in a pro-

ject designed to develop measures of community needs and community
impact of education programs. The Cooperative for the Advancement
of Community-Based Education (COMBASE), an association for which
Gollattscheck has been board chairman, and NCHEMS are working
together closely on a project "to explore ways of evaluating community
outcomes." In the first two areas, the AIDP project is providing considerable help, especially for the large component to improve long-
range planning and governance. Gollattscheck sees the entire AIDP
project as a way of "helping us improve our skills at meeting student
needs."

Vice-president Young viewed the planning component of the
AIDP project as essential. It is his view that the "academic end of
the enterprise is real good—we are doing a great job." On the support
end, however, Young thinks some work is needed. An important aspect of the AIDP project is the management-information system,
which "is going to assist us in developing our management system."
According to Young, "an absence of information is causing problems."
He also feels that another management need at Valencia is for long-
range planning. The AIDP proposal expressed the relationship between these needs as follows:

> A major planned change in Valencia Community College's
> planning process involves a centrally coordinated system-
> ization of information and data through a Management In-
> formation System. The college has made considerable
> achievement in its development during its short history;
> however, decisions and planning have occurred on a "best
> information available" basis. One of the major program
> components of this proposal deals with short-range and
> long-range planning (Program Component III) (Valencia
> Community College, 1976, p. 1).

Historically, planning has been a fragmented activity, reflecting
the functionally differentiated organization structure:

> Although no college-wide planning function presently
> exists, several groups within the college participate in
> the planning process for institutional development. Par-
> ticipants range from the faculty member who plans and
> develops a new course of study to the president who, with
> the college administration and college-wide governance
> structure, devotes time to long-range planning (Refined
> Plan, p. 72).

The need for a new, more coordinated planning process was the result of structural changes, particularly, completion of the East Campus in 1975 which added a third campus to the college. As a result of this change the college anticipated modifying its long-range planning process to include participants from the east location. The implementation of a more coordinated management system is not an easy process. Valencia Community College is using the five years of the AIDP grant to make this transition. Simultaneous to the need for more coordination between campuses, there is a need for more delegation to campuses, particularly in their budgeting processes.

In only the first year of its AIDP grant, Valencia is in the early stages of implementing a new management system. The AIDP project at Valencia is being implemented through a committee process involving administrators, students, and faculty in various aspects of the implementing process. For the implementation of the component, the director of planning reports through the AIDP steering committee to the AIDP coordinator and president. Each component has a committee assigned to it. Administratively, the director reports to the vice-president for instructional services. At present, the committee system is just getting under way.

Kenneth Wagner, director of institutional planning for the past year, has been overseeing the implementation process for this component. He described the situation when he started as follows: "When I took over, the project had parts but no infrastructure. My main objective was to create a communications infrastructure." He worked on the implementation design for the refined AIDP plan. He spent most of the first year working with committees, trying to define the types of information the college needs in its data base. Wagner, who used to teach college courses on management information systems, has found some of the process frustrating. As he puts it, "Because of the state of professional development here, some people didn't know what a quantifiable objective was." Because the AIDP plan calls for the implementation of management by objectives and the state-legislated program planning and budgeting systems (PPBS), also a component of the AIDP proposal, the development of more sophisticated management skills within the campus administration is seen as important.

As part of the implementation process, VCC has a series of workshops on campus. McManis Associates conducted a workshop on MBO at VCC the week prior to the site visit. Approximately 50 people attended. The reactions to the workshop, at least on the part of those interviewed, were mixed. Change in the administrative styles of people at the college is likely to be slow. Even though the college is young, those involved in the college administration have been successful and probably will maintain old patterns as long as they continue to be successful. At the end of summer 1977, Kenneth Wagner resigned to take a position with another institution. Successful implementation of new management practices will depend on the flexibility of those already involved in administration.

Gloria Raines, vice-president for instructional service, played a major role in the development of the MIS data base. By the start of the 1977-78 school year, Valencia planned to have completed the first step in data base development. By that time the college planned to have computerized information systems for: student records, including basic demographic data, student course history, and transfer work coming to the college; the personnel system, which will have developed an on-line system that would integrate information from applications; and finance, which includes on-line accounting procedures. However, a committee is trying to define broader collegewide information needs.

Implementation of other parts of PME and MIS systems has not always gone smoothly. One faculty member involved with the MIS committee observed: "There needs to be more coordination between this and other committees. Some things that this committee will do will have broad implications." Regarding MIS, Dean Richburg, a member of the AIDP steering committee, admitted that there have been "problems getting this off the ground." He is aware that part of the frustration of faculty and others involved is that development takes time, and the administration has had difficulty explaining this lag.

In addition to the management of collegewide affairs, some attention has been given to campus-management needs. The West Campus is the most complex of the three campuses. The implementation of MBO procedures is most applicable to this campus. Dean Richburg describes a yearly planning process with each department chairman that is similar to an MBO process. Each year he and each department chairman establish the goals for the department. At the end of the year they assess the program before establishing new goals.

At present, Valencia Community College can be viewed as a complex institution with diverse management needs. The campuses are at different places on the development continuum. The West Campus has a need for more formalized procedures and structure, while the two newer campuses are striving to maintain their flexibility. The administration is trying to develop a collegewide system for coordination. Implementation of a more coordinated management system appears to be taking some time at Valencia.

STRUCTURE AND MANAGEMENT

This analysis suggests that there is a dynamic relationship between structural development and institution-management needs. The previous chapter categorized the case institutions into developmental categories and defined a set of measures that could be used to predict development phases. When the management systems used and implemented by these same institutions are analyzed according to the proposed developmental model, the analysis suggests that the proposed model needs only slight modification.

Table 6.1 presents a brief summary of the management systems one can expect to find at institutions in the first four developmental phases. The management characteristics observed in the case institutions are similar to those in the hypothesized model. Based on this analysis, one can predict the following about the basic management needs of institutions in each developmental phase:

Phase I institutions operate most effectively with informal management systems;

Phase II institutions need to establish more formal planning and management procedures and systems to maintain existing programs;

Phase III institutions need to establish a delegated planning and management system and formal procedures defining the operations of administrative officers; and

Phase IV institutions need to establish planning and management systems that are capable of coordinating the activities of diverse subunits (departments, schools, colleges, and campuses) and of establishing systemwide programs.

The difference between this newly hypothesized relationship between structural development and the model originally proposed is that standardized administrative procedures become important earlier in the developmental sequence than was originally thought. According to the general model in Chapter 4, standardized policies and procedures were needed during phase IV. Based on the case analyses, it appears that administrative procedures are needed for the functional subunits during the delegation phase, and that systemwide procedures are needed in the coordination phase. Otherwise, the original model appears accurate.

The institution-management needs identified in Table 6.1 are dependent on the phase of structural development. A college or university will not experience the management needs of an organization in a later developmental phase. For example, a phase I institution will not have the same management needs as a phase II or phase III institution. The structural complexity and size of the organization

TABLE 6.1

Phases of Management Development

Phase	Management Focus	Management System
I	Creation of new programs	Information management system with administration and faculty collaborating on program development
II	Defining long-term direction and maintaining existing programs	Systems established for long-range planning, program development, and day-to-day decision making
III	Delegation of administrative responsibilities to organizational subunits	Systems established for subunit management, and administrative procedures defined for administrative subunits
IV	Coordination of subunit activities	Development of systemwide planning and management procedures, systemwide program development, and systemwide objectives and priorities

affect the type of management system that is needed. If management effectiveness is the desired outcome, then attaining a balance between the phase of structural development and management system should be the objective of either institutions or interventions by external funding agencies.

In addition, there is some evidence in the case studies to suggest that management needs emerge in a fashion similar to Maslow's (1954) needs hierarchy for individuals: the needs of the prior stage must be met before a new set of needs emerges. Therefore, the management systems described in Table 6.1 function as plateaus at which an institution's management system might be most effective. To reach this plateau, the management needs associated with prior developmental phases also must be met. If a college or university is undermanaged, which often is the case in higher education, then unmet management needs may have to be addressed incrementally. The cases of Xavier University and North Carolina A & T illustrate this point. Xavier's characteristics in the late 1960s and early 1970s were similar to phase III organizations. Yet Xavier had to establish more formal planning and management procedures and a system for maintaining existing programs before it could address the need for delegation of management responsibility to schools and departments and for more formal policies and procedures. Once North Carolina A & T addressed the management needs of the prior phase and established a delegated system and formal policies and procedures, the need to establish co-ordinating mechanisms quickly emerged. These needs are now being addressed even though the institution had many of the characteristics of phase IV for some time.

CONCLUSIONS

Structural development and management effectiveness appear interrelated in some interesting ways. Based on the analysis of the management systems at these five institutions, several tentative con-clusions have been drawn about this relationship. Institution-manage-ment needs can be viewed developmentally; as a college or university becomes more complex structurally, its management needs increase. This chapter examined several examples of institutions considered to be in different developmental phases. The management needs identified by these institutions and the types of management systems they have implemented can be differentiated according to the four phases of structural development outlined previously. Based on this analysis, it is possible to construct a model of the most appropriate manage-ment system for institutions in each phase, if one assumes these institutions are well managed.

The model constructed as a result of this analysis is similar to the initial model of structural development and management effec-tiveness proposed earlier. Four distinctively different plateaus of institution-management needs and corresponding management systems were identified. These plateaus, which indicated the predominant management needs for each developmental phase, must be attained if the institutions are to increase the efficiency of their resources use and planning and to improve their other indicators of management effectiveness. Although there is not enough evidence to be certain, the case studies suggest that attaining this balance between structural development and management development will improve management effectiveness.

Finally, it appears that management needs are additive. Insti-tutions in more advanced phases have to address the management needs of the prior phase, if they have not already, before they can address the needs of the current phase. The best evidence for this assertion is that institutions in structurally complex phases addressed the management needs of more than one phase: Xavier had to improve its long-range planning and systems for maintaining programs before the need to delegate planning and management practices surfaced; North Carolina A & T experienced greater needs for coordination once it improved its delegated management system; and Valencia Community College, an institution that has grown rapidly, is simultaneously addressing the need to delegate budgetary and other responsibilities to the campuses while it is developing a more coordinated management system.

This method of examining the relationship between structure and management appears to be an exciting new avenue for addressing the problems of management effectiveness in higher education. In the next two chapters a third element, external interventions, is added to the framework. The institutions in this study have been funded by the largest federal program designed to improve college- and university-management systems. With this general model as a basis, an examination will be made of the relationship between the federal intervention program and management and information-system needs identified and addressed by the campuses as part of their AIDP projects. This analysis is used to propose a general model for external interventions designed to improve institution-management systems.

7

MANAGEMENT INTERVENTIONS

Management development in colleges and universities, especially improving the academic management, is a dynamic process. Specified or cookbook approaches to management improvement are of limited value because it is difficult for them to account for unique qualities in the local settings. At the same time, there is a need for management-intervention frameworks that help college administrators determine the types of management systems and intervention processes that are likely to be successful. Unfortunately, management development is a new subfield in higher education. In recent years there has been a steady flow of literature proposing new approaches to planning systems (Kieft, Armijo, and Bucklew, 1978), information systems (Baldridge and Tierney, 1979; Bassett, 1979) and strategies for improving training programs for college administrators (Argyris, 1980; Mayhew et al. , 1974; Webster and Shorthouse, 1976). Until recently, however, there have been few frameworks to help guide administrators' decisions about the types of systems and training they are likely to need.

This chapter suggests and explores the implications of three management-intervention frameworks: one for formal management systems, a second for management training, and a third from the institutional change process. These frameworks were developed as part of the initial study of exemplary Title III institutions, and elaborated on in subsequent articles (St. John, 1980c; St. John and Weathersby, 1980). The three frameworks are explained and verified using data from the restudy. Also, a phase V, collaborative organization structure is discussed here. While the original study and the subsequent restudy of exemplary Title III schools excluded large university systems due to the eligibility criteria for Title III, examples of phase

V organization structures were available for analysis in subsequent research on public colleges in Missouri (St. John, 1980a; Norris and St. John, 1980). This research is used to speculate about the applicability of the three frameworks for phase V institutions. Since the Missouri study dealt more with the issue of information-system automation than management per se, this discussion remains speculative.

MANAGEMENT-SYSTEMS INTERVENTION

Based on the analysis of the management interventions at the case-study institutions, it was possible to suggest a general model for interventions designed to improve college or university management. Table 7.1 breaks down the general concept of an institution-management system into four components: planning, managerial, evaluation, and inquiring systems. These components are defined as follows: planning systems refer to procedures for systematic institutional and program planning; managerial systems refer to day-to-day decision systems; evaluation systems refer to systems for evaluating progress toward planned outcomes; and inquiring systems refer to the data bases and information retrieval systems used by the other three systems. All the institutions funded by AIDP undertook development efforts in these areas. Consequently, all the case institutions had experimented with these management components. Combined, these four components suggest a useful scheme for systematically categorizing institution-management needs.

This model views management development as an additive process; management systems can be most effectively created by building on prior management developments. If an external funding agency intends to establish objectives for management development in colleges and universities, such objectives should be based on the management needs institutions actually experience and build on the nucleus that already exists within these institutions.

Phase I Management-System Interventions

According to the model, phase I institutions should develop: planning systems that emphasize short-range planning, informal-collaborative managerial systems; evaluation systems that provide information about external trends; and inquiring systems that are largely informal and interpersonal, relying on the judgments of organization members. St. Mary's Junior College, especially during its first decade, characterized the management developments needed by a phase I institution.

TABLE 7.1

Intervention Model: Development Matrix for Planning, Management, Evaluation, and Inquiring Systems

Phase	Planning	Managerial	Evaluation	Inquiring
I. Creation	Short-range program planning	Informal-collaborative interaction, task-oriented management	Market studies, supply-demand studies, knowledge of educational trends	Informal, interpersonal judgmental, consensual
II. Direction	Add: Long-range planning capacity	Add: Formal systems for maintaining existing programs	Add: Assessment of program impact, students/faculty attitudes, etc.	Add: Standard format reports of transactions; functional budgets; annual reports; some computerization
III. Delegation	Add: Department and college-based planning capacities	Add: Delegate management responsibilities to administrative units; formalization of management policies and procedures	Add: Assessment of subunit performance on stated objectives	Add: Unit cost analysis; seeking comparative data on costs, work loads, and performance data; computers required
IV. Coordination	Add: Systemwide planning, priority and goal setting	Add: System of coordinating diverse subunit activities and initiating coordinated activities	Add: Prioritizing and assessing competing systemwide objectives	Add: Objectives expressed as programs (PPBS attempted); simulation models to evaluate alternatives; program costs analysis; extensive computerization
V. Collaboration*	Add: Formal collaborative planning processes between functional and central administrations	Add: Systems for showing management responsibilities between subunits and central administration; matrix management possible	Add: Assessment of system achievement of combined subunit and central objectives	Add: Decentralized information systems; evaluate policy impact on subunits; evaluate central policy options; extensive distributed computerized systems

*Phase V systems are speculative and have not been formally studied.

From its founding in 1964 until the initial long-range planning effort in 1973, St. Mary's was managed as a creative enterprise committed to innovation. Both the founding president and first vice-president, who managed the college in collaboration with the faculty, were committed to change, and the pace of change was rapid. Faculty and administrators were aware of trends in higher education and worked closely together on a number of innovative proposals successfully submitted to funding agencies. St. Mary's has retained many of these qualities while making a concerted effort to improve its management system.

Doane College and the new campuses of the Valencia Community College system also illustrated these same characteristics. However, since Doane and St. Mary's have transitioned to phase II and the VCC campuses were not included in the restudy, there is not sufficient data to give a detailed explanation of the development of phase I systems at this time.

Phase II Management-System Interventions

According to the model, phase II institutions should add planning systems that stress long-range planning, formal managerial systems capable of maintaining programs, evaluation systems capable of assessing the impact of programs, and standardized inquiring systems. The recent management developments at Doane College and St. Mary's Junior College illustrate phase II management developments.

Doane College

By 1973-74 Doane College had accrued a significant deficit as a result of faculty enrollment projections. Two major changes have helped Doane make a necessary transition to a more stable organization, both academically and financially. The first was a transition in the curriculum toward a blending of career development with the liberal arts, a combination that has attracted enough students to stop the enrollment decline.

The second was an improvement in the institution-management system. It was clear that Doane needed means of predicting enrollment realistically and of managing the college's scarce resources.

In 1980 Doane still was confronted by difficult conditions. In May 1980, as the college president looked ahead, he observed the following factors:

1. There are fewer high school graduates in our region.
2. A high percentage of the graduates go to some post-secondary education [program].

3. A higher percentage of those in postsecondary education will seek technical training and skills for the job market.
4. Many will seek the most practical at the cheapest cost.
5. There is no evidence of the public sector declining or slowing growth.
6. Items one to five threaten Doane and must be dealt with.

The same memorandum from Phil Heckman to the Doane trustees observed:

> We began a happier and easier time in 1973, beginning with the board decision to pledge its aggregated gift and to challenge others. From that came the elimination of deficit, the career Development program, the five-year AIDP grant, the enrollment rise, the Writing Institute, faculty improvement, etc.
>
> We must make some decisions again, courageous and important. The next spurt cannot be driven by a new sacrificial board campaign. We've never come down from the last one. No, it will call for understanding of the mission, the possibilities, and the courage to attempt better ways. *

In spite of the fact that its initial AIDP grant ends in 1981, Doane faces the new decade with an improved management capacity, one that blends formal systems and the personal commitment of faculty, students, and administrators. The result is a capacity to make difficult decisions in academic and administrative areas.

The academic component of Doane's AIDP project (ADVANCE, as it was called locally) illustrates the developing capacity of the college to maintain and improve existing academic programs. Over the five-year period, each of the five academic divisions was systematically analyzed by external consultants and existing faculty—one faculty member from each division received a year of release time to work on the curriculum-development effort during the grant. This led in some cases to major revisions in the academic programs; it even stimulated a streamlining of the academic structure in one instance. As Vice-president Osterhout observed in the restudy questionnaire, these changes "may have stimulated the merging of the fine arts and humanities divisions. "

---

*See Appendix for reference.

Doane also has been able to integrate academic planning into its overall planning process, which was described as follows:

Insofar as the specifically academic portion [of the planning process] is concerned, one should note two facts. First is the widespread involvement of faculty in the entire process. This includes faculty representation on the Central Planning Team and a preponderantly faculty group, the Analytic Studies Team, reviews the plan each year; plus individual task forces on specific areas of need. Secondly, each academic division develops long- and short-range objectives each fall as the plan is developed. This process works better in some divisions than others. The academic vice president works carefully with each division in this process, as well as develops academic affairs office objectives that transcend the individual disciplines represented within each academic division.

The institutional research office has played a significant role in the development of evaluation systems capable of assessing student and faculty attitudes, as well as gaining assessments of program impacts. The experience with the institutional research office was very successful at Doane; in fact, the 1978 external evaluation report questioned the original AIDP plan to reduce this office to a half-time position, as assistant to the president after two years, since this function had proven so useful at getting evaluative information to the planning committee. Additionally, development of the automated information system took considerable refinement. These efforts have proven satisfactory at Doane. These developments are discussed more in the next chapter.

St. Mary's Junior College

In 1978 St. Mary's College secured a second AIDP grant. The college was nearing completion of its initial grant at the time of the original study. While the initial AIDP project had been highly successful in most areas, the college experienced difficulty with the design and implementation of its PME system. The second AIDP project placed more emphasis in this area; consequently, these capacities were more highly evolved than they were previously. The recent management-system improvement at St. Mary's illustrated the systematic developments described in Table 7.1.

The planning function at St. Mary's is headed by an administrative team composed of members of the major administrative areas, including the academic dean. The academic-planning process is now described as being "almost complete." The planning process involves individual faculty in goal setting and the review process. The process of setting institutional and academic goals for the college also involves faculty as active participants. Goals are set at all levels, from individual faculty to the institution as a whole. Fiscal planning is now on a five-year horizon, with "core" (or "sure") budgets set "for two years in advance of the next year's actual budget." Overall, the planning effort has been intensified:

> New directions are now incorporated into annual and three-
> to five-year objectives. Fiscal support is tied to a demon-
> stration of particular project's relevance to the college
> mission and goals in advance of project initiation. This
> was not true in the past when many seemingly good ideas
> were funded on the merit of the idea alone rather than in
> terms of the fit of the idea with the college.

This shift from sponsoring creative ideas based entirely on their substance, to evaluating new proposals based on an overview of the college's overall direction, signifies a major change in emphasis at St. Mary's. Previously, the college seemed governed on creative principles; now it is trying to integrate its creative activities with the overall direction of the college. The development of systematic day-to-day management processes also is more evident at St. Mary's.

The development of managerial systems at St. Mary's is proof of the emphasis the college now places on program maintenance. The management of AIDP projects illustrates this new emphasis. Mary Broderick, acting dean and AIDP coordinator, describes this shift as follows:

> Under the first grant which ended in 1977, AIDP activities
> were supervised out of the Office of Educational Develop-
> ment. This presented a number of problems in that efforts
> were well along before they came under the regular struc-
> ture. . . . Under the second grant, which began in 1977,
> all AIDP activities are supervised from their inception by
> the regular administrators who will be responsible for
> carrying on the effort post-AIDP. Integrated fiscal and
> project evaluation approaches were designed to allow for
> this early integration.

The planning team also oversees the day-to-day management process. It meets regularly to guide a process that increasingly involves faculty formally in both planning and management decisions. The new process involves everyone in goal setting and review. Understandably, "some are more enthusiastic than others." However, "there has been no apparent covert or overt resistance; the attitude seems to be that this is what we have to do if we are to remain vital. " The process of evaluating the achievement of annual objectives is tied into the overall process. In addition, the college has continued to refine its strategy for developing its information system, which will be discussed later.

St. Mary's is still in the beginning stages of its management-development effort. As a young institution with a commitment to remain small, the college initially showed a cautious attitude about its management-development effort. However, in recent years the college has emphasized these efforts. In fact, the AIDP coordinator ranked the planning, management, and evaluation system as the most important component in the institution's overall advancement program.

Phase III Management Interventions

According to the model, phase III institutions should develop: decentralized planning systems; delegated managerial systems; evaluation systems that assess the ability of organizational subunits to attain their planned objectives; and computerized inquiring systems that have reliable costs, workloads, and performance data. The management-development efforts at Xavier University of Louisiana illustrate phase III developments.

Xavier University of Louisiana

Xavier University has used Title III to make essential changes, both academically and administratively. It is not an overstatement to say that the infusion of Title III funds over the past 15 years has helped move the college from a primary concern about survival, to a primary concern about qualitative change and development. As the current SIDP coordinator, Mary Ellis, put it:

Title III began at a time in Xavier's history when it was suffering with great financial need. In these years, its very survival was at stake. The institution was capable of raising funds for status quo maintenance, but not for growth. Title III made growth possible in those crucial years. As time has passed, the funds for planning and for implementation of programs to meet the growing needs of minority students trying to make their way in a highly competitive society have been the difference between failure and success.

Title III has been integral to the development of a new management philosophy at Xavier. The AIDP coordinator has served as planning officer; she reports directly to the executive vice-president, who is responsible for the operations of the college. This combination, in her view, "has had excellent results." The integral involvement of the coordinator with the daily operations "allows the management by objectives philosophy of SIDP to be broadly assimilated throughout the university through the planning process." The result has been:

Under AIDP, Xavier has developed a full set of measurable institutional goals for the first time, and in our planning process, each department of the university is responsible for helping meet appropriate goals. What began as a management philosophy for AIDP activities served as a model which has become the operational philosophy of the planning process.

Formal planning processes at Xavier begin with the central planning group and extend to the organization subunits, which are required to relate their planning to university goals. The result is a decentralization of planning responsibility within an overall, institutionwide framework. The academic component of the planning process was described as follows:

Academic planning is incorporated into the overall planning process. Academic deans as well as elected faculty members serve on the Planning Team which reviews all university plans and submits them to the President with its recommendations. All academic plans, from the departmental level on up, are expected to forward the university's goals and objectives as established by the Planning Team.

Improvements in the planning process are viewed as integral to improvements in the day-to-day management at the university: "Because of the strong planning function, there is a growing sense of interdependence among the various areas. Communication is better both into and out of the planning process; therefore, there is a better understanding of the total needs/directions of the university." Two aspects of the management-development process are seen as important. One is the improvement of policy and procedures. Recently the university completed procedure manuals for the registrar's office and for both administrative and academic computing: "The implementation of these procedures has greatly increased efficiency and effects are felt throughout the institution." A second area has been management training, particularly at the middle management levels; the assisting agency "has been used to present management training workshops for mid-management staff." These campus-based workshops are considered important "in making these areas function more efficiently." During 1980-81, efforts will be made to extend "the training both upward to sharpen/invigorate skills [of] top level management, and downward to the department chair level."

The management-development activities have had a direct effect on the academic program as well; evaluations and curriculum studies play a vital role in this process. At the time of the restudy, the faculty was "at the point of adopting a very comprehensive and rather sophisticated system of evaluation which has been discussed over the past several years." This is the direct result of workshops that considered the issues of faculty effectiveness and faculty evaluation. In 1977, during the initial site visit, Xavier was in the midst of a curriculum study. The results are described below:

> The reform that will have the greatest impact is without doubt the revised Core Curriculum for the College of Arts and Sciences which will be implemented in August 1980. This new curriculum is one of the results of the curriculum study supported by AIDP funds and conducted by the faculty of the college during the period [from] spring, 1975, through spring, 1979.
>
> It seems pretty safe to say that without Title III funding to support our four-year-long curriculum study, we would not be ready to implement the kind of core curriculum that goes into effect this fall. By providing for released time for faculty in various departments, a thorough study and discussion, extending over several years, was made possible and out of this finally emerged, although not without struggle, the common agreements as to goals and means of reaching them that were needed to win general faculty and administrative support.

In summary, Xavier University appears to be using an integrated approach to planning, management, and evaluation that both decentralizes these functions to operational units, and encourages the reexamination and strengthening of existing practices and programs. Involving faculty and middle management in the planning and study processes has enabled those involved in the functional areas to identify methods that can improve the effectiveness of their own practices. Their management-development efforts also have led to an increased formalization of the university structure, as well as to increased sophistication of college-management systems.

Phase IV Management-System Interventions

According to the model, phase IV institutions should develop: systemwide planning capacities; managerial systems that coordinate the subunit activities; evaluation systems that prioritize and assess systemwide objectives; and inquiring systems capable of expressing programs as objectives. Recent developments at VCC and NCA&TSU illustrate the types of developments required of phase IV organizations.

Valencia Community College

VCC moved full force into the coordination phase when it became a multicampus system in 1974. Prior to that, all the college's activities had operated on one campus; both the campus-based and continuing education activities had been housed in the West Campus academic departments. When the college became multicampus, the central administration moved off campus, the Open Campus was formed, and planning began for the East Campus. The movement by the college toward the coordination phase has not excluded the possibility that the three campuses, the major organizational subunits, might remain in prior developmental phases. The management-system implementation process described in the previous chapter details the intended management outcomes at VCC. Their continued efforts illustrate the phase IV systems developments described in the development matrix.

Both academic and fiscal planning have developed in a centralized fashion during the AIDP project at VCC. On the administrative side, the planning system is highly dependent on the information system: "Title III funding has provided the college an opportunity to develop an integrated management information system. As such, the planning function is far more sophisticated and integrated into the ongoing operation of the college than it was prior to Title III funding." The emphasis on automated information has opened the planning process to more participants: "The management-information system has improved communication and the sharing of information throughout the college by college management." In the three years since the original study, when Valencia was instituting its automated system, the progress with MIS has been substantial; it is discussed in depth in the next chapter.

The academic planning system has developed a systemwide approach as well. The curriculum and instructional development center has been a catalyst or source for centralized academic planning. A major function of the CID center is to give a few faculty release time each year to develop new curriculum or instructional innovations. VCC has a collegewide curriculum committee that "approves changes submitted by faculty members who have developed their materials in the curriculum and instructional development center." As a result, the college has been able to approach the curriculum-development process on a collegewide, as well as on a campus-by-campus, basis. Evaluators have described the CID effort to improve the college's curriculum as highly successful.

While much of the day-to-day management at Valencia is handled at the campus level, and thus is decentralized, the college also has developed a centralized managerial process. A recent external evaluation report describes the centralized management function as follows:

> The Valencia approach to MBO shows a centralized flavor. Its strength lies in the creation of a number of special task forces to cover the diversity of interests that obviously exist among various college constituencies. Its weakness is that it does not lend itself to implementation of these objectives. If institutional objectives are set, the college must establish ways of measuring attainment of them. Highly centralized objectives such as those set by this institutional model must, in turn, be translated into supporting departmental and divisional objectives so that they can be carried out at the various implementation/support levels. If this is the intent, this can be accomplished by adding a block to show MBO input into the budget formulation process.

Since VCC has approached its management-development effort from a centralized perspective, the challenge remains for the planning and management system to become more useful at the operational levels, for example, the campus, departments, and administrative units. However, VCC has done the basic system work necessary for an operational information and planning system. As the external evaluation report puts it: "Increasing the understanding of MIS increases its usefulness and durability. In the last year of AIDP, the college should focus its resources on those activities which will integrate MIS into the fabric of the college and make it indispensible." In fall 1980, VCC was entering the last year of AIDP funding.

VCC has emphasized a coordinated and integrated approach to development. The following response to a questionnaire item asking the AIDP coordinator to rank the importance of AIDP activities, reveals the strengths of this integrated approach:

> The Valencia AIDP application represented a comprehensive, integrated approach to college development. . . . Consequently, it is extremely difficult to rank any one

activity as being more or less important than other activities. For example, the short-range/long-range planning component which provided for the development of an adequate institutional research function provides information on the personal assessment and goal setting system. This information allows appropriate refinements and changes as needed to make the system more successful for students. Therefore, to argue that one is more or less important becomes an academic exercise and not a utilitarian effort.

VCC also uses information generated in evaluation processes in both planning and management. For example, a reading of successive AIDP external evaluation reports shows how the college has adjusted to programmatic plans based on the feedback it has been given by external evaluators. In fact, college administrators seem to seek both internal and external evaluative information that can be used for planning. Regarding the weaknesses of Title III, the AIDP coordinator observed: "A possible weakness may have been staff organization as well as shortages in the Title III office in Washington. For example, the institution did not receive a site visit until the beginning of its fifth year. However, the use of outside external evaluators offset potential weaknesses in this area."

The management-improvement activities of VCC have had a centralized flavor. This was purposeful; the original AIDP proposal called for this emphasis. At the same time, attention has been given to the management needs at the campuses, as the prior chapter indicated.

North Carolina A & T

The management-development effort at North Carolina A & T State University should be viewed in context. As a predominantly .black, public campus in the South, A & T has been the subject of conflicting state and federal policies. At the time of the original site visit to A & T in summer 1977, the author concluded that the university's future success was highly dependent on the outcome of OCR review; also, at that time the college was beginning to encounter income-expenditure deficits. Since then, the University of North Carolina (UNC) system has been involved in a court battle with the federal government over its desegregation plans. Additionally, in 1980 the UNC system initiated "a study to assess the administration of the system's five predominantly black colleges" (Chronicle of Higher Education, June 16, 1980, p. 12). Financial problems at A & T were cited as a reason for the study: "The financial problems at A & T State University were brought to light in a report from the State Auditor's office, which found the institution's fiscal office 'essentially unauditable', with overdue bills totaling nearly $700,000" (Chronicle of Higher Education, June 16, 1980, p. 12).

In contrast to the problems A & T has encountered in the state, the university, like many other predominantly black colleges, has long enjoyed substantial Title III support. In 1977 when the author visited the campus, A & T had an AIDP grant and supplemental Title III grant. In 1979 the college finished the supplemental grant and started a new, three-year SDIP grant. This discussion will emphasize only the types of management developments at A & T; the subsequent discussion in the overview speculates about possible reasons for the financial problems. However, it should be noted that this discussion is intended only to illustrate the applicability of the management-intervention model and not to criticize the A & T administration. The administration is caught in a complex political milieu that involves conflicting federal and state pressures, and even conflicting pressures from the federal government (if the Title III program and the OCR review are considered).

The development of a planning function at A & T has progressed on two fronts: a delegated planning system has been implemented involving academic and administrative units; and a centralized planning office has been given responsibility for developing campuswide plans. In the questionnaire, the academic-planning process was described as follows:

> Yes, the University does have a formal process for academic planning which was initiated on an AIDP/Title III grant in 1974. A Planning Office was organized, staffed, and a program is currently implemented to provide leadership in short-term and long-term academic planning. The structure is initiated by the Chief Academic Officer and the Director of Planning. The Planning Office staff coordinates and consolidates planning reports and insures that input is provided by all departments and schools.

A second thrust in the planning effort has been toward the development of a centralized administrative planning process. The planning office has been responsible for MIS development (discussed later) and for defining a universitywide planning model. At the time of the original study, planning was entirely delegated, and the new planning model was viewed as a way of prioritizing objectives. The most recent evaluation report describes the following accomplishments in the development of the planning model:

> A long-range Planning Committee has been established;

A university planning guide has been signed, developed, and distributed;

A planning process was designed that links planning to budgeting;

Training sessions have been coordinated for university administrators in using the planning guide;

The goals and objectives of university schools, divisions, and offices have been refined and updated;

A planning calendar has been developed to provide for the development of long-range university planning during 1979-81.

The development of a coordinated planning function is still under-way at A & T; some of the PME activities in the new Title III grant will continue this effort. Willie Ellis, the AIDP coordinator, described an emerging "shared concern about planning over the short and long haul. "

The day-to-day managerial activities at A & T have continued to emphasize a delegated approach. Academic departments, chairs, deans, and other senior faculty are given responsibility for imple-menting new academic projects under Title III. One effect of this approach was described by Ellis as follows:

New faculty in general don't create a substantial change nor impact on senior faculty. However, there are some exceptions. Most of the Title III activities are headed-up by senior faculty members, but quite often, new faculty members are part of the projects. As you would expect, the new faculty are burning up with new and innovative ways to teaching and learning. However, they are often caught up under the influence of more traditional super-visors who want to hold onto the traditional approaches.

The current structure was considered adequate for meeting the reporting requirements under Title III. However, the Title III coordi-nator observed: "Title III has had some difficulty in procuring finan-cial statements from the fiscal office. " The Title III program at A & T appears quite successful at meeting milestones for most of its pro-grams; it also routinely conducts evaluations of its Title III efforts. It is not clear from the restudy how this information is used to gener-ate development priorities. It also appears that most developments emphasize a delegated structure-building approach to institutional development and a near absence of centralized development priorities.

Phase V Management-System Interventions

The management-system developments proposed for phase V institutions are still speculative, as the fourth phase is the last phase for which there was evidence in the case studies or the restudy. However, in another study, a fifth phase was identified (St. John, 1980a). During this phase, new organizational arrangements are necessary to develop collaborative management between centralized and decentralized units. According to the model, phase V institutions should add: formal collaborative planning processes between functional and central administrations; systems for sharing management responsibilities between subunits and central administration; systems for assessing achievement of combined subunit and central objectives; and distributing information systems capable of evaluating policy impacts on subunits, as well as assessing central policy options. Since the subsequent study emphasized these developments, phase V systems are described in more detail under MIS developments in the next chapter.

MANAGEMENT TRAINING

The general management-development model has been used to suggest the types of management training that are most likely needed by institutions in each phase (St. John and Weathersby, 1980). Table 7.2 summarizes this scheme. It builds on the additive approach to management systems suggested earlier. Just as the management systems associated with each phase add to and complement the developments of each prior phase, this schema suggests that management-training needs become more sophisticated as institutions increase in complexity.

Phase I Management Training

According to the model, phase I institutions need staff training in problem solving, brainstorming, curriculum design, and program development. Training in these areas, along with education and training in areas of instruction, is considered basic to institutions in all phases. Since a basic purpose of higher education is instruction, and most colleges use traditional student–faculty-based approaches to instruction, faculty development can be considered a basic training activity of most institutions, regardless of developmental phase. All the case-study institutions were able to fund faculty-development activities as part of their Title III programs, which activities are described below:

TABLE 7.2

Management-Training Needs by Development Phase

Phase	Management Focus	Management Training
I	Creation of new programs	Staff training in problem solving, brainstorming, curriculum design, and program development
II	Defining long-term direction and maintaining existing programs	Add: Top management training in long-range planning techniques, accounting and personnel management procedures
III	Delegation of administrative responsibilities to organizational subunits	Add: Training of middle managers in formal management techniques, including management by objectives and formal systems development
IV	Coordination of subunit activities	Add: Training of academic and administrative managers in team-building techniques, systems and policy analysis, and priority and goal-setting techniques
V	Collaboration among decentralized organizations	Add: Training of central administrative personnel in systems maintenance, decentralized systems design, and consulting as support techniques

At St. Mary's College, faculty-development activities included travel to meetings and workshops, special in-house presentations, seminars, and individual assistance from the faculty-development coordinator.

Doane College's faculty-development efforts used two approaches: faculty were aboe to take off-campus internships in a new area to strengthen the college's career emphasis, and were given special summer appointments to develop new courses and curriculum.

Xavier University used Title III faculty-development funds in a variety of ways: to sponsor campus-based training and workshops, to send faculty to off-campus workshops and professional meetings, to support faculty research activities, and to provide release time for faculty involved in developing new courses and instructional approaches.

North Carolina A & T State University maintains faculty-development programs that allow faculty members (13 from 1974-78) to pursue graduate work toward a doctorate for two years, and that involve faculty in in-depth experiences at workshops, seminars, and on- and off-campus in-service education experience.

Valencia Community College has concentrated its faculty-development efforts on the curriculum and instructional development center, which has allowed ten faculty to receive 60 percent release time each year for in-service training sessions, seminars, and the development of new teaching strategies, which they work on a specific curriculum or course project.

Phase II Management Training

In addition to special training for faculty in instructional and curricular areas, phase II institutions need training for top administrators in long-range planning techniques, systems, development, and formal accounting and personnel-management procedures. Some of this type of training is for administrators to advance in their careers, and therefore is not always identifiable as a separate program. The administrative staff training opportunities the two phase II institutions took advantage of illustrate this emphasis.

At Doane, consultants work with the planning team on the development of the long-range planning process. In addition, specialized training opportunities were pursued for: the vice-president for development and his staff, who took advantage of professional training clinics in the field; members of the admissions staff, who attended training sessions and used consultants to assist in their recruitment efforts; and the business affairs staff, who pursued specialized training in computer technology and accounting procedures.

At St. Mary's, there was a concentrated effort to improve planning skills: the AIDP coordinator and president attended seminars and workshops and undertook site visits that emphasized institutional planning. Other management-training opportunities included computer-related seminars, workshops, and site visits by the AIDP coordinator and the vice-president (who also serve as treasurer and business manager). Additionally, the director of admissions and the coordinator of extended programming attended seminars on recruiting and program marketing.

Phase III Management Training

According to the model, phase III institutions need to add training programs for middle managers—deans, department chairs, and program directors—in formal management techniques, including management by objectives and formal systems development. The management-training program at Xavier University illustrates this emphasis.

During the past two years, Xavier has emphasized management training for middle management. Its AIDP-assisting agency has provided on-campus workshops for professional administrators in functional areas (business, personnel, and so on) and for academic deans. Plans for the current year include management training for senior administrators and department chairpeople. These seminars have emphasized objective settings and evaluation skills development.

Phase IV Management Training

According to the general management-development model, phase IV schools are likely to need specialized management training for central administrators in areas such as team-building techniques, systems and policy analysis, and priority and goal setting. It is not entirely clear from the restudy results that training in the area of team building was obtained at the phase IV institutions. However, both institutions emphasized management training, particularly programs oriented toward improving the skills of senior and middle managers. These efforts illustrate some of the more sophisticated training needs of phase IV institutions.

North Carolina A & T has made a concentrated effort to provide management training at all levels of the university. Six senior administrators were involved in the Harvard Institute of Educational Management, an intensive summer program providing management training to senior college and university administrators. Also, several administrators were involved in American Management Workshops, and a management firm was employed to train department chairpersons in communication. Campus-based seminars have been held for faculty and administrators in human relations, management of time, and management by objectives. Throughout the restudy and case-study data, there is evidence that A & T has emphasized management training and that Title III funds have been critical in this effort. For example, Title III has provided funds necessary to hire an EDUCOM consultant to provide training in the use of the EDUCOM financial-planning model.

VCC has utilized Title III funds to provide management training for senior and middle managers in management-by-objectives procedures that support institutional goals. Two separate sessions were held with deans, department chairmen, and vice-presidents in the development of institutional objectives and individual management objectives. The college also has strategically used training opportunities to improve the skills of central administrators. For example, the director of the CID center participated in a number of staff opportunities at Miami-Dade Community College. These activities have afforded the opportunity to gain additional expertise in her role, enabling her "to share these experiences with faculty who have participated in the CID on a release time basis." This example represents an emphasis on increasing the skills of central administrators in analytic and team-building skills, in addition to the need for training of middle managers.

Phase V Management Training

Since the case-study institutions did not include examples of phase V institutions, there were no examples of training programs in these settings. However, the model suggests that phase V institutions have to develop the support services required by decentralized organizational structures. While many administrative support services, such as word processing or more formal planning and management functions may be decentralized, it is still necessary for central administrators to maintain certain support and coordinating services. In the computing area, for example, administrators will need training in decentralization in systems design, training techniques, and support of specialized capabilities that are too costly to decentralize or duplicate. In other administrative areas, such as academic program review and planning, central administrators need training in policy planning and evaluation techniques. For example, the emphasis for senior academic administrators in very complex organizational environments often shifts from review of actual programs to establishing review guidelines to be implemented by campuses, schools, and colleges.

Overview

The restudy results have elaborated on the management-training framework developed from following the original study. This framework suggests only the types of management training that are likely to be encountered in institutions that are attempting to develop effective management systems; it does not suggest the means for attaining these outcomes. There is an increasing number of management-training options available to higher education institutions. These include: consulting firms that provide campus-based training programs; short-term institutes and workshops that take individuals away from the campus for short periods of time for training purposes; and professional training programs run by universities and professional associations. This framework can be helpful to institutional administrators who are deciding which management-training options to use.

The analysis of the restudy results suggests that management-training needs do become more sophisticated for complex institutions. Certain types of training, particularly in the academic areas, are basic to all colleges and universities. However, the types of management training administrators need appear to be tied to the complexity of the institutions and the sophistication of the management systems that have been implemented.

INSTITUTIONAL CHANGE STRATEGIES

In addition to suggesting an intervention model, the analysis of the AIDP projects at the case-study institutions, when coupled with the analysis of their structural development and management, was used in the original study to suggest general institution-development strategies. Since the study results revealed that the effectiveness of different institution-management systems varied according to an institution's developmental phase, it seemed logical that change strategies also would vary according to developmental phase. There is evidence in the case studies and the restudy to suggest that this is so. A comparison of the developmental strategies used by the case institutions reveals the dynamic relationship among change strategy, management needs, and formal structure.

Phase I Change Strategies

The case studies include no examples of phase I institutions as direct recipients of AIDP funds, although there are examples of phase I institutions contained in the case studies: the Open and West Campuses of Valencia Community College were involved in the VCC's AIDP project. Phase I institutions are oriented toward the creation of programs and informal management systems. Based on these facts, one might assume that the most appropriate development strategies for these institutions would be oriented toward program planning and development. In fact, these were the primary management activities at both VCC campuses, but since they were not direct recipients of AIDP funds, it was difficult to reach specific conclusions about how this general strategy would work.

Even though there were no examples of phase I institutions in AIDP (most of those institutions may be excluded by the Title III eligibility criteria), there is some reason to assume that phase I institutions might make good use of intensive developmental support. New institutions that are technologically more advanced, such as VCC's Open Campus or the few examination degree programs, may be in need of initial start-up support. In the long run, these institutions may be more efficient and may provide more services of similar quality and at less cost than traditional institutions. These are the types of programs that often are supported by another federal program, the Fund for the Improvement of Postsecondary Education.

Phase II Change Strategies

Direction-phase institutions have more formal organization structures and management systems than creative-phase institutions. Consequently, an intensive institution-development effort should have some structure, yet allow for the informal and collaborative processes that take place in these organizations. Both phase II institutions receiving AIDP funds illustrate development strategies that provide some structure, but still rely on the creativeness of the informal system.

At St. Mary's during the initial AIDP project, a steering committee was formed to implement the AIDP project. The committee, which consisted of the coordinators of the various AIDP activities, worked collaboratively on the development effort: they met weekly to talk about the entire program and about specific activities; they shared their expertise, provided each other needed interpersonal support, and consciously worked changes through the system. They developed a six-phase implementation process that worked toward integrating successful new activities into the system. During their second AIDP project, St. Mary's shifted the focus of its planning group from innovation to long-term and short-term planning. The membership of the group changed from AIDP activity coordinators to key administrators. The planning group now oversees the AIDP effort, the planning effort, and the day-to-day management system.

Although the composition was different, the general-strategy employed by Doane College during the initial study was similar. One of the vice-presidents served as AIDP coordinator. He and other members of the planning team, the primary management group in the institution, oversaw the implementation of the AIDP project. They worked collaboratively, trying to use all their expertise to solve problems as they arose. In addition, they periodically formed ad-hoc groups to tackle specific problems. These groups involved diverse organizational members in program planning and development. At first this was an informal process, but at the time of the site visit, the planning team was going to integrate the ad-hoc task force approach into the planning cycle. This strategy continued to evolve at Doane since the original study.

There were some differences in the strategies the two institutions used in their development effort. At Doane, the planning team was the primary management group; at St. Mary's, the original steering committee was formed specifically to handle AIDP and was not formally a part of the top administrative group. Later, St. Mary's strategy changed to include senior administrators. However, this occurred only after the organization structure stabilized. In both cases, the same elements were present: a team of people took responsibility for implementing the AIDP project; and in each case, strategies were developed to work changes into the system.

Phase III Change Strategies

Phase III institutions have organizational structures that are more functionally differentiated than either phase I or phase II institutions, which places greater management needs on middle-management levels that may not exist at less complex institutions. In phase III institutions, an effective development strategy has to work through the delegated structure, involving middle managers in the implementation process. The original case studies provided two examples of phase III institutions that have received AIDP funds, both of which have employed development strategies that involved middle managers in the change processes.

North Carolina A & T is the more complex of the two institutions. Although it is currently transitioning to a more complex developmental phase and therefore can use different developmental strategies, the strategies it has used during the first three years of the AIDP project have been successful and represent the types of change processes that are effective in delegated institutions. At A & T, responsibility for implementing each of the activities is delegated to a coordinator who is a dean, department chairman, program director, or faculty member. These people oversee the implementation process, and there is little coordination between them. The AIDP coordinator and assistant coordinator assume responsibility for the entire project. A & T continued this delegated development strategy during its subsequent AIDP grant.

Xavier University employed a similar development strategy at the time of the original study. The AIDP coordinator worked closely with the executive vice-president on coordinating the AIDP effort.

Responsibility for each of the activities was delegated to an activity coordinator, who assumed responsibility for its implementation. Judgments about the success of these activities, and decisions about whether they should be continued after AIDP or terminated early because of lack of success, rested with top administrators. This strategy has continued at Xavier. At the time of the restudy, the activity directors were monitored by one of three area coordinators (the academic dean, dean of students, and executive vice-president) who had responsibility for cultural enrichment and student services, academic projects, and administrative activities.

Both strategies start with the assumption that to be a success, a change process has to integrate the new activities into the system. In a functionally differentiated system, this requires involving middle managers—a level of decisionmakers that does not exist in less complex organizations—in the change process.

Phase IV Change Strategies

At coordination-phase institutions, the primary management-development task—developing coordinating capacities—is more complex than the management focus at institutions in prior phases. Phase IV institutions need development strategies that involve representatives from functional subunits in the implementation process for new activities that affect their operations. Like phase III institutions, they also require that an individual take responsibility for the implementation of specific activities. However, these activity coordinators are more likely to be part of the central administration rather than middle managers.

Valencia Community College provides the clearest example of a coordination-phase institution. Each of its AIDP activities is designed either to enhance coordination of subunit activities or, if it is a new program, to improve the activities of two or more subunits. Each activity was implemented in a coordinated fashion, with a committee composed of members from different campuses overseeing the implementation process. In addition, each activity has a person responsible for its implementation. For example, the CID center, designed to improve the instruction programs in the college, has a director who works closely with faculty from the different campuses; the center itself rotates between the East and West Campuses. The management developments at VCC under AIDP, those activities designed to enhance the coordinated-management system, are coordinated by individuals as well, usually the director of planning or the vice-president of instructional services. This strategy appears to have been highly successful at VCC.

North Carolina A & T made use of central administration for implementation of activities that were intended to develop a centralized capacity. The implementation of the academic-advising activity is an example of this emphasis. In the administrative area, the MIS component and planning activity were coordinated by the planning officer. In most instances, however, A & T used a decentralized implementation strategy.

According to the developmental model, coordinated developmental strategies are effective for phase IV institutions—an assumption illustrated by these examples. Phase IV institutions appear to need developmental strategies that allow for coordination between subunits and provide the leadership needed for implementation.

CONCLUSIONS

The analysis of the AIDP projects at selected institutions suggests that the developmental approach has several implications for management-system interventions in higher education. AIDP was designed to enhance the institution-development process. It has lacked a conceptual model of development that would maximize the effectiveness of AIDP funds and provide a framework for evaluation. The general model presented in this text can be used to develop such an evaluation and intervention framework. It can be used as a basis for a general management-systems intervention model, for suggesting a framework for addressing management-training needs, and to suggest general intervention strategies for institutions in different developmental phases.

The analysis of the institution-development programs at these institutions showed variations, according to their developmental phases, in the types of management developments that were implemented. Less complex institutions (those in the direction phase) tended to use AIDP funds to improve both their long-range planning processes and program maintenance capacity. Although there was some variation in the way they approached the development of management-information systems, it was apparent that these institutions did not have high demands for computerized information. Schools in a medium range of complexity (delegation-phase institutions) tried to implement delegated management systems and had relatively high demands for computerized management-information systems. Schools that were more complex (coordination-phase institutions) used AIDP funds to improve their capacity to coordinate the activities of diverse organizational subunits. These institutions experienced high demands for management information and needed the most sophisticated information systems.

These findings can be used to suggest an external intervention model, with phased plateaus for institution-management systems. In this chapter, plateaus were proposed for planning, management, evaluation, and inquiring systems. Based on the analysis in the three chapters, it is possible to suggest a scheme that predicts the types of developments in these four areas that institutions in each phase might need. This model can provide a basis for planning intervention strategies, which is considered in detail in Chapter 9. It also can be used to suggest ways of improving programs designed to aid college management, which is the subject of the final chapter.

8

MIS INTERVENTIONS

The information revolution brought about by rapid and recent developments in computer technology, including the availability of less expensive computer hardware, has left college and university administrators with some difficult decisions about the uses of automated management information systems (MIS). This chapter develops a framework to help guide administrative decisions about, and planning for, MIS development and automation. It takes into account institutional size and complexity, internal management needs, and the relationship between MIS development and other institutional planning, managerial, and evaluation (PME) systems. The assumptions on which the framework is based are:

The basic pattern of MIS-computerization costs into, and perhaps through, the 1980s is already well established. The costs of computerization can be expected to remain relatively constant (adjusting, of course, for inflation), because hardware costs are decreasing, while personnel and software costs, including systems development, are increasing.

The design of management information systems should take into account the internal management needs of the institution. Information-system development, to be effectively implemented and utilized, must be approached within a context that considers other institution-management systems, especially the PME systems operating at the institutions.

The characteristics of an institution, especially its size, complexity, and history, are critical factors in determining management needs. The larger and more complex the institution, the more sophisticated its management needs are likely to be.

There is no "one best" or "most appropriate" management or information system for all institutions. The internal needs of institutions dictate the degree to which PME and MIS developments are needed; the need for more sophisticated systems is often an outgrowth of the successful implementation of less sophisticated systems. Therefore, systems development and modification should be viewed as a fluid process with future needs determined largely by past developments.

Three research steps were used to design the MIS-development framework. First, the general management-development model, derived from the literature on industrial and educational management, was tested and elaborated on by examining in-depth case studies of management-development efforts at a few institutions funded by the Developing Institutions Program, which is part of Title III of the HEA. Second, using the indicators for phases of structural development proposed in Chapter 5, the public higher education institutions in Missouri were grouped into five distinct developmental phases, and their MIS needs were examined. Finally, as part of the restudy, an MIS-development questionnaire designed for the Missouri study was used to gain information on MIS developments at the case-study institutions; these results are used here to elaborate on the implications of the model. The results suggest that a differentiated approach to the task of MIS development is needed in higher education, and that systems design should be considered within the context of the overall management needs of an institution.

THE MISSOURI STUDY

The Missouri Department of Higher Education recently conducted a comprehensive study of computing at state-supported higher education institutions. By 1975, 26 states had conducted or planned a statewide planning effort for higher education computing (Heydinger and Norris, 1977). Missouri had not undertaken such a planning effort, and therefore provided a natural setting to examine how computing has evolved in the institutions without the influences of statewide coordination. The study results have been analyzed and used to explore the implications of the general management-development model for MIS development.

The study results from the public institutions in the state were available for analysis. Five survey instruments were administered to each public institution and system office; one examined the status of MIS development. The MIS-development questionnaire asked about the status of MIS development in eleven areas:

Planning, management, and institutional research;
Financial management applications;
General administrative service application;
Auxiliary service applications;
Logistics and related services;
Physical plant operations;
Admissions and records applications;
Financial aid applications;
Library applications;
Other administrations applications; and
Hospital applications.

This survey asked questions about the relevance of computerization for several specific systems in each area, the status of these systems (manual, computerized, combined manual and computerized, under consideration for development, or in production), and the processing mode for computerized systems (batch, on-line, or combined batch and on-line). Institutions also were asked to identify the five top priorities for systems development and the major factors limiting implementation.

The institutions were grouped into categories according to the quantitative indicators of structural development identified in the prior study. Each category then was analyzed for the status of MIS development. Two general findings extended the limits of the general model. First, although some important differences were observed between institutions in phase I and phase II (which are described in the following section), computerization of administrative systems is considered relevant in both phases. Second, a fifth category of institutions was identified in this study. The large state institutions were not excluded as they had been in the prior study of exemplary Title III institutions due to the program's eligibility criteria.

An important caution should be kept in mind when interpreting these findings. The entire management system was not examined in the Missouri study. The original study emphasized the interrelationship of management systems, while the Missouri study examined MIS development only. However, the types of MIS development that have taken place at the Missouri institutions in each phase are, with the exceptions noted above, highly compatible with the general model. The analysis suggests a cohesive framework for decisions about MIS development.

The restudy used the MIS questionnaire developed for the Missouri study with some additional questions specific to their Title III programs. The combined results suggest a relatively viable framework for MIS development in higher education.

MIS-DEVELOPMENT FRAMEWORK

The five-phase structural-development model provides a useful conceptual basis for identifying and grouping the MIS-development needs of diverse higher education institutions. It also provides a framework for addressing those needs. The results of the MIS-development survey are described below for the institutions grouped by structural-development categories. The discussion considers the results of this analysis in five areas: the applicability of MIS systems, appropriate computer environment, MIS-development priorities, factors limiting MIS implementation, and factors encouraging MIS implementation. These areas are summarized in Table 8.1. An overview for the MIS needs of institutions in each phase is supplemented by a discussion of the MIS-implementation process and the case institutions.

Phase I MIS Intervention

MIS development for very small, phase I institutions poses a unique set of problems with a relatively limited range of satisfactory solutions. The main problem is that systems in some key areas, such as finance and student records, are important for the operating systems, but the cost of implementing in-house automated systems often is beyond the financial means of these institutions. The solution usually is to contract with an outside firm or institution to maintain those automated systems that are needed. A business manager from a phase I institution included in the Missouri study explained this situation: "We have a very satisfactory arrangement with a local service bureau to handle our requirements for administrative financial data and student personnel records. The total annual cost is less than the salary of one trained operator; thus we have no interest in acquiring an in-house computer. " These institutions can often afford to operate with entirely manual systems.

Very small colleges, with low enrollment and limited financial resources to devote to management development, are faced with basic issues when making decisions about administrative computing. Basic operating systems, such as student registration and grade reports, often can be managed efficiently in a manual mode. These schools usually have registrars or admission officers who know most students. However, when automation is necessary for financial or student record

TABLE 8.1

MIS-Development Framework

Phase	Applicability of MIS Systems	Computer Environment	MIS-Development Priorities	Factors Limiting Implementation	Factors Encouraging Implementation
I	Relevant in limited areas, particularly student records and financial management	Computer support for automated MIS beyond means of institution	Automation of a few systems as appropriate	Local environment not sufficient to develop and maintain automated systems	Contractual arrangements with other institutions or firms
II	MIS development likely in some areas (student records and finance) and is considered relevant for systems in most areas	Likely to have some computer development; either small special-purpose machines or part of a network	Initial systems may be planned in several areas with student records, finance, research, and financial aid being priority areas	Numerous problems emerge related to developing new systems (from scratch or adapting old systems); personnel, money, and machine access are key problems	Develop computer access (contractual, minicomputer, or network access); identify most important MIS priorities
III	MIS moderately well developed with mixture of automated and manual systems in most areas; automation is relevant in most areas	Likely to have computing: either CPU mainframe (medium-sized machine), mix of small machines, or network access; instructional computing likely	Initial systems in operation in several areas and specific system-development priorities well identified	Personnel for systems development key limitation; money and software limitations; specific hardware needs (disk space, terminals, etc.) a possible limitation	Training students in systems development and programming helps with personnel limits; following overall systems-development plan also important
IV	MIS moderately to well developed; automation relevant for most systems in all areas, operating systems are probable in most areas	Likely to have active computer environment; large mainframe, operate as part of central computer network, or mixture of network and local computers	Automation important in most areas; priorities include change to on-line systems; modification of existing systems as well as developing new systems	Personnel and money are key limiting factors, especially finding personnel with specialized expertise necessary to modify and update existing systems	Staff allocation and training decisions are critical; individuals with required expertise are limited; training non-D. P. personnel to maintain and operate systems also important
V	Automates systems essential to management of system; centralized systems and distributed systems in production	Complex computer environments with distributed hardware and distributed data processing in diverse administrative subunits	Refinement and updating of systems already in production; data base maintenance important factor	Personnel is identified as the most critical problem, finding people to develop and maintain distributed processing systems	Staff training and development; exchange of personnel for training purposes, and develop compatible data definitions and processing systems

systems, external assistance, rather than in-house development, is likely to be the most cost-effective solution. For small campuses that are branches of large colleges or systems, these data-processing needs usually can be handled by the parent campus or the central administration. For single-campus institutions, contractual arrangements with a local university or a consulting firm may provide the most cost-effective solution to computerization problems. The restudy did not include an example of a phase I institution.

Phase II MIS Interventions

Phase II institutions are more complex than phase I institutions and so have a more complex set of management-information needs. Some computerization of administrative systems is relevant, and in-house maintenance of those systems can be an appropriate solution. Contractual arrangements with an outside firm or institution also remain a possibility. The two key issues for these institutions are: first, deciding what is the most appropriate hardware solution (small special-purpose machine, network access, or contractual arrangements); and second, identifying the most appropriate MIS-development priorities. These institutions also need to recognize that the costs of developing and maintaining automated systems may outweigh the benefits in many instances. In short, phase II institutions are likely to be in the initial stages of system automation.

Automation decisions are slightly more complex for small phase II colleges than for any other institutional group. They have automation needs, usually for both financial and student systems, but their needs are not so complex as to require sophisticated simulation models. They require simple operating systems that will cut back on administrative costs, rather than complex, data-driven analysis systems that are costly, in terms of staff support, to maintain. A key guide for administrators at phase II schools should be whether installation of the new systems will require collection and automation of more types of data then are needed to meet operating and planning needs. These basic student and financial data can provide the information necessary for relating personnel and program decisions to enrollment and cost information. Other types of information, such as data about student and faculty attitudes, can be gathered and analyzed on an ad-hoc basis as necessary. Fortunately, there usually are a variety of hardware options available to small colleges in the initial stages of computerization: contractual arrangements, microcomputers, or network access (in most states and regions in the United States). Decisions about computer hardware options also should take into account instructional-computing needs. The case-study institutions provide two examples of phase II institutions undertaking MIS interventions.

St. Mary's

At the time of the original study, St. Mary's Junior College was in the initial stages of MIS development. Most of its systems were manual; in fact, an objective of the original AIDP grant was to define the types of manual systems that were needed. When necessary, particularly when special survey results needed to be analyzed, the University of Minnesota computer system was used; SMJC had an account with the university for this purpose. The restudy results show that while St. Mary's sophistication in the MIS area has improved, its basic orientation has remained the same, with an emphasis on combined manual and automated systems without an in-house computer. The college has shifted its computer use from the University of Minnesota to the religious order, but its emphasis has remained the same. As AIDP coordinator Mary Boderick describes it:

> Extensive exploration of the appropriateness of computerized MIS/TIS has led us to conclude that our present approach of manual in combination with certain specialized use of the Sisters of St. Joseph Administrative Center computer is right for us. Size is the key. We have only 750 students and a staff of approximately 125 persons.

St. Mary's has at least four combined manual and automated systems in two areas: admissions and records applications and financial management applications. Additionally, it has two other administrative systems (test scoring and alumni records) and one in planning, management, and institutional research (institution-coding structure). In fact, St. Mary's considers automation possibly applicable in some other planning, management, and institutional research applications. Its priorities for MIS development are improved registration, improved enrollment reporting, scheduling, and alumni records. All these systems are under development. The order has provided St. Mary's the necessary technical assistance; in particular, the college is cooperating with the College of St. Catherine (another Sisters of St. Joseph college) on the adaptation of existing systems.

The computer environment at St. Mary's is simple: it has one local minicomputer, which is used for instructional purposes. For administrative computing, someone drives three miles to a Sisters of St. Joseph administrative center to use the order's machine.

AIDP has had a significant impact on the MIS-development efforts at St. Mary's. The most important impact was in clarifying data need: "We are finally gaining clarity on MIS needs as a result of the goal setting/goal review process being established collegewide. Now we see what data we need to measure goal achievement. Before we were unsure as to what we needed data for." Automated systems are considered relevant at St. Mary's "only in those areas where the time/ staff costs for preparing for materials for computerization does not, at a minimum, exceed the costs of computerization." St. Mary's realizes that "many formulas" and "the actual experience of other institutions" does not apply because of its size. As a result, most of its systems are manual. St. Mary's recognizes that its approach has been cautious and deliberate.

> We have been cautious about automation because of our size. Now that we are able to see more of the cross-department interaction factors, we are beginning to see a few areas where additional automation could assist us in planning of particular interest right now in simulation of alternative staffing scheduling patterns as we shift with evening and weekend programming.

Doane College

Doane College has placed more emphasis on MIS development than St. Mary's. At the time of the original study, Doane had acquired a local computer (DEC/PDP 11/34) through donated funds, and then added to its hardware capability with AIDP funds. As part of its AIDP grant, Doane undertook ambitious MIS-development activities that included computerization of historical college records as well as implementation of standardized modeling systems. At the time of the site visit, some administrators expressed doubts about the value of these activities, which also were questioned in the first external evaluation report.

Doane has been highly successful with most of its MIS-development efforts, especially in its operating systems. The college has several systems in production in both financial management and admissions and records applications. In addition, the college considers computerization relevant in most administrative areas. One or more systems are in production in planning, management, and institutional research, physical plant operations, financial aid, library applications, and other administrative applications operating systems use all three modes: batch, on-line, and combined batch and on-line. Some systems are combined with manual systems. Its priorities for development include budget preparation, enrollment forecasting, student aid evaluation, facility inventory, and class schedules. The college also has made use of purchase packages.

Doane's experience with attempts to develop simulation models for budget and enrollment forecasting has not been as successful as its other MIS-development activities. As part of its final AIDP plan, Doane proposed several NCHEMS packages. This experience has not been successful so far. The following comments from the most recent external evaluation documents this:

> In our original evaluation, we cautioned that the entire
> NCHEMS software package has a number of problems
> inherent in it which would make its useful application
> difficult. The College has now written off its efforts to
> implement the NCHEMS materials, and is now exploring
> instead alternative decision making models such as
> PLANTRAN or tying with the EDUCOM system. The one
> NCHEMS package that the College might wish to use would
> be the induced course load matrix (ICLM), which is a rea-
> sonably satisfactory student flow analysis indicating which
> courses are taken by which majors.

Throughout the MIS-development process, Doane administrators have maintained a realistic perspective about MIS development. This balanced, but optimistic, view is still evident: "Although we have not accomplished as much as we set out to do so in our original plan, we feel we have made substantial progress and it has created a need in the eyes of our administrators to continue our efforts in MIS develop-ment." In fact, college administrators recognized that relevance of computer systems is not entirely determined by economic variables:

> Prior to obtaining our own computer, we had an on-line
> rental arrangement with a local industry and our input
> and only data processing hardware on campus was a key
> punch. Even on that level we began to see opportunities
> for data processing in our administrative system and we
> have ever since continued to stride toward further auto-
> mating our operation.

> Early on, we learned that in very few cases did we actu-
> ally save labor, but we greatly improved our access to
> information and the speed it was obtained. There seems
> to be no end to increasing interest in the computer and
> currently we project a continued enlargement of our use.
> For a long time we were hampered by the limitations of
> our hardware but now we feel it has reached a point where
> we can continue adding programs for some time.

Overview

The St. Mary's and Doane examples illustrate the diverse range of opportunities in the area of MIS development that phase II institutions encounter. There are some basic similarities, particularly in their emphasis on the student record and financial systems, which appear to be most critical. Phase II institutions have an opportunity to choose the most appropriate way of meeting their administrative-computing needs, ranging from contractual arrangements to in-house development. Other automated administrative systems, even simulation models, are possible, as the Doane example illustrates; however, these may be most appropriately viewed as enhancements that do not result directly in cost savings. Instead, savings may be realized through improved planning and management decisions. Judging from the evidence in these studies, the degree to which simulation modeling is applicable to phase II institutions is still uncertain.

Phase III MIS Intervention

Phase III institutions are likely to have already faced the problems of initial computer-systems development. Automated systems are considered appropriate in several areas. These institutions also are likely to identify specific limiting factors, as well as specific systems-development priorities. Computerization is, by necessity, an important part of the overall administrative-management system at phase III institutions.

These medium-sized colleges and universities, usually between 1,800 and 5,000 students, have complex administrative data-processing needs. Unless they are part of a large multicampus system, they usually lack the financial resources to maintain large and well-staffed computing facilities. They need basic operating systems as well as more sophisticated systems in areas such as student financial aid, general administrative services, and institutional planning and research. They also need a capacity to relate financial data to student data, or to cross-check student records with financial aid information. This requires easy access to reliable, up-to-date information. Institutional researchers need easy access to diverse types of data to respond in internal and external inquiries. This situation is further complicated by a lack of trained personnel (programmers, analysts, and so on) and problems retraining these people once they are hired. These colleges need to train and employ students as a partial solution to their personnel needs; they also need to realistically evaluate their computer hardware needs. Access to a large network with some local capability, as opposed to developing or purchasing all systems to operate on in-house computers, may be the most cost-effective alternative. The restudy provided one example of the MIS development at a phase III institution, Xavier University.

Xavier University

Xavier University of Louisiana was experiencing significant problems with its computer operations at the time of the original study. In 1977 Xavier had both an administrative center (with an IBM 1130) and an academic center (with a Honeywell 68/80), as well as two miniprocessors in the math science department and network access for the personnel (to IBM 370/165) and library computing. In 1980 Xavier continued to have a relatively complex computing environment, but had consolidated the two computer centers, installed new machinery (HP300) to replace the two smaller machines, and had instituted new procedures to improve the management of computer operations.

Automated MIS is considered important to the university information system. Automated systems are in production in planning, management, institutional research, financial management applications, physical plant management, and admissions and records. Additionally, automated systems are being developed in financial aid, and the library has access to a three-college system (Xavier, Loyola, and Dominican) in New Orleans, through a national library catalog system. Automated systems at Xavier are mostly on-line.

Title III has had a significant impact on the MIS-development efforts at Xavier. Mrs. Ellis, Xavier AIDP coordinator, suggested that MIS automation would not have happened without Title III support, and that the national program remains crucial in the untimed developments of the automated systems. She considered automated information "essential to the management system." While the college has manual systems in some areas, automated systems are considered appropriate in most areas. Interestingly, automated resource requirements modeling was the only area explicitly considered not relevant for automation.

Progress in the MIS-development efforts has occurred faster than anticipated during the past two years. In fact, the university has had to install additional memory to its system because automation has proceeded faster than scheduled. In addition to memory (for example, disk space), the key factor limiting MIS development is personnel. The university has had difficulty hiring and retraining programmers. A source of the problem is the low pay schedule at the university. Administrators have chosen not to pay higher salaries for computing because they do not want to get these salaries out of line with other administrative salaries. This makes recruitment difficult; the college has lost trained personnel for the same reason.

The integrated academic-and-administrative-computing center has allowed for a more conscious strategy to improve academic computing. Administrators recognize that to integrate computing into the instructional process, existing faculty need to be trained in instructional applications. An objective of subsequent Title III proposals will include faculty training in this area. During the past two years, use of the academic-computing services has more than doubled.

Phase IV MIS Interventions

The Missouri study included three types of institutions in phase IV: large branch campuses in the University of Missouri, large regional universities, and multicampus community college systems. This is the most dominant category in the public sector. In spite of the diversity in the types and purposes of these institutions, there were major similarities in their administrative data processing and MIS-development needs. All areas of MIS computerization were considered relevant, one or more automated systems were usually in production in most areas, and in most instances systems modification and refinement were a higher MIS-development priority than creating new systems. Phase IV institutions have highly complex administrative structures with sophisticated management needs.

Large, coordinated college and university systems have complex administrative-computing environments. Most already have developed basic operating systems, need new systems in other areas such as physical plant or hospital applications, and need to update their basic financial systems to accommodate increased demands. In addition to these complex operating-system needs, they can make use of student flow and financial models that will help central administrators relate enrollment information to student-enrollment patterns. It is possible that the program-budgeting model or other financial-planning models have already been attempted. However, staff limitations, especially training needs, often impede the development of new systems and slow the implementation of already developed ones. It is practical to train administrators and staff in functional units—colleges, campuses, student-service divisions—in the maintenance of operating systems. For these schools, maintenance of administrative-and-academic-computing systems (on one or multiple machines) requires paying attention to hardware costs. Investment in small machines often can save on hardware costs, if the system's compatibility problems can be overcome. The restudy provided two examples of MIS interventions in phase IV institutions.

North Carolina A & T State University

North Carolina A & T State University is in the midst of an MIS-development process that it considered necessary. A & T is dependent on automated systems. As Edwin Bell, director of planning and coordinator of the MIS-development activities, described it: "The volume of transactions and the complexity of reporting have grown to the point where manual systems are no longer appropriate. " Bell also noted in the MIS questionnaire responses that:

> AIDP has been the primary support for MIS development at N. C. A & T State University. It has supported the acquisition of both computer hardware and software as well as the staff related to the development of an integrated administrative data processing environment. The state has provided no support for MIS development. Without AIDP the process could not have started.

A & T has a relatively complex computer environment that includes a local CPU (a digital 1070), access to a regional central unit (in the IBM 370 series), and 80 terminals. A & T has three or more operating systems in planning, management, and institutional research, financial management and applications, and admission and records applications. It also has at least one system in production in general administrative services, logistics and related services, and student financial aid. Operating systems are on-line, batch, or combined, with a high portion of on-line systems. The top priorities for development include financial accounting systems, accounts payable system, management support system (financial planning), data directory system, and outcomes assessment. The university also is implementing the EDUCOM financial-planning model. Automated MIS is considered relevant in all areas except hospital applications, which is not applicable. State acceptance of contracts and money is cited as the most crucial factor limiting MIS developments.

The AIDP project has helped the university make effective decisions about MIS development. The following examples were cited in the questionnaire:

> A five year administrative data processing plan has been developed through AIDP. The plan describes the goals for administrative data processing, the needs for functional areas, the management structure that is required, the technical plan for specific activities, and the budget plan. . . . Also a series of management audits were conducted through AIDP support and the logical data bases for the functional areas of the University were completed with AIDP support. . . . A feasibility study is being completed about the implementation of an on-line data dictionary-directory through support from AIDP.

The external evaluation of the AIDP project at A & T noted some organizational problems confronting the MIS-development activities:

Two additional comments need to be made here. First, a possible problem has developed between people working on the MIS and those in the computer center. The difference is one of philosophy as to how and to what extent the data base of the University should be developed. The Advisory Committee should address it and resolve it. The consultants also remind the University of previous recommendations regarding a restructuring of the reporting relationship of the Computer Center which we believe would help this problem. . . . The second comment regards the needs for the chancellor to take action on the proposed management plan for MIS which is now before him. We understand this will be acted on soon.

The need for coordinated administrative development at A & T was cited earlier. This same organization dilemma seems to be affecting the development of the MIS system at A & T as well. However, it is apparent that the university is making substantial progress on its MIS-development activities, which were getting under way at the time of the site visit in 1977. At that time the MIS function was being reorganized; the director of MIS had left the university, in part due to the plan development of the system, and this has since been made a responsibility of the director of planning. The progress since that time has been substantial, although more organizational adjustments may be necessary to accommodate the continued adjustment of automated administrative data-processing systems.

Valencia Community College

Valencia Community College has made rapid progress on the development of its automated MIS. At the start of the AIDP project in 1976, the college began initial efforts to identify automation needs and develop a plan for its implementation. At the time of the site visit in 1977, after the first year of AIDP, a collegewide committee was meeting to identify management-information needs. This exercise seemed successful at exposing this group, which had representatives from the campuses and the central administration, to the range of information needs facing the campus. At the present time Valencia Community College appears well on the road toward developing an integrated MIS that is useful to the college administrators.

Valencia Community College has a relatively large central computer (IBM 370/138) with 24 terminals and four printers. This system supports multiple in-production systems in the following areas: financial management applications, general administrative service, applications, and admissions and records. Two systems are in production in planning, management, and institutional research and other administrative applications. Systems are currently under development in financial aid administration, library, admissions, financial management, and planning, management, and institutional research. The top MIS-development priorities are: financial systems, personnel/payroll, financial aid, facilities and budget analysis/preparation. Personnel is considered the major factor limiting development; this includes "financial support [money] for personnel, and training of user personnel to utilize the system." Valencia Community College has made extensive use of externally developed systems, usually from other community colleges; it has had high levels of success with these adaptations. The student systems are mostly on-line, while the financial systems are mostly batch.

There are still manual systems at Valencia. However, even these have an automated flavor. These systems include:

> The admissions systems is primarily manual, however, once the individual is admitted all demographic data is translated to the computer network. . . . Some of the state reports are manually prepared, however, computer listings and data is utilized in preparing the reports. . . . Research reports are prepared manually, however, the computer is used for statistical analysis of data.

Continued MIS development is needed at Valencia Community College. However, it is viewed as part of the integrated MIS plan, which Title III has supported:

> The Title III program has identified the need for integrated systems, and these are being developed to form the Valencia Community College MIS. The need for developing additional transactional information systems (computer systems) has, also, been identified, and the institution is planning development in this area. The need for institutional research has, also, been identified in Valencia developing needed research for decision making, e.g., productivity models, cost analysis models, etc.

The external evaluators of the AIDP project at Valencia Community College have commented on the high level of success. However, there are organizational problems: "At the present, the Vice President for Instructional Support seems to be driving the system development aspects of financial information. This is a tribute to strong leadership. While no one knocks success, one wonders what happens when the system changes or the key mover is promoted." The evaluators also observed that the system can become more functional:

Just as the responsibilities for outcomes must follow functional lines, so too must the responsibility for systems definitions. Even though an initial system may be designed by the technical staff, it has been shown again and again that the system cannot be maintained and it will not be utilized unless there is adequate ownership for the effectiveness of the system residing outside data processing; that is, within the operating department.

Valencia, while it has made ample progress on the initial MIS-development activities, is now encountering the need to decentralize the system. However, there has been significant progress in the MIS-development effort during a relatively short period. Automated information is now considered critical to the central administration and is of increasing importance to the campuses.

Overview

NCA&T and VCC illustrate the importance of automated information at phase IV institutions. In both cases, central administration and functional subunits are seen as users of automated information, and administration of computing resources is as important. The re-study of exemplary Title III institutions reaffirms the basic characteristics observed in the Missouri study, except these two institutions did not have the extensive prior history of MIS development evident at the Missouri institutions.

Phase V MIS Intervention

Phase V institutions are the most complex observable organization structures in higher education. In Missouri public higher education there are two examples: the University of Missouri system, when analyzed as a whole, and the Columbia campus of the university, the flagship campus of the system. They both differ from phase IV institutions; in addition to centralized MIS systems and facilities, they have other distributed MIS systems and facilities. In the case of the university system, the campuses maintain automated MIS systems along with the central administration. At the UMC campus, there are five computer centers, three of which do extensive administrative data processing.

The extremely large campus or university system has a distinctly different set of administrative-computing problems than other higher education institutions. In addition to supporting the multiple users and systems through a centralized system, the central computing facility has to support (or at least coordinate) the activities of other administrative-computing centers, campuses, hospitals, or research offices. MIS-development priorities often include refining and updating existing systems, as well as developing specialized capabilities such as student flow modeling and induced-course-loan analysis. These more sophisticated systems are essential for cost-conscious management decisions, both by central administration and by campus administrators and college deans.

Decisions about which systems to operate centrally and which should be decentralized can be critical to administrators in both the central administration and major subunits. Staff training, for both central administrative personnel and operating unit personnel, is important; staff exchange programs between operating units and central administration are a definite possibility. System compatibility also is a major concern, and therefore standardization of reporting dates and data-element definitions across subunits is important for both operations and management. There were no examples of phase V institutions included in the restudy.

CONCLUSIONS

This chapter has proposed an MIS-development framework for higher education institutions that considers MIS needs within the context of institution-management needs. If one assumes that the costs of automation are likely to remain relatively constant during the next decade, with decreases in equipment costs being offset by increased personnel and software costs, then it seems that institutions should base their MIS-development decisions on their overall management-information requirements rather than on the hope that automation costs are going to decline suddenly. In this context it is important for institutions to identify the types of MIS developments that are most appropriate, rather than attempting to develop the best possible system. The cost of finding, retaining, and training personnel to develop and maintain basic operating systems is a critical factor for most institutions. Most importantly, administrators need to determine the types of information systems that will help them make critical decisions about enrollment and finances.

Higher education administrators and federal and state policymakers need to take a more sophisticated, indeed a differentiated, approach to the development of administrative-computing systems. Too often administrators at very small campuses will attempt the development of sophisticated systems, without giving the necessary attention to the development of basic systems. Government policymakers, usually trained as administrators in large university systems, are likely to encourage this singular approach. They often assume coordinated systems are best for all campuses and college systems; their experiences and observations usually support this assumption. Increasingly, higher education administrators, both at the state and campus levels, will have to utilize a differentiated lens when planning administrative-computing systems.

During the initial study, it appeared that the same smaller campuses were being encouraged by the Title III program staff to implement sophisticated MIS. In recent years it appears that those same institutions have had the freedom necessary to develop systems that met local needs. If this is the case, then the Title III program may be adjusting to the different MIS needs campuses are experiencing.

This analysis suggests that two concerns are critical to the development of administrative-computing systems in higher education. First, in spite of the decreasing price of some computer hardware, the overall costs of automation are high, especially when personnel and system maintenance costs are considered; therefore, colleges need to make cost-effective decisions about systems acquisition, planning, and development. Second, the types of MIS development needed by a given higher education institution are dictated by its structure as well as by its actual management-information needs. Both these factors suggest that a differentiated approach is necessary.

9

IMPLICATIONS FOR INSTITUTIONS

Management development is a dynamic and essential process for colleges and universities. The current condition of higher education, the financial constraints and declining pool of traditional students, increases the importance of planning for future activities and managing existing (often scarce) resources. Most institutions no longer have the fortunate situation, common during prior decades, of being able to expand when new programmatic developments were needed due to an ever-expanding potential clientele. Instead, colleges and universities are confronted by a condition that requires conscious planning about how new programs can be developed when resources are scarce, how existing programs can be modified to meet changing student needs, and how existing structures can be streamlined and made more efficient.

This chapter considers the implications for colleges and universities of the study of management-development activities at exemplary Title III institutions. All the case institutions were, at some point during the past decade, confronted by basic operational problems; some even confronted the issue of survival. At the same time, these institutions were able to focus their planning efforts on the important tasks of identifying new directions, as well as improving their operational management. These challenges are facing most colleges and universities.

The case-study institutions were able to secure external funding from the Title III program and to use these funds and various external consulting services to improve the quality of college- and university-management systems and of their academic programs and student services as well. This chapter focuses on the implications of this study for the internal process of management improvement. First, however, the concept of management development that has emerged during this study is considered.

AN EMERGING CONCEPT OF MANAGEMENT DEVELOPMENT

This study started with a concept of college management that was fundamentally different from most research on this subject. Most current research on college management starts with the assumptions that sophisticated management is needed by colleges and universities, and that the objective of research should be to identify the factors that encourage or limit implementation (for example, Baldridge and Tierney, 1979). This study started with a different assumption: college-management improvements are necessary due, in part, to the new condition, but the types of systems that should be implemented and their degree of sophistication are determined by the characteristics of the organization (its size, structure, and history), rather than the characteristics of the proposed system. In practice, the two research approaches produce some similar findings about college management, such as identifying the importance of needs assessment and the difficulties in adapting systems from large institutions in small college settings. However, the implications of the results take on different meanings because of the differences in the assumptions underlying the research. Due to the conscious emphasis on basic research on college development used in this study, the results have contributed to a broader concept of management development in higher education.

The most obvious finding, and the one that has the most direct implications for institution-based management-development efforts, is that college-management needs vary according to a campus's size, structure, and history. Based on consideration of these facts, management-development plateaus can be identified that predict the types of management improvements colleges and universities are likely to need. These developmental phases are related directly to size and structural characteristics that can be estimated by quantitative indicators, but that are more accurately diagnosed by examining the history of a given college or university. Once an institution's phase of structural development is diagnosed, it is possible to predict the types of management and information systems it will probably need, although not to determine the specific systems.

This research also has interesting implications for an emerging concept of management development. In a sense, the approach to a development model used in this study is analogous to the biological development of an individual and the cognitive developments that correspond with this change. In other words, there is some similarity between the development of an organization and the development of a person, especially in the sense that Piaget (1971, 1977) describes the process of cognitive development of an individual. The challenge for the researcher is to identify the types of formal systems that correspond with organizational needs. The challenge for the college administrator is to identify and implement appropriate management procedures and systems, just as the challenge for educators is to identify and utilize instructional materials and processes that are appropriate for a child's cognitive capacity rather than to promote the development along the cognitive continuum, which is a natural development process (Groen, 1978). The analogy between the individual and the organization is useful in explaining the limitations of the management-development model as well.

Just as a cognitive development is not the only way an individual child develops, structural development is not the only type of development a college experiences. Within psychology there are concepts of human development, or evolution of the individual, in areas other than cognitive development, including theories. These include concepts of moral development (Kohlberg, 1975), ego development (Lovinger, 1970), and human motivation (Maslow, 1954). These theories are concerned with the qualitative development of the individual. Just as it is possible to construct theories or models of qualitative development of the individual, it is possible to envision concepts of qualitative change in organizations, particularly in colleges, since they attempt to have a positive impact on the development of individual students. Management development may be related to aspect change in the organizational development, just as cognitive development may be related to other aspects of human development. (Kohlberg, for example, bases his theory of moral development on Piaget's stages of cognitive development.) At the very best it would appear that effective management is necessary to identify alternative futures and to construct ways, organizationally, of achieving those futures.

Increasingly, higher education administrators are concerned about institutional quality and the capacity of their management and planning systems to improve their qualitative and financial conditions Table 9. 1 suggests one possible relationship between effective management and the qualitative development of colleges and universities. The study of exemplary Title III institutions has identified the types of management and information capacities in colleges and universities in different phases of structural development are likely to need if they are to develop effective management systems. Table 9. 1 suggests a possible role for a college-management system in the qualitative development process. The proposed stages are hypothetical, although they are similar to stages proposed in an earlier Title III study by Hodgkinson and Schenkel (1974). Balderston (1974) proposed a direct relationship between management and qualitative change when he dis-

TABLE 9.1

Possible Relationship between Effective Management and
Qualitative Development of Colleges and Universities

Stage*	Characteristics	Management Role
I Low Range	Institutions challenged by the most basic issues of survival and problematic daily operations	Improve basic decisions about finances and operations
II Medium Range	Institutions making uneven progress toward financial viability and educational goals	Improve capacity to plot long-range future and determine short-range operating needs
III High Range	Institutions making steady progress toward achieving fiscal and educational goals	Improve capacity to determine program needs and capacities to have positive impacts on students
IV Distinctive	Institutions capable of defining short- or long-range goals and directing resources (human and fiscal) toward goals, which include consideration of impacts on community	Improve capacity of institution to relate institutional decisions to community and social needs, and to weigh decision options in this context

*The term "stage" is used here to describe qualitative plateaus for college development to distinguish this concept from the structural-development concept explored in this book, which uses the term "phase" to describe plateaus of development. This distinction is consistent with the individual-development literature, which uses the concept of "life phase" to describe changes related to age and life structure and "stage" for internal changes (for example, ego development or moral development).

tinguished among management for survival, management for stability, and management for excellence. These interrelated concepts suggest a dynamic relationship between management development and qualitative change.

Four stages of qualitative development are suggested in Table 9.1. Low-range institutions are challenged by the most basic issues of survival and confronted by problems with their daily operations. The role of effective management in this context is to help the college make basic decisions about financial and college operations. An institution in any phase of structural development can be challenged by these basic issues. A small college that loses its line of credit at a local bank will be not able to pay faculty or insure current prospective students that the college will be open next semester. The same severe financial conditions can confront the largest institutions. While there are not examples of this in higher education, there are recent examples of large companies (such as Chrysler) or large cities (New York) that have had these problems. It is conceivable that the same conditions confront a large university campus of a college system. In these instances, it may be in the interest of government—state, local, or federal—to bail the institution out of trouble, which was true in the case of Chrysler. However, small colleges will not have this luxury.

The second stage for institutions is medium range, in which they make uneven progress toward financial viability and education. In the new conditions of financial stress and declining enrollment, many institutions of all sizes are confronted by these issues. The role of an effective management system, in this context, is to improve the capacity of the institution to plot its future, as well as to improve to short-range, day-to-day operations. Several of the case study institutions were struggling with these conditions during the period of the case study and before.

The third stage, according to this scheme, is high range. Institutions in this stage have a capacity to make successful progress toward their fiscal and educational goals. The role of an effective management system for stage III institutions is to improve the capacity of the institution to evaluate program needs and their capacity of the institution to evaluate program needs and their capacity to have a positive impact on students. This is a level of qualitative development most colleges and universities strive to attain. At this level they are meeting basic survival needs and are capable of using resources in a strategic way to impact on students.

Some institutions not only have a commitment to excellence, but also a capacity to achieve it; they not only have a positive impact on the development of their students, but they also have a substantial role in their communities if not in society. The institutional purpose and values are shared among the immediate college or university community, as is the awareness that their activities—their roles in instruction, research, and service—make a significant contribution. Again, size and structure are not necessarily major factors; a small Reed or Swarthmore is as likely to have these qualities as a Harvard, Stanford, or University of California. Age may be a factor, at least somewhat, to the extent that it takes time for an organization to develop these qualities. The role of effective management, in this context, is to improve the capacity of the institution to relate institutional decisions to the broader social role of the institution. This is true even for a counterculture institution, such as Black Mountain College (Duberman, 1972), which has an alternate community to serve.

This qualitative-development model is proposed to help round out the management-development concept explored here. It is more than an afterthought; it is based on years of research on and experience with college development and management. The purpose of management development, after all, is not simply to implement new or sophisticated systems, but to enhance the capacity of institutions to meet their basic organizational needs and to improve qualitatively. The concept of management being proposed here is based on a view of management as a basic thinking and analytic capacity that is necessary if a college or university community is to deal effectively with both the operational demands placed on the organization by its history, size, and formal structure, and the striving for qualitative improvement in organizational life. Both dimensions are important in the development of college-management systems.

While there are two developmental continuums (structural and qualitative), a college usually experiences its evolution as a singular process, with both structural and qualitative issues influencing the ebbs, flows, and crises of organizational life. * From the perspective of the individual college, both dimensions are (or should be) important in the task of management development, which gives a college or university the capacity necessary to achieve its qualitative goals. At the same time, the structure of a college limits the types of management improvements that are likely to be successful. The process approach to management development, outlined below, suggests strategies that colleges and universities in different structural development phases can use to develop viable management systems.

---

*Again, one must consider the analogy to individual development: Erickson, for example, has developed a concept of individual life cycles that includes both the structural and qualitative domains. In the long term it may be possible to develop integrated concepts of college development. However, in the short term this distinction is important to planning.

A PROCESS APPROACH TO MANAGEMENT DEVELOPMENT

This study reveals that management development is a dynamic and fluid process, that future management needs are often determined by the outcome of prior attempts to improve management. Old systems need to be updated, new needs often emerge when old problems are finally solved, and changes in the organization, the addition of new programs or people, can be a catalyst for new ideas and directions. The study also reveals that management improvement is an ongoing process, that it is not a simple matter of implementing a new system and then forgetting about it. New people need to be trained in the use of old systems, oldtimers need to learn to use new systems or to change habits so they can be implemented, and most systems need to be modified and adapted to meet local needs. This is usually the case whether the system being implemented is for planning, managing, evaluating, information, or some combination.

Institution-development, management-development, and change and planning methodologies proposed for higher education often have common components. Webster and Shorthouse (1976), in their review of the state of the art of management development and training in higher education, propose the following steps: assessment; planning; pilot testing; implementation; and evaluation. Schien (1969) suggests a cycle for process consultation: problem formulation; generating proposals and solutions; forecasting consequences; action planning; action steps; and evaluating outcomes. Bergquist and Shoemaker (1976), in their institution-development model for small colleges, propose the following steps: assessing the institution and its environment; clarifying institutional mission and goals; developing analytic and projective models; developing and testing strategies for stabilization or change; implementing strategies; and monitoring effects and possible redesign. The NCHEMS model for academic and program planning suggests the following steps: needs assessment; planning assumptions and context for planning; and implementation and operation participation (Kieft, Armijo, and Bucklew, 1978). In general, institutional change strategies have similar steps or elements.

For the purpose of this chapter, which is considering the implication of the general model for institutions, five key elements critical to a successful management-development or institutional change effort will be examined. These are:

Assessment of the organization and the need for management improvement;
Goal Formulation to identify critical targets for management-development efforts;
Implementation activities that allow for the selection, development, and adaptation of systems to meet local needs;

<u>Evaluation</u> of the implementation process and outcomes to de-
termine ways the management systems can be improved; and
<u>Reassessment</u> of organizational and management needs.

These elements reflect a commonality with other change strategies. In fact, institutions choosing to consider the strategies in each
of these areas outlined below may decide to add a step—such as pilot-
testing or monitoring and redesign—to evolve a development strategy
that meets local needs. The argument here is simply that the way an
institution undertakes each of these steps should be compatible with
its structure and management needs. How the intervention frameworks
outlined in the prior two chapters can be used to inform institution-
based management-development efforts will be considered below. The
following discussion of these strategies is general, emphasizing differences in the way colleges and universities in varying phases of
development should approach the task of management development.
Specific information about the types of systems that should be implemented has been discussed in the prior two chapters.

Assessment

Assessment of organizational needs is a critical first step to
any change effort. While this statement may sound simpleminded,
research on college-management development suggests that the lack
of prior assessment is often a major problem. Baldridge and Tierney
(1979) point to the tendency of administrators to use their own pet
projects, the tendency to be superficial, and the availability of external funds as a stimulus, as the factors that limit adequate needs
assessments. Based on this investigation, a fourth factor should be
added: a lack of basic knowledge to guide assessments of college-
management needs. It is in this area that this study is potentially
most useful, as it has identified basic relationships between organizational characteristics and college-management needs.

A needs assessment should begin with an analysis of a college-
organization structure; particularly an analysis of its phase of structural development, which will allow for a comparison of the types of
systems that are likely to be needed with those that are actually in
place. This can lead to an assessment of whether new systems are
needed, or if existing systems should be refined instead. The quantitative indicators of structural development, shown in Table 5. 3, are
a starting point for such an analysis. It is also important to review
what is known about the history of the institution, particularly the
major reorganizations, program additions and changes, and prior
management-development efforts. This initial analysis—which could

be done by a president, planner, institutional researcher, or other administrator with a knowledge of the organization—can be a starting point for the design of an assessment strategy.

Needs assessments are an important starting point for a management-development effort. If done well, they put the management needs of the college into a perspective that includes an understanding of the nature and future of the college as an organization. The needs-assessment strategy a college uses should vary according to its phase of structural development. Table 9.2 outlines the assessment strategies that seem most appropriate for each development phase.

Phase I Assessment Strategies

Small colleges in the process of forming a curriculum must assess the needs for the proposed program and the curriculum requirements for these offerings, as well as identify individuals who can undertake the initial curriculum-development efforts. There were interesting examples of these types of assessment activities in the case studies.

Provost Evans at VCC East Campus spent a year assessing the needs for a new campus. He brought outside experts to the campus to share ideas about what a new community college might do, and he visited other community college campuses that were attempting to do something different. This assessment was important in forming an initial idea of the type of campus he wanted to develop.

When Sister Anne Joachim took over as head of a small hospital nursing school, she began with an assessment of need for such school. She used her knowledge about the allied health fields and her impressions of the future of the health-training needs to form the idea for a junior college. She solicited help from some of the faculty in the nursing school, which was closing, and from the religious order, which could provide some moral but not substantial financial support, to begin the process of putting this idea into action.

When Phil Heckman came to Doane College in 1966, it was a very small liberal arts college. There seemed to be a bright future; there were plenty of prospective students and financial support to build new buildings. He decided, based on this assessment of the college's condition, that it should grow to 1,000 students. The fate of the college since this time is described in a prior chapter. This action catapulted the college into a new phase of organizational life.

The most basic and important kinds of needs assessments for all colleges are assessments of the need for academic-program services. It will be increasingly important for college and university administrators to find ways of modifying existing programs to meet new needs, as Sister Joachim did at St. Mary's and Phil Heckman did at Doane College. This, in part, is an intuitive process; it involves

TABLE 9.2

Management Needs-Assessment Strategies

Phase	Strategy
I	Identify market needs; organizational, curricular, and program requirements; individuals with interest and expertise to offer courses
II	Add: Assessment of program maintenance needs; needs for program mission change; and needs for formal management of academic programs
III	Add: Assessment of management needs of organizational subunits (departments, divisions, colleges, administrative units); need for uniform policy and procedures; and need for new, refined, or changed programs
IV	Add: Assessment of coordination needs; central administrative capacity to define centralized programs and services; need for coordinated programs and centralized services; and need of capacity to analyze systemwide policy options
V	Add: Assessment of systemwide organizational and program needs (usually at a number of campuses); collaborative strategies that involve central administrators and functional subunit representatives in planning and management; and capacity of existing strategies to meet new needs

using available information to form an idea about what might work. All colleges need people, administrators, faculty, and students who are interested in assessing program needs and finding ways of putting them into action.

Phase II Assessment Strategy

In addition to assessing the needs for an academic process, a phase II college (in fact, a phase II organization can be a large department in a university) also must assess the organizational requirements for maintaining programs, the need for formal management systems, and perhaps the need to change the mission of the organization. In practice, the initial need for assessments of this sort is a critical point in organizational life. For organizations that have reached phase II, there is need for ongoing assessment of this type. Again, there were colorful examples in the case studies.

To that point the college had operated with a short-range perspective, one that emphasized innovative courses and programs and involved faculty in identifying new directions for the school. The long-range planning effort began with the first real assessment of the college as an organization. The college identified a number of key issues—the need to limit growth, to remain innovative, and to maintain current programs—as a part of the planning effort, which began with a needs assessment for the college.

Doane College was confronted by a drastic financial situation in the early 1970s. Suddenly the market had changed, student interest in liberal arts curricula (especially at small rural colleges) had waned, enrollment had declined, and fiscal deficits resulted. While the college had a long-range planning effort in place, the new condition called for a much more in-depth look at the college and its future prospects than had been possible in the past. The assessment that resulted included examination and reflection about all aspects of the college and its mission. Substantial changes in both the structure of the college and its mission resulted.

Phase III Assessment Strategies

Since phase III colleges are larger and more complex than phase I or phase II institutions, the appropriate types of need assessments are also more complex. In addition to needing assessment of the direction of the organization as a whole, there are numerous components, or organizational subunits, that have assessment needs as well. The management needs of major organizational subunits should be considered, as well as the need for uniform policies and procedures and the need to refine, change, or add programs. The study again included interesting examples.

The transition of Xavier from religious to lay leadership was accompanied by financial problems and enrollment difficulties, followed by a relatively successful period of enrollment growth. In this context, it was necessary to undertake a detailed examination of the workings of the organization. In administrative areas, program assessments were done of all major academic programs (of the departments in arts and science, and of the college pharmacy and the graduate school). In the administrative areas, the need for routine procedures was examined.

VCC West Campus experienced an organizational jolt when the central administration moved off campus in 1974 as the college became multicampus. The campus administration began to examine the administrative and support needs of academic departments that had lost a major portion of their activities; the off-campus program had suddenly become the responsibility of the Open Campus. Also, the administrative needs of student-affairs units, the major administrative units left on campus, were examined.

Phase IV Assessment Strategies

The types of assessment strategies required by phase IV organizations are, again, fundamentally different than the prior phases. In particular, these organizations should assess the need for coordination, centralized services and program coordination, and system-wide analytic activities. The case studies provide a few examples of phase IV assessments.

When Valencia Community College transitioned from a one-campus structure to a three-campus structure, the college undertook an extensive assessment process. While some of the assessment activities included strategies associated with prior phases, as the discussion of the VCC campuses above so clearly indicates, the predominant assessment activity was an examination of collegewide needs and the needs and opportunities for coordinated development. As part of their AIDP-planning process, they examined the full range of college needs from faculty and curriculum development to central planning and management needs. The needs-assessment process included a dialogue across the college, which involved numerous faculty and administrators.

For North Carolina A & T, movement into the coordination phase has been more gradual. However, their assessment activities have identified the need for coordinated development. The original AIDP included the design of a university-advising center as one example of the centralized services strategy. Also, the external evaluators of Title III in their early reports pointed to the need for coordinated planning and management activities, which was an information source the university administrators used to adjust the direction of their development activities.

Phase V Assessment Strategies

Phase V organizations are extremely large campuses, large multicampus systems, or statewide systems. Their assessment needs are more strategic and specific. In these cases, assessments of systemwide needs usually involve collaborative approaches due to the large number and diversity of organizational units involved. Again, the computing area provides an example. None of the case-study institutions was this complex.

In 1978 Missouri was one of a relatively few states that had not undertaken a statewide planning effort for computing. When such a study was initiated, it was clear that a detailed assessment of the current situation was necessary. A variety of existing data sources were used, including: program-enrollment information collected in the statewide information system; the state-level analysis of the responses to a recent national study, the Fourth Inventory of Computing in Higher Education; and studies conducted in other states. A variety of new survey instruments also were developed: an MIS survey, a survey on academic compiling, a survey of academic deans, and one of college presidents. This diverse information was necessary to gain a composite picture of need for computer hardware, networking capability and support services, instructional computing, and manpower training (Missouri Department of Higher Education, 1979).

Goal-Setting Strategies

Goal-setting strategy, as used in this context, refers to the way planning or goal setting should be structured, rather than to the form or purpose of the activity or to the actual specification of goals or objective statements. Regardless of the process used, the objective of a goal-setting strategy is to set a direction and identify targets for development. The author's bias is toward goals that are specific enough to identify the direction a campus or program is supposed to move, but not so specific as to include statements about the actual systems or packages that are to be implemented. Management development is an incremental process that often requires adjustments in the course or specific program that is chosen. The challenge to the planner is to identify goals that are general enough to allow for this adjustment as programs and systems are implemented, yet specific enough to provide targets, guidelines, or directions to the administrator, faculty, or students responsible for the implementation process. Table 9.3 outlines suggested strategies by structural development phase.

Phase I Goal-Setting Strategies

Goal setting in the small college or a newly developing program tends to be impressionistic and intuitive; but it is perhaps most successful if approached collaboratively, with ample dialogue about possible directions and anticipated needs. Informal dialogue helps, especially when gathering diverse student opinions. At the initial stages of starting a college or when running a small, creative program, there is also some advantage to giving faculty freedom to set their own curricular goals, or to setting guidelines for individual faculty to use in curriculum-development efforts.

There were examples of this goal-setting approach in the case studies. Both of the new VCC campuses were run with a flexible orientation. When faculty were hired at VCC East Campus, they were

TABLE 9.3

Goal-Setting Strategies

Phase	Strategy
I	Informal collaborative process to identify courses, program goals, new directions, and organizational needs; use of committees for planning purposes a viable option
II	Add: Formal planning group of key change agents to review organizational deficiencies, needs, and strengths and to identify management and program-development targets
III	Add: Delegated planning system to identify operational goals/objectives for major administrative and academic units
IV	Add: Centralized planning capacity to identify coordinated systemwide objectives and priorities; goals can be expressed as programs; and task forces can be used for specific planning problems a viable option
V	Add: Collaborative goal-setting strategies involving central administrators and campus/college administrators

encouraged to think creatively about the college curriculum and the courses they taught. At the Open Campus, the staff had considerable freedom to identify topics for short courses of in-service programs. St. Mary's and Doane also exhibited these characteristics during their early years. In each of these cases, the goal-setting process for the campus as a whole was handled by a few key administrators.

Phase II Goal-Setting Strategies

Phase II institutions need to formalize the goal-setting process, especially in areas that concern the process of management and information-systems designs and development. Usually a small planning group, composed of key administrators, is necessary to analyze available information, perhaps to guide the actual assessment activities. Initially, goals are usually vague; often they can be expressed as needed capacities, such as long-range planning, management information system, and so on. While these general statements are useless to larger, more complex institutions that have these systems in place, the general statement of capacities as goals is necessary to get the small campus without a history in this area started in the management-development process. As time progresses and the planning group becomes more experienced with the planning process, these statements can become more specific; in fact, for a small college, a planning group that meets routinely can be a key part of the day-to-day managerial process, especially as goals get translated into action. The struggle of the phase II schools to develop planning capabilities is described in detail in the text. The experiences of Doane and St. Mary's (and even Xavier during an earlier period) with the right system for planning and with actual formation of a group to do the planning, illustrate the importance of this process and its problems. The NACUBO planning model may provide a useful starting point for a small college in the initial stage of developing a planning effort; it did for Doane and Xavier. Both Doane and St. Mary's have continued to refine their planning processes and the role of the planning group. The planning group remains important for both campuses, however, as a mechanism for identifying problems and setting goals for management and academic programs.

Phase III Goal-Setting Strategies

Phase III institutions need to foster goal-setting activities in different decision centers within the organization. Both academic and administrative subunits need goal-setting capabilities. Again, the case studies included several examples: VCC's West Campus strengthened the planning capabilities of academic departments; Xavier emphasized improvements in the goal-setting capabilities in both academic departments and schools; and North Carolina A & T went through an elaborate goal-setting process involving academic and administrative units. In these organizations, a central planning team can set the context for the goal-setting process in the organizational subunits.

Phase IV Goal-Setting Strategies

Phase IV needs a capacity to identify coordinated, systemwide objectives and priorities. It is also possible that goals are expressed as programs or services. Task forces, teams providing representation for major organizational subunits, can be involved in the goal-setting process for new program areas. For example, at VCC committees or task forces, with representatives from the different campuses, were used to plan the MIS system and the other AIDP components. These were later implemented by the central administration, but they provide service to the campuses.

Phase V Goal-Setting Strategies

In phase V systems (very large campuses or systems) it is necessary to design collaborative goal-setting or planning strategies that involve campus administrators and central administration (possibly systemwide or state-level administrators). The Missouri computer-planning efforts again provide an example. While there was a complex environment in Missouri, with several campuses having well-developed computing capacities, there were several unserved (or have-not) campuses and no organizational capacity within the state to address the needs of unserved institutions. The initial planning group, with representatives from state agencies and public and private colleges, identified several areas where cooperation development was necessary—continued technological development, instructional computing, MIS development, improved financing, and statewide planning for computer services and hardware—and proposed to the state coordinating agency an organizational strategy for addressing these needs (St. John, 1980b). A survey of college presidents was used to assess the appropriateness of potential statewide objectives (Missouri Department of Higher Education, 1979).

Implementation Strategies

Implementation strategies should also vary for different organizational contexts. The research on the management-implementation processes at the case-study institutions certainly illustrates these differences. Table 9.4 summarizes the appropriateness of different management-implementation strategies for organization in each phase of development. A brief overview of these strategies follows.

Phase I Implementation Strategies

The heart of the academic process in colleges and universities is the freedom to teach and to learn. Therefore, the objective of academic management within the very small college (or the academic department in a large college or university) should be to provide the opportunity for dialogue, collaboration, and formal and informal interacti ns among students and faculty, as well as the opportunities to attend or teach courses. Teaching and learning are the essence of implementation in an academic setting. Very small colleges, especially those with an emphasis on innovation, need this freedom. The critical role of the one or two key administrators in this setting (the president of a small college, or the chairperson of a large department) is to take charge of the necessary day-to-day managerial problems that plague any organization. At times it is also necessary to pull faculty and students together, perhaps through task groups or an existing committee structure, to identify program and course needs or to evaluate limitations of existing approaches. This was the management-implementation strategy that was used as the administration of the phase I schools studied here.

TABLE 9. 4

Implementation Strategies

Phase	Strategy
I	Informal, collaborative institutions among faculty and students; emphasis on organizational and interpersonal problems and conflict resolution
II	Add: Administrative team to set direction for implementation and monitor process; representation of students and faculty possible; necessary to involve key administrators responsible for implementation
III	Add: Delegation of implementation responsibilities to key administrators and faculty in major subunits; subunits held accountable for implementation process
IV	Add: Coordinated implementation strategy using teams or working groups to implement new systems; teams may involve subunit representatives (as appropriate), but probably are headed by central administrators Drop: (As necessary) delegated implementation strategy, especially if it creates excess duplication
V	Add: Specialized support and training organizations (or networks) to work with campus and system administrators on design of implementation strategies

Phase II Implementation Strategies

In the small phase II organizations, it seems appropriate to use a small administrative team to oversee and monitor the management-implementation process. Usually a few administrators have responsibility for the management-development projects, for example, information systems, institutional research, and so on. Key administrators with implementation responsibilities for management projects should meet regularly to review progress, as well as to consider the interface between systems. For example, it is important to make sure that studies by the research office are used by other groups, that the design of automated systems take into account reporting needs, and that academic managers understand the purpose of these more formal systems. Since these activities usually involve only a few administrators in a small college, as well as a small number of staff with implementation responsibilities, a small committee can oversee management implementation relatively easily. It is also possible to involve some students and/or faculty in these processes;

this is especially important if their perspective is considered important to the management-development process. However, it is critical that those with implementation responsibilities be involved. Both Doane and St. Mary's provide examples of this implementation strategy; in both cases the planning group also retained implementation responsibilities. The combining of these planning and implementation functions may have a lot of payoff for the small college, since it is the easiest way to develop widely shared knowledge about the uses and limitations of the formal management systems.

Phase III Implementation Strategies

Phase III colleges and universities have developed implementation strategies that involve appropriate subunit administrators in implementing and monitoring management-development activities, as well as provide the necessary accountability for the implementation process. Xavier provides an excellent example of this approach: academic administrators in colleges and departments had responsibility for implementing the academic management-by-objective process, while directors of administrative units (business, computing, development, and so on) had responsibility for working with their staff on the implementation of improved management practices. To be successful, management-development activities will involve a large number of administrators, including middle managers, a level of management that may not exist at smaller phase II organizations.

Phase IV Implementation Strategies

Phase IV colleges and universities have a more complex organizational environment in which to implement new management systems. There are more colleges, schools, and possibly campuses that create trade-offs in the design-management systems that do not confront smaller organizations. For example, is it more effective to implement modest cooperative education programs at each undergraduate school or campus, or to create one centrally that works with students from a variety of fields? Similar questions can be asked about faculty development, curriculum development, and management and information-systems development. As phase IV colleges become more adept at coordinated approaches, they will choose the centralized approach when it is cost-effective. The implementation process in these situations will usually involve working groups with representatives from the campuses or colleges involved, but will be headed by central administrators. Both phase IV campuses included in this study made use of this strategy. A & T used it primarily for coordinated academic services, such as advising and cooperative education. Valencia tried to use it for academic and formal management activities, from student services to curriculum and MIS development. A college or university that is transitive from phase III to phase IV will probably use both strategies, which is the case at North Carolina A & T.

Phase V Implementation Strategies

Management-systems implementation in phase V systems involves a contradictory strategy: it is necessary to centralize and decentralize, as appropriate, to develop the defined capabilities. The use of networks and other specialized training and support organizations is a viable approach. The critical issue facing these management improvements is how to use existing expertise, which is usually decentralized, to address a common set of problems. The Missouri computing facilitating network provides a good example (Norris and St. John, 1980). The planning group in Missouri recognized that computer hardware was limited in the achieving of statewide objectives; instead, there was a variety of service and training needs across the state, in public and private institutions, that limited complementation. The purpose of the facilitating network that is being implemented is to organize a people-based network across the state that can address these deficiencies.

Networks and other collaborative implementation strategies may be an increasingly important mechanism in higher education for institutions adjusting to the changing growth condition. These may be an outgrowth of statewide, systemwide, or consortia planning. However, strategies that utilize expertise from numerous settings will undoubtedly be an option for starting programs with scarce resources.

Evaluation Strategies

Evaluation is a critical part of the management-development process. Persons implementing new management systems, procedures, or processes, or designing, programming, or documenting automated information systems, need evaluative information to guide their activities. Those who are responsible for the implementation of these systems, the directors, deans, or executive officers, need evaluations (perhaps from external sources) to make effective decisions about when to refine, modify, or discontinue a particular activity, program, or management practice. The involvement of the case-study institutions in Title III increased the types of evaluative information available to the institutions. These institutions were required to perform routine internal evaluations as part of the Title III monitoring process and to use an external evaluator to report on the AIDP project each year. Table 9.5 suggests the types of evaluative information that can enhance the management-development process for institutions in

TABLE 9.5

Evaluation Strategies

Phase	Strategy
I	Collect evaluative information about students and courses that can inform decisions about curriculum, academic programs, and student services. Informal exchange between students and faculty important
II	Add: Evaluation and monitoring of enrollment, finances, and student progress; standard and routine collection procedures become important
III	Add: Evaluation capacity in program and service areas; data-collection procedures oriented toward information needs of program
IV	Add: Coordinated evaluation capabilities that generate data about systemwide objectives as well as objectives of subunit (program, department, colleges, campus). Standardized formats increase in importance
V	Add: Strategic evaluations that assess impact of collaborative programs; utilize results of campus evaluating and conduct specialized studies

each phase. The challenge for administrators responsible for implementations is to use the type of information to make effective decisions of the management-development process.

Phase I Evaluation Strategies

Phase I colleges should collect and utilize information about students and courses that can be used to inform decisions about curriculum, academic programs, and student services. Dialogue among students, faculty, and administrators can be an important information source, as can data collected on a routine and/or ad-hoc basis. Certain basic student characteristic data are necessary for any college or academic program; usually these can be collected as part of a registration or admission process. It is important to utilize these data, at least to generate summary reports that can inform administrators and faculty about enrollment and student characteristics. Also, at times there is a need for ad-hoc surveys of students or alumni to gain insights about new and old programs. All the schools included in this study made efforts in these areas. This type of basic datum should be the basis of a college or university evaluation system.

Phase II Evaluation Strategies

Phase II colleges need more routine and standardized reporting and evaluation procedures than the very small phase II school. Standard accounting procedures, enrollment monitoring, and data about student progress in different academic programs are important. Since program maintenance is a major factor in phase II colleges, increased emphasis on standardizing and utilizing information is necessary. The changes in the use of evaluative information between phase I and phase II are subtle. These changes include increasing the sources of information and improving the way information is collected, maintained, and utilized. Recently, both Doane and St. Mary's have placed considerable emphasis on the development of their MIS systems. Most colleges collect certain basic types of student information for reporting to external agencies as well as for the routine tasks of admission and registration. Routine reporting and evaluation are more important in phase II institutions, where is is important to evaluate the progress toward planned outcomes and the effectiveness of the implementation process. For example, at St. Mary's, evaluations of the planning and management process led to revisions in the composition of the administrative team.

Phase III Evaluation Strategies

Phase III institutions need to develop evaluation capabilities in major organizational subunits, schools, colleges, large departments, and administrative offices. The most obvious new need for evaluative information is for projects implemented within organizational subunits. A variety of strategies can be utilized to get evaluative information to subunits and to develop an evaluative capacity within subunits. A central MIS system can produce computerized reports for subunits, programs can maintain records of ongoing activities, external evaluators can be used to evaluate achievement of program goals, or ad-hoc surveys can be used. Regardless of the strategy, purpose remains relatively constant regardless of the specific evaluative strategy; to evaluate progress toward goals established within the academic and administrative subunits.

Phase IV Evaluation Strategies

In addition to the evaluation capabilities outlined above, phase IV institutions need a capacity to evaluate programs toward system-wide objectives as well as subunit objectives. A major and recurring decision for phase IV organizations is whether to approach the development of new programs or services centrally, rather than in a decentralized mode. The two phase IV institutions included in this study have been developing capabilities to generate this type of information:

at North Carolina A & T, the planned EDUCOM financial-planning model will add the additional model capability necessary to evaluate universitywide policy options; at VCC, a variety of systematic approaches, including PPBS and centralized MBO, have been used to generate evaluative information collegewide policy decisions.

Phase V Evaluation Strategies

Phase V systems need the added capability of evaluating the impact of collaborative approaches, which are more strategic. Since phase V systems are extremely complex, they need evaluation capacities that examine the impacts of programs, services, and policies on users. For example, a state-level management-development program might use a model similar to the one developed in this book to evaluate the impact of the program on funded institutions.

Reassessment

Periodically, possibly every three to five years, a college should reassess its management and other developmental needs. This is far more than an evaluation function. It is necessary for managers to take a step back and ask whether the systems implemented have generated new management needs; whether the goals established when planning for the management-development effort are still appropriate; what new developments or goals are needed; and how the existing structure and systems can be changed, modified, or refined. Since the environmental conditions facing colleges are changing rapidly, as is knowledge about college management, it is wise to plan for reassessment. Also, the case studies indicate that the successful implementation of management systems often leads to new management capabilities.

ORGANIZATIONAL REDESIGN

The structural-development approach has a variety of implications for the redesign of college and university organizational structures. As enrollment drops during the next two decades, institutions will be increasingly confronted with difficult decisions about cutting back on programs and administrative overhead to reduce costs and improve the effectiveness of operations. If large enrollment drops are experienced over an extended period, which is a likelihood for many colleges, then more dramatic shifts in academic and administrative structures will be necessary. It is possible to consider the issue of organizational redesign as part of the overall management-development process.

Unfortunately, the question of organizational redesign, particularly as it relates to understanding the implications of enrollment decline, is not yet well enough understood. There are no useful frameworks to guide administrative decisions about when to cut programs, merge administrative units, or make more drastic changes in the structure of organizations. However, the structural approach does provide a framework to guide research in this area. It also provides a perspective from which to view the types of organizational redesign issues colleges and universities are likely to face.

Most colleges reach points in their history when it is necessary to streamline their administrative and/or academic structures. Three of the case-study institutions took steps to streamline their organizational structures during the period of the study: St. Mary's Junior College cut back the size of its development office when its fundraising plans had not been realized; Doane College merged two of its academic divisions in an attempt to reduce operating costs; and Xavier University combined its academic and administrative computing centers. Each of these moves provides an example of reducing the complexity of the organizations while remaining within the same developmental phase; each added to efficiencies by reducing overhead without altering operations in a negative way. These types of organizational adjustments—combining programs, merging functions, or reducing the size of administrative units—will be increasingly necessary for colleges that are adjusting to shifts in student interests at a time when enrollment is not growing.

Large enrollment drops will probably require more drastic shifts in organizational structures. These more dramatic changes can be equated with downward movement along the structural continuum; to moves from a more complex to a less complex phase of structural development. This is an area in which the structural approach has enormous potential. The quantitative indicators of structural development discussed in Chapter 5 provide a starting point for this type of organizational analysis. When enrollment drops below the minimum levels for a given organizational phase, then it would be appropriate to consider cutting back in other areas: reducing the number of chief administrators, which would imply combining of administrative functions; cutting or merging schools and colleges, which would lead to reduction in administrators, support staff, faculty, number of programs; and closing of campuses in multicampus systems.

CONCLUSIONS

The Title III program, when viewed from an institutional perspective, is an external intervention program that involves securing both external grant funds and using consultants and external assisting agencies. A major argument of this book, which is indeed substantiated by the results of the study and the restudy, is that intervention programs such as Title III should be strategic and make use of a differentiated approach in the funding process. At present, most external programs are not designed with this differentiated lens; usually they are designed to implement sophisticated management techniques, such as MBO and MIS. They are more appropriate in some settings than in others, as the intervention frameworks developed here illustrate.

This study and others, particularly Baldridge and Tierney (1979), show that while external funding can help colleges and universities with basic management improvements, there is a tendency for institutions to undertake unnecessary activities. One reason is the availability of funds, which colleges sometimes go after whether needed or not. Another is the lack of adequate needs assessments prior to the grant-application process. The regulation and monitoring procedures used by external funding agencies also encourage this behavior; to secure funds, institutions sometimes find they must include projects in their proposals they might not need.

If institutions undertake adequate needs assessments before they apply for external funding, or as a final step in the application process, then funds can be used for the specific types of management improvements that are needed. The amount of knowledge about management development available to college administrators is increasing, which improves the range of options and opportunities available. However, it also increases the number of choices that must be made in order to develop an effective management system. This chapter has suggested a process approach to the task of management development. The components of the process are the same for colleges at all points along the structural-development continuum. The specific strategies for each phase vary, however, since the types of management and intervention strategies that are most effective for different colleges and universities appear highly dependent on their size, structure, and local history. The challenge for administrators is to identify those strategies that are most appropriate for their local setting.

An adequate management-needs assessment can also be the starting point for an internal change process. This chapter has proposed a management-development process that includes assessment, goal formulation, implementation, evaluation, and reassessment. At first, the strategies suggested here may seem simplistic, and perhaps they are. Sometimes the most appropriate change strategies are the simple ones that use common sense. Simplicity should not be confused with simplemindedness, however. There is a tendency in higher education to confuse the obvious, to make problems more complex than they really are, and to impose solutions that are either too complex or unnecessary.

Colleges can attempt management improvements that are too complex, as some of the examples in the case studies indicate. They can also use change strategies that are more complex than necessary. For example, the author once consulted briefly for a small college funded by AIDP that was using a highly sophisticated change strategy with numerous task groups to implement AIDP activities, an implementation strategy appropriate for a phase IV institution. A problem developed, however, because progress was not adequate in the judgment of the AIDP coordinator, the activity directors, and the president. Upon reviewing the college and its history, it became apparent to the author that more delegation was necessary since the college was in a transition from phase II to phase III, but that the extensive involvement of faculty and administrators in the elaborate implementation process was taking too much energy from the limited number of available people. Instead, a simpler approach was needed: an administrative or change-agent team could have managed the implementation process with some delegation of implementation responsibilities to academic or administrative officers. This strategy eventually evolved; however, the conflict may have caused the AIDP coordinator to move on before he might have otherwise.

It is also possible to retain simple strategies for too long. The North Carolina A & T case study illustrates the need to move beyond the delegated development approach in a setting where more coordinated development is needed, for example, a campus transitioning from phase III to phase IV. At A & T, the adjustments to their new condition have been slow, perhaps because of the institution's continued success with the delegated approach, as evidenced by the continued Title III support and recognition as an exemplary Title III institution. However, the university now is also confronted by financial and political difficulties that suggest a more sophisticated strategy is needed.

Administrators, as well as students and faculty, need to acquire informed perspectives about the development of their institutions. For the past several decades it has been possible for most institutions to grow. As a result, many administrators had high aspirations for their institutions, particularly for increasing the number of students and programs, if not for changing the status of their institutions from two-year to four-year status, from four-year to university status, and so forth. The aspirations of administrators will have to shift away from growth and program expansion and toward other types of college development. Improved management can play an important role in redirecting institutional aspirations. Indeed, effective management has an important role to play in the qualitative development of colleges and universities. At the very least it can enhance the prospects of institutional survival. It is hoped that it can also help colleges develop distinctive roles.

10

IMPLICATIONS FOR POLICY

If a single overarching conclusion were to be drawn from this research for public-policy purposes, it would be: if the goal of public policy, at the state or federal level, is to fund management interventions that improve the capacity of colleges to plan for their future and to manage their existing resources wisely, then the objective of funding programs should not be to implement sophisticated management systems; instead, the sophistication of management systems that are funded should be oriented toward addressing local needs. Public programs and private philanthropy can play a vital role in assisting institutions with management-development activities. Such programs can even enhance prospects for self-sufficiency of institutions in times of financial stress. However, there is a fine line between strategic assistance and creating a dependence.

This is the most critical dilemma facing management-intervention programs that provide external financial support. Providing funds to a college or university that is making a critical transition, particularly in a time of financial stress, can be a delaying mechanism providing extra (or replacement) funds rather than encouraging necessary and basic change in existing practices. Unless the funds are given strategically—that is, funding those projects that are most likely to have local benefit and that would not be undertaken without this support—then external funding is likely to have little effect. In the public-policy arena this dilemma confronts federal institution-assistance programs, like Title III, and state agencies that monitor and make recommendations on the budgets of public institutions. In policy context it is important to make decisions that support local needs as well as the public interest.

This chapter considers the implications of this study for public policy. First, it addresses the general policy issues raised in the research, particularly the implications of the study for institution-assistance programs designed to help institutions making critical transitions necessitated by financial problems. Second, it considers specifically the implications of the research for the administration of the Title III program. Finally, it addresses in a general way the issue of public policy and research on historically black colleges; this issue is important because the history of Title III is so closely tied to the federal efforts to assist black colleges with their development.

PUBLIC-POLICY ISSUES

A variety of new issues face postsecondary education policy in the United States due to dramatic shifts in the demography of higher education and the financial condition of colleges. Most public policies, even those designed in the 1960s and 1970s, have been oriented toward growth by expanding both access to new clients and the range of support service institutions provide. A policy focus that supports growth, if continued during an era when colleges are declining in enrollment, could have disastrous effects. At the very least, such policies would lead to inefficiencies for the public and for colleges. At the most, it may push colleges further down the road toward financial problems, if not closure. It is now time for a critical examination of public policy and for dramatic adjustments to both the focus of existing policies and the regulations that govern their implementations.

These broader issues are raised because public decisions about the financing of programs designed to improve the management of colleges need to be examined in this context. The HEA Title III program is only one of numerous state and federal programs that are making this adjustment. Title III was originally oriented toward helping colleges grow. When the original legislation was being debated, it was generally argued by the program's supporters that out-of-the-main-stream institutions would be vital to the public in meeting the needs of an expanding student population. The program's funding criteria and the rhetoric used to justify the program over the years have been growth oriented. Title III has probably had less effect on increasing student enrollment and other activity levels than student financial aid. Comparisons of activity levels at funded and nonfunded institutions show no discernible differences (Weathersby et al. , 1977). This suggests that Title III may not have increased outputs; what it may have done is create a dependence (GAO, 1978b). Some of the most critical battles over 1980 reauthorization of the HEA centered around Title III and its funding criteria. Essentially, institutions now seeking Title III funds argued that the funding base should be broadened, while those that already had been funded tried to insure their continued funding. Throughout the debates, there remained a problem: in spite of past arguments that Title III would create a set of developed or unfunded institutions, in practice the program has not achieved this goal; it has created dependence rather than independence.

The problem with a growth orientation is more than rhetorical. The program regulations for Title III have supported expansion of services, such as adding new academic programs, student services, and management systems at funded institutions. Expansion alone will not help a college reach self-sufficiency, especially if enrollment and related income (for example, tuition and/or state support) are not increasing. The financial problems at North Carolina A & T, documented in prior chapters, are only an illustration; after all, A & T has done better than many other Title III institutions, according to the judgment of program staff, in effectively using its Title III funds. At the very least, the management of Title III at the federal level should adjust its funding and monitoring processes so that they reflect an orientation toward this new condition.

Policymakers also are faced with a more basic question: should new institutional-assistance programs be created to provide support for financially troubled institutions or to institutions adjusting to this new condition? In spite of the emphasis of this entire book on public interventions that have this purpose, the author would argue that it is far more important to adjust existing policies and programs so that institutions can deal with this new condition. The advent of new programs will not have a positive impact without adjusting existing state and federal policies to deal adequately with the new conditions. However, one cannot avoid the question with this indirect answer. The direct answer may be simpler: it is probably necessary to design intervention programs that accomplish this purpose or at least make this attempt. The language of the Education Amendments of 1980, which reauthorize the HEA, reflects this intent. The amended Title III now starts with the following statement:

Findings and Purposes
Sec. 301(a) The Congress finds that—
(1) many institutions of higher education in this era of declining enrollments and scarce resources face problems which threaten their ability to survive;
(2) the problems relate to the management and fiscal operations of certain institutions of higher education, as well as to an inability to engage in long-range planning, recruitment activities, and development activities;
(3) the solution of the problems of these institutions

would enable them to become viable, thriving institutions of higher education; and

(4) these institutions play an important role in the American system of higher education, and there is a strong national interest in assisting them in solving their problems and in stabilizing their management and fiscal operations.

(b) It is the purpose of this title to assist such institutions through a program of Federal assistance (House of Representatives, 1980, p. 26).

This language recognizes the importance of management and planning at financially troubled institutions and its role in solving their problems; the purpose of the legislation is now "to assist such institutions through a program of Federal assistance." This legislative reorientation suggests that the Title III program should change, that it should help colleges and universities deal with this new condition. This will require a better understanding of the financial health of colleges and the types of public interventions that can help colleges improve their financial condition. The study of exemplary institutions can help inform the Title III program in the same very basic ways; it also suggests a new direction to policy research on the financial condition of colleges.

The design of a strategy to improve the condition of struggling colleges and universities should accommodate differences in institutional characteristics—such as size, structure, and local history—that will influence the success of interventions. It should also be sensitive to the range of services that funded institutions provide. It is unlikely that during a period when all students are faced with more options and choices among institutions and programs (an unavoidable result of the decreasing applicant pool) that it is effective for public policy to encourage schools to expand. There is little reason to expect sudden increases in the number of students attending a given institution just because it has implemented a new program or a series of new programs.

The results of this study show that the types of management systems colleges should implement are determined in part by their characteristics. The research also suggests that the number of programs and services a college can support and remain financially stable may be influenced by these same factors. If enrollments are not growing at a funded institution, the Title III program should not encourage the institution to expand the number of its academic programs and student services. In these cases, the program's strategy should be oriented toward redirecting existing resources and faculty efforts. Three of the institutions included in this study—Doane, Valencia, and Xavier—emphasized changing and modifying existing programs as part of the

AIDP projects. The management-development efforts at these schools were partly directed toward improving the capacity of current faculty to change existing curriculum, rather than toward adding new programs and services.

It is in this area that this study raised only questions that are important to public policy: What are viable ranges of programs and services for institutions? How can public policy and institution-assistance programs be designed to encourage colleges to support a reasonable range of programs and services, rather than encouraging expansion when this is not a financially viable option? Answers to these questions are important not only to the design of effective intervention strategies, but also to the refinement of other state and federal policies as well. For example, state funding formulas for state institutions need to consider these questions, in addition to the level of appropriation per student. Otherwise, state financing may add to inefficiency if incremental increases are used, or run the risk of financial crises if formulas only are used. Without addressing these questions, public policy runs the risk of adding to institutional inefficiencies at one extreme, or dismantling viable structures at the other.

It is in this area that the differentiated approach proposed in this book may have the most potential for public policy. The quantitative indicators of phases of structural development may be a useful starting point for research that identifies ranges of services and programs for colleges that take structure and size into account. It is entirely possible that the relationship between size and range of services is not linear, especially on the downward slope; as colleges decrease in enrollment, it may not be reasonable to expect them to reduce the number of their academic programs to complement this decline. Instead, there may be plateaus that provide some elasticity during this downward movement. In other words, as long as institutions remain in certain size ranges, or developmental phases, it may be reasonable for them to continue to offer a particular range of services. However, large enrollment declines or declines from one plateau to another may require more drastic cuts in programs. The quantitative indicators included in Chapter 5 may be a starting point for research that addresses this question.

Certainly public policy must be sensitive to these issues; indeed, the design of intervention or institutional-assistance programs that are intended to assist colleges with their adjustments to the new conditions must reflect these concerns. Otherwise, these programs may add to institutional difficulties. Thus, the answer to the question of whether such an intervention program should be created is a cautious and calculated one: such a program probably should be tried, but in order to implement it effectively, better knowledge is needed about the range of programs that institutions can support while still remaining financially healthy. The research cited here can help redirect policy in the area of management-systems improvement, but it is not able to add insight about this larger issue. The larger issue, like the research on college management, has implications well beyond the HEA Title III program.

IMPLICATIONS FOR TITLE III

The study of exemplary Title III institutions has direct implications for the administration of Title III at the federal level, especially for the program's funding of management-development activities. Before detailing these, a word of caution is necessary. This study, and the prior evaluation of Title III conducted by Weathersby and associates, did not include research on Title III program administration. While there is a federally funded study now under way that is examining the administration of Title III, this discussion does not have the benefit of those results. Nor did the author have access to program officers or program files, except the Title III monitoring files on selected institutions, when he was conducting this research. Therefore, the consideration of the implications of the research are based entirely on observations and interviews with institutional representatives about the Title III administration and the effects of the program. Nonetheless, this research does have implications for the administration of Title III.

As might be suspected from the fact that exemplary institutions were the subject of this study, the case-study institutions enjoyed generally positive relationships with the Title III program staff. There are several reasons for this. First, they were among the groups of institutions funded by Title III. During the period from 1971 to 1974, the application-to-award ratio, which was about 2 to 1 for Title III, was higher than for many federal programs (St. John, Tingley, and Gallos, 1977). Also, among those institutions receiving Title III funds, the selected institutions were among a small group considered exemplary by Title III program staff. For these reasons, the observations made in this study about Title III program management probably represent the more positive attributes of Title III. If one had investigated the institution-development efforts at less successful institutions, the findings may have been different. In spite of these limitations and the fact that a relatively small number of Title III schools were studied, the results do provide some interesting information about the administration of Title III. In particular, the study results suggest that the differentiated approach to management development is most appropriate for an external intervention program such as Title III, which is designed to improve college-management systems. They also suggest that the Title III administration has gone through significant changes in its approach to management improvement.

During the initial period when AIDP was started and when two of the institutions in this study (NCA&TSU and St. Mary's) were funded, Title III's approach to management development seemed laissez-faire: management improvements (PME and MIS) were required, but the program did not impose standards about what should be included. St. Mary's, funded in the initial year of AIDP, included little emphasis of management improvement. A few years later, the intervention strategy used by Title III apparently began to change. Doane College, which applied for AIDP during the program's initial year, was not successful until the third year and its third proposal. While the initial proposal did not emphasize formal management systems, the third one did; in fact, Doane administrators pointed out that to be funded, sophisticated management-improvement activities had to be included. St. Mary's also began to receive criticism from Title III program officers in the second and third year of funding because of the lack of emphasis on management-systems development.

At the time the case studies were conducted in 1976-77, the Title III program, especially AIDP, was emphasizing sophisticated management, especially MBO and computerized information systems. Two agencies, McMannis Associates and University Associates, had contracted with USOE to provide technical assistance to AIDP institutions. While these agencies provided a variety of services, their training activities in the management area emphasized MBO and other sophisticated management approaches. Although these approaches made some sense given the needs for program accountability at the federal level, the effects of these standardized approaches were not uniform. For example, in the author's study results it was found that the larger institutions (Xavier, NCA&TSU, and Valencia) found these approaches helpful—in fact, each campus arranged for this type of training activity locally—while the smaller institutions (Doane and St. Mary's) did not find them of value.

By the time of the restudy (summer 1980), it appeared that Title III was taking a more flexible approach. There have been some changes in the relationship between ED and the primary assisting agencies, due in part to responses made to criticism by the Government Accounting Office and other external evaluators (data on the specific nature of the changes were not available). Also, the colleges seemed to be experiencing less difficulty with the Title III program administration. The small institutions seemed to have more flexibility with respect to choosing less sophisticated approaches or discontinuing systems that did not work. The larger campuses continued with their more sophisticated projects. One Title III coordinator expressed satisfaction with a site visit from the Washington Title III program staff. Site visits were not frequent earlier due to budget limitations. Evaluators often pointed to a need for more direct interactions between campuses and program staff. In fact, the author found site-visit reports, when available in the program to be some of the more insightful and useful documents about the campuses.

The direction of this more recent shift in the administration of Title III is not clear. A number of current events will probably influence the refinement of program administration at the federal level: the HEA reauthorization suggests some programmatic changes; the current evaluation efforts may provide useful data about program administration; and there is new leadership in the administration of Title III. The effects of these shifts are still uncertain. In spite of this uncertainty, there are specific areas in which the study can inform the administration.

The Title III program and other management-improvement programs providing special assistance have three general functions: preapplication assistance and dissemination; making decisions about which institutions and projects to fund; and monitoring and evaluation of funded projects. If a differentiated approach is to be implemented, then the activities in each of these must reflect this emphasis.

Preapplication Functions

The major preapplication activities for the Title III program are eligibility determination, dissemination of program information, and assistance with applications. The implications of the research for each of these activities are discussed below.

Eligibility

Eligibility has been a continual source of frustration for the administrators of Title III. Two factors have contributed to this conflict. First, the eligibility criteria have until recently remained growth oriented, when the prospect for growth has declined, especially for the type of institutions that seek Title III funds. Second, eligibility criteria have never been distinguished from funding criteria; as a result, eligible institutions have tended to view the program as an entitlement.

A recurrent problem for Title III program staff has been the need to identify the types of institutions or consortia the program should fund. In spite of the consistent use of growth-oriented eligibility and funding criteria from 1965 until 1979, the actual types of funding arrangements approved by Title III have changed considerably. Initially, all funded institutions had to be in a cooperative arrangement with a more "advanced" institution, a group of "developing" institutions, or an assisting agency. Many institutions that have been historically funded by Title III depend on these cooperative relationships. Therefore, Title III eligibility criteria must acknowledge this complex and diverse situation. The criteria should identify institutions with special developmental needs; however, they should not be implemented in such a way that groups of institutions with obvious needs are automatically excluded. Eligibility criteria will undoubtedly be reviewed as a result of the recent reauthorization. These criteria emphasize low Education and General Purpose expenditures per student and high BEOG awards per student. Regulations implementing these criteria should acknowledge the diversity of institutions that can use Title III funds. The eligibility system should recognize that as long as consortia are funded, some member institutions may not meet eligibility criteria. Further, numeric criteria used to identify eligibility should be applied in a way that recognizes the diverse types of cooperative arrangements that already exist in higher education. While the misuse of federal funds should certainly be avoided, strict applications of numeric criteria may exclude some types of institutions Title III is most able to help.

The Title III program has historically overemphasized the importance of eligibility and underemphasized the importance of establishing funding criteria. By using a single set of criteria to make eligibility and funding decisions, Title III has encouraged eligible institutions to view Title III as an entitlement. While many institutions may be eligible and even deserving of special developmental funds, decisions about which of these institutions to fund should be based on the quality of the proposals and on the appropriateness of the specific interventions proposed. Title III must identify the types of interventions that are likely to be effective in different situations and establish funding criteria that are sensitive to these factors. Social science research on the change processes in colleges and universities and on the effects of Title III can inform this process.

Dissemination

Title III program decisions about funding, particularly about the types of projects that should be funded in different settings, can be made easier by an effective information-dissemination process. In the management area, the program can disseminate to prospective applicants precise information about the types of management developments that are likely to be successful in different settings. Such information could be published as a background or as supplemental information for program applicants. The model for management- and information-systems development included in the prior chapters could be the starting point for such information. The problems facing Title

III require more basic changes than disseminating information that communicates a differentiated approach: they require a shift in the philosophy of the program and the types of assistance it provides in the application process.

Application Assistance

While the 1970s saw a drastic shift in the condition of higher education due to decreased public support, complex financial conditions, and slowed growth, these factors are likely to worsen in the 1980s when most institutions probably will experience enrollment declines. Title III has the potential to aid institutions making critical decisions about the management of decline and the financial, legal, and human consequences of closing. However, this would require a reassessment of Title III's traditional aims. Historically, the program operated under the assumption that its role was to help institutions reach a developed condition even if development was not well defined. Implementation of this policy has meant that some types of management, student services, and academic developments have been more likely to be funded than others. A shift in program design so that it enables institutions to deal with this new condition will require emphasizing and revitalizing existing curriculums and services rather than adding new functions. In some instances colleges may simply need financial support to plan for closing. If a new program philosophy is adapted, the application-assistance process will need to emphasize a new set of principles to encourage institutions to attain self-sufficiency rather than dependence. Title III program staff have always provided assistance to institutions in the application process. In fact, final AIDP plans usually reflect considerable input from program staff. While AIDP no longer exists as a distinct program, Title III will continue to support multiyear development efforts. The involvement of program staff in this application assistance process should emphasize a qualitative, goal-oriented approach rather than the current quantitative milestone-oriented approach.

Funding Decisions

Funding decisions are a critical part of the Title III program. These decisions relate to which institutions and projects to fund. Movement away from the growth-oriented model requires recognition that all colleges and universities are developing institutions; that even Harvard, Yale, and the University of California must continue to cha change and improve their services, programs, and administration, especially during periods of severe financial stress. Equally important is the recognition that there is no size, program mix, or level of funding that constitutes a developed institution. All institutions have to adjust to changing environments, to changes in client needs, and to competition from other providers of educational services.

Perhaps due to past discrimination or to acute enrollment problems, some institutions are less well equipped to deal with stressful financial conditions. As a strategic-intervention program, Title III can help these institutions make necessary programmatic and management adjustments, or could even help some to deal with the human, legal, and financial problems institutions encounter when they decide to close. However, during a period when the number of institutions needing these services is increasing, Title III cannot achieve these outcomes if it is viewed as an entitlement by institutions that meet eligibility standards. Such an approach avoids the most crucial challenge: encouraging funded institutions to adjust to the new condition. The research on the effects of Title III shows that a differentiated approach to funding is needed. In the management area, there is clear evidence that the sophisticated management approach favored by Title III is not always the most appropriate solution to institution-management problems. While there has not been developmental research on the other areas funded by Title III (academic programs and student services), there is a growing body of research that suggests institutions can overdevelop academic programs and student services, and thus add to their financial problems (Balderston, 1974; Cheit, 1971; Weathersby and Jacobs, 1977). Development of a funding strategy that does not encourage overdevelopment will require evolving clear concepts of the types of development outcomes that are likely to be successful in academic and student-service areas, as well as in management, and then using these to guide decisions about which projects to fund.

Monitoring and Evaluation

The study of exemplary Title III institutions did not focus on the monitoring and evaluation process at the federal level. Instead, it focused on the actual developmental activities undertaken by the case institutions. However, the study results do have some implications for the monitoring process.

The most obvious area in which the study results could lead to improved practice is in increasing the sensitivity of the program staff to the types of change processes that seem appropriate in different institutional settings. The study suggests that the sophistication of the institutional change process should be congruent with the complexity of the local institution. The same may be true for the monitoring and evaluation process. It is probable that more sophisticated monitoring strategies are appropriate for the larger and more complex campuses funded in the program, while simplified approaches may give smaller campuses the freedom they require. A federal monitoring strategy should take into account the proper use of and accounting for federal funds; therefore, certain accounting procedures may be necessary in all instances. Other monitoring strategies, such as the use of detailed milestones for all activities, may be more appropriate for larger campuses where the need for routine approaches is obvious. For smaller campuses, the program officers may find it easier and more constructive to be flexible in the monitoring process. While this might introduce ambiguity to the monitoring process, it may be necessary to give colleges the flexibility they need when implementing new systems or when developing formal procedures for the first time. A second area in which improvement can be made in these functions is cooperation between Title III programs and other agencies. There has been a contradiction in Title III's policies about cooperation: the institutions funded by Title III have been encouraged to cooperate with each other, but the administration of the Title III program has not cooperated with other government agencies concerned with college development, particularly state agencies. Regarding the reauthorization of HEA, one state commissioner of higher education has argued about Title III:

> Title III, the program for developing institutions, has to date been a direct federal/institutional program operated without state involvement or reference to state plans and priorities. In some cases, this has led to federal and state concerns operating at cross purposes, particularly at public institutions. Even in the case of independent institutions, the states at least should be informed of developing institutions applications and grants and given the opportunity to comment on these in the light of state planning priorities. In the case of public institutions, state involvement should be more direct (Arceneaux, 1979, p. 25).

This conflict between state planning and the priorities advanced by the Title III interventions is bound to become more complex unless cooperative arrangements can be integrated into the Title III application and award process. This is especially true for the southern and border states subject to the desegregation regulations being implemented by the Office of Civil Rights (OCR). As a result of the Adams decision, these states have been required by ED to submit plans that call for changes in the funding and enrollment patterns of public sector institutions. Title III has funded many of the historically black institutions in these states that are most directly affected by these plans. In order to avoid conflict between the requirements of two agencies within ED or conflict between state and federal require-ments, increased cooperation will be necessary.

Even in those areas not affected by the Adams decision, in-creased cooperation between states and ED is important. A continuing criticism of Title III (GAO, 1975, 1978a; Weathersby et al. , 1977) has been that the Title III staff have not made enough site visits to institutions as a part of their funding decisions. If the federal govern-ment cannot afford the expense of these visits, as has been argued in the past, then the Title III program staff could at least solicit reviews of proposals from state officials who are closer to the institutions. This problem was at least recognized in the 1980 Education Amend-ments that reauthorized Title III, which required that funded projects not be in conflict with their state's plans for public institutions. This creates an opening for more cooperative efforts.

PUBLIC POLICY AND HISTORICALLY BLACK COLLEGES

The direct challenge of desegregation is just now beginning to be felt by traditionally black colleges. While the 1954 Brown decision has had direct effects on the administration of public schools during the past quarter century, its impact on postsecondary education has not challenged the basic structure and purpose of black colleges. How-ever, the 1977 Adams court order is likely to have a dramatic impact on higher education generally, and on black colleges particularly, in the next 25 years. (See Haynes, 1978, for a critical analysis of the Adams case.) It is too early to predict what the eventual impact of the Adams decision will be on American higher education, but some fundamental changes are already apparent, including:

> A much more direct and active role for the courts in higher education policy and planning (including the recent Tennessee decision to merge two urban universities);
> A more active role by the executive branch of federal govern-ment in state-level higher education policy and planning (includ-ing the requirement that Adams states submit plans for approval by the federal government); and
> As a consequence of both factors, there is an increased state regulation of public institutions and a possible resulting de-crease in institutional autonomy.

Certainly the OCR desegregation regulations have received much attention in the higher education literature. Unfortunately, the quality of insights gained from this literature is not reflected by its volume. Only after a quarter century are researchers beginning to understand the impact of the Brown decision on elementary and secondary education. It would be shortsighted to assume one can now accurately predict the impact of the Adams decision and the federal efforts to desegregate higher education. While recent research, including the results of this study, can inform policymakers about the effects of public policy on black colleges, there is a need for more basic and applied research in this important area. More research is necessary to outline the potential impacts of policy decisions on the quality and development of these institutions.

In the late 1950s and early 1960s, historically black colleges encountered their first threat from integration. Faced with the increasing enrollment of black students at historically white colleges, black colleges were hard hit by enrollment and financial difficulties at a time when most of higher education was still expanding. At that time black leaders were among the primary advocates for a federal program to aid struggling colleges. The eventual result of their lobbying efforts, the Title III program, is a tribute to black leaders' commitment to their institutions, as well as to leadership of President Johnson and then U. S. Commissioner of Education Francis Keppel. Title III funds have been used primarily to aid predominantly black colleges. While the original legislation did not require these funds be set aside for black colleges, the program's administrators sent a significant portion of Title III funds to black colleges; also, black college leaders have been an important lobbying force for Title III. However, as more institutions encountered financial and enrollment difficulties in the 1970s, the number of institutions competing for Title III funds increased. In addition, some of the organizational and programmatic relationships between black institutions and the Title III program have recently been criticized; a Government Accounting Office report (1978b) suggests that Title III not be continued because of problematic relationships among the institutions, assisting agencies, and the federal government. Despite this, black colleges and their allies in the legislative and executive branches of the federal government still have the necessary foundations of support for the Title III program. In fact, the recent reauthorization of Title III insured that a substantial portion of funds would be set aside for black colleges. As the conference report on the bill put it: "Each fiscal year the amount available under part B for institutions with special needs that historically serve substantial numbers of black students will not be less than 50 percentum of the amount received by such institutions in fiscal year 1979" (U. S. House, 1980, p. 37). There are three parts of the new Title III program, and each will doubtlessly provide aid to black colleges.

One significant effect of the Title III program has been the improvement of planning and management systems at black colleges. This study of exemplary AIDP institutions documents that black colleges have been nationally recognized for their leadership in developing more refined management practices in higher education. One institution diagnosed as being in severe financial difficulty in the Hodgkinson study (Hodgkinson and Schenkel, 1974), Xavier University of Louisiana, made a significant turnabout by 1977, largely as a result of AIDP support. Xavier developed a planning and management model that adequately tied realistic enrollment projections to fiscal management. The situation at Xavier continued to improve in the late 1970s. This dramatic change in one institution illustrates the developing capacity of black colleges to deal with a difficult environment and to develop appropriate management systems.

A second area in which black colleges have shown leadership, partially as a result of Title III support, has been the development of institutional research capacities within institutions that have scarce resources (Holmes, 1979). Because financial resources are often limited, institutional research officers in black colleges and universities have had to find innovative techniques for providing timely information to decisionmakers. One administrator who was responsible for a black college institutional research office described her experience as follows: "The operation of the institutional research unit at Fayetteville State University, especially during its formative years, was successful and has remained so as a result of using more creative approaches to solving problems in the absence of adequate financial resources" (Holmes, 1979, p. 8).

Thus in spite of a difficult and perhaps adverse situation, black college leaders have seized the HEA Title III program as an opportunity to improve their institutions, especially as regards planning and management capabilities and institutional research functions that will be essential for dealing with a new set of conditions. Coping with court-ordered desegregation in the public sector of higher education is, at best, a creative challenge. Fortunately, planning and research functions will give black colleges an opportunity to maximize the potential of this situation.

Most of the literature on the impact of black colleges on their students has been anecdotal; it consists primarily of the description of experiences of those who attended these institutions. With the advent of institutional research offices in black colleges during the past decade, the potential for generating new types of information about the impact of black colleges on their students is enhanced. Black colleges have special missions that add to the diversity in American higher education:

For certain culturally and racially different groups, access

to higher education and participation in its fullest benefits
have been realized through the existence of special interest colleges—the Catholic, Women's, and Historically
Black Colleges (HBC's), to name a few. The dissolution
of traditional barriers which necessitated the origins of
these colleges have not lessened their impact or raison
d'etre. They may no longer be avenues of primary access
to higher education for their traditional clientele. However, their role in commitment to the educational attainment and progress of their perspective groups remains
unabated. They continue as insurance against barriers
which might restrict full opportunity and attainment while
contributing to one rich fabric of American higher education (National Advisory Committee on Black Higher Education, 1979, p. xvii).

One challenge for researchers concerned about the future of
black colleges is to document the special qualities black colleges contribute to their students. In particular is the challenge to identify the
ways in which these colleges have a qualitative effect on the cultural
development of their clientele; this might include such varied research
topics as basic skills development, socio-emotional change, and leadership development. This type of information, gathered in a systematic fashion, will be helpful to institutional administrators and state
and federal policymakers who are considering basic policy issues
that affect the future of black colleges.

Another area in which research can help inform the change process resulting from the Adams case, is through the detailed examination of the changing roles of courts and public policymakers in planning
for desegregation, which is likely to have a substantial impact on the
future and development of black colleges. At center stage is a very
basic question: What approaches to planning for desegregation and for
monitoring compliance are likely to have the most positive impacts on
black colleges? While this is an important question, little is known
about these potential impacts. Further research should compare institutions in different Adams states, as well as examine the development of predominantly black colleges in states not affected by the
Adams decision.

Within the federal government there is an increasing concern
about coordination of federal programs that affect black institutions.
In August 1980 the Carter administration started an initiative, Executive Order 12232, which may lead to an increased emphasis on providing federal support to historically black colleges by most federal agencies. This action, coordinated by the secretary of education, involves
each federal agency in a process of reviewing its goals as they relate

to black colleges; perhaps it will lead to a more coordinated federal posture if this constructive attitude is maintained by the Reagan administration. At the same time, there is a need to take an in-depth look within the Education Department at possible contradictions in ED programs that affect black colleges. The OCR review and Title III are the most obvious examples, but the Minority Institutions Science Improvement Program (MISIP) is also administered by ED, and several student-assistance programs have a direct impact on the student services and academic programs at historically black colleges. It is also apparent that there are possible contradictions in the regulations for these programs. For example, MISIP, which requires 50 percent minority enrollment for institutions to be eligible, may cause problems for historically minority institutions that cease to have 50 percent minority enrollment due to successful desegregation. The probable impacts of the desegregation process on all federal programs, as well as its impact on the institutions, should be of concern to federal policymakers.

CONCLUSIONS

During the next decade state and federal postsecondary policy in the United States will face the critical task of adjusting to conditions of financial stress and enrollment decline. Current public policy and programs, those oriented toward both institutional and student support, will have to be adjusted to take into account this new reality. Social science theory and research has an important role to play in the policy-adjustment process; new knowledge about college change and development can inform policymakers about the potential impacts of alternative policies. This study has focused on the impact of one federal program, HEA Title III, on college and university development.

The HEA Title III program has the potential of assisting colleges with basic adjustments to the new condition, especially in the area of management development. Its key finding is that management improvement does not always mean that sophisticated management should be implemented. Instead, the sophistication of a college's or university's management needs is dependent on its size, structure, and history with management systems, as well as on the external conditions the college faces. Those colleges that implement management systems and processes that are appropriate for their own situation are most likely to deal effectively with the new condition. Title III and other management-intervention programs can enhance the prospect of college survival, renewal, and continued development by funding appropriate management interventions. To account for the varying needs of institutions, Title III will require a more differentiated approach than has been used by its administrators in the past.

This study has also raised questions for public policy. First is the question about the relationship between effective management and the qualitative development of colleges and universities. As the prospect for quantitative decreases in numbers of students, services, and programs becomes a reality, the attention of college and university administrators will shift to qualitative improvements in existing programs, to improvements in the impact of programs on students, and to increasing their impact on the communities. Improved institutional planning and management has an important role to play in the qualitative development of colleges and universities, but these relationships need to be explored, particularly in the area of relating financial decisions to the process of academic management. The larger concern about the role of management in the qualitative development of colleges and universities also needs to be explored further.

This study also raises questions about the applicability of the structural-development approach to a range of questions facing public policy. In particular, what are the implications of the structural-development model for public policies and programs that have an impact on the range of programs and services of colleges and universities? One of the major issues facing higher education policymakers at all levels is that current policies still encourage institutions to expand their programs and services. Students' costs have been rising faster than the costs of providing educational services (as measured by the higher education price index and other indicators). Some have argued that this trend is the result of an institutional tendency to meet increasing aspirations with increased student fees (Weathersby and Jacobs, 1977). Certainly state and federal student-aid programs create an incentive for institutions to use student income to finance expansions. The structural-development approach provides another perspective to view the relationship between the characteristics of colleges and universities, the range of services and programs they support, and their productivity. Because of changing financial conditions, policymakers must be concerned about efficiency in education.

Finally, this book raises questions for change-oriented college and university administrators. Can basic research on the structural development of colleges and universities be used to improve college-management systems? The prior chapter speculates about the implications of the structural-development model for management-development efforts. As the focus of college administrators shifts from creating new structures to improving the quality of programs and services, will the necessary attention be given to the development of effective management systems?

BIBLIOGRAPHIC NOTES ON CASE STUDIES

Case studies of the five selected Title III-funded institutions were prepared as part of the initial study for the U. S. Office of Education. These documents are available through the ERIC (Education Research Information Clearinghouse) system. Information from these documents, with supplementary information from the MIS survey and Title III impact questionnaire, and from additional documents supplied by the institutions, were used for illustrative purposes throughout the text. Specific references from the case studies and additional sources used for this book are listed below for each institution.

DOANE COLLEGE

I visited Doane College on July 9 and 10, 1977. People interviewed included:

Phillip Heckman, president
Willard (Bill) Grosz, vice-president for development
David Osterhout, vice-president for financial affairs
Donald J. Ziegler, vice-president for academic affairs
I. E. Pappy Khouri, director of admissions
Bill Pallett, director of institutional research
Robert Thomas, dean of students
Edward Watkins, director of career development
R. E. Dudley, chairman, education division, associate professor
L. E. Dodd, associate professor, education
R. M. McCallister, chairperson, social sciences division; professor, psychology
E. J. McPartland, associate professor, political science
D. S. Deines, instructor, business
Robert A. Dobson, chairperson, board of trustees; president, Dobson Brothers Construction Company, Lincoln, Nebraska

Other references supplied by the U. S. Office of Education and Doane College include:

Allen, H. S., Goldenstein, E., and Johnson, R. External Evaluation Report I to Doane College (1977).

248

Doane College. AIDP Internal Evaluation Report (1977).
Doane College. AIDP Refined AIDP Plan (1977).
Doane College. Five-Year Plans (1970-77).
Doane College. Minutes from Planning Team Meetings (1977).
Doane College Catalog (1977).
Upton, M. The Doane of Tomorrow (1977).
AIDP Consultant Reports (from Richard Hogetts, Wayland
 Gardiner, Ralph Tyler, James Johnson, R. Strafford North,
 Robert Pitcher, Theodore Miller, Donald Hoyt, and Richard
 Ireland).

In addition, numerous pamphlets and booklets on the career-
development program were provided by Doane College. As part of the
restudy, Doane completed both survey instruments as well as supply-
ing numerous background documents. The following documents are
referred to in the text:

Allen, H. S., Goldenstein, E., and Johnson, R. External Evaluation Report 2 to Doane College Advanced Institutional Development Program, 1978.
Allen, H. S., Goldenstein, E., and Johnson, R. External Evaluation Report 3 to Doane College Advanced Institutional Development Program, 1979.
Heckman, P., Material for Spring Meeting, Doane College
 Board of Trustees, May 15-16, 1980.

ST. MARY'S COLLEGE

I visited St. Mary's Junior College on July 28 and 29, 1977.
People interviewed included:

Dr. Carol Peterson, vice-president, educational development,
 evaluation, and research, and AIDP coordinator
Sister Anne Joachim Moore, president
Dr. Thomas G. Scheller, senior vice-president and treasurer
Dr. Marcia S. Hanson, director, technical education
Dr. Roger Claesgens, associate professor and coordinator,
 continuing education
Dr. Lawrence Demarest, associate professor and AIDP evalua-
 tion coordinator
Sister Mary F. Heinnen, associate professor and program co-
 director, new program development
Dr. Mary Broderick, assistant professor, development and
 research.

Other references from USOE files and St. Mary's Junior College included:

Peterson, C. Institutional Goals and Development Priorities, interim working paper (August 1977).

St. Mary's Junior College. Annual Report (1977).

St. Mary's Junior College. Advanced Institution Development Program, Final Plan (June 1974).

St. Mary's Junior College. Revised Plan for Planning, Management and Evaluation.

St. Mary's Junior College Bulletin, 1977-79.

St. Mary's Junior College. Report of the Long Range Planning Committee (1973).

St. Mary's Junior College. The Student Handbook (1976-77).

St. Mary's Junior College. The Future Begins Tomorrow (pamphlet).

U. S. Office of Education. Monitoring and Evaluation Files for St. Mary's Junior College AIDP Grant.

In addition, St. Mary's provided numerous reports and correspondence regarding AIDP activities, including the results of several evaluations. St. Mary's also supplied both survey instruments.

XAVIER UNIVERSITY OF LOUISIANA

During a June 23-24, 1977 visit to Xavier University, the following people were interviewed:

Anthony Rachal, Jr. , executive vice-president
Clarence Jupiter, director, development services
Joseph C. Rice, coordinator AIDP, coordinator of planning
Sister Mary Veronica Drawe, university dean
Bhagwan S. Gupta, director, fiscal services
Sister Florence Kuhn, SBS
John Goode, private consultant, John Goode Associates
Bill Katzenmeyer, private consultant, associate dean, graduate school, Duke University

Materials supplied either by the campus or through USOE files:

Bobowski, R. C. Gert Town's Good Neighbor, American Education, August-September 1976.

Rachal, A. M. Keynote Address, Educational Staff Institute, Hampton Institute, August 8, 1973.

Rice, J. C. AIDP a Winner at Xavier! Xavier Gold, 1, 1977, 7-14.

Jupiter, C. A Proposal to Reprogram AIDP Funds for a Comprehensive Resource Management Program at Xavier University, 1977.

Haskins and Sells (CPA). Xavier University of Louisiana Financial Statements as of June 30, 1976 and Auditors' Report.

Xavier University of Louisiana. Gleanings: Section A, A Brief Historical Sketch; Section B, Traditions, September 1966.

Xavier University of Louisiana. Occupations of the Graduates of Xavier University, Class of 1928 through Class of 1965.

Xavier University of Louisiana. Xavier: Where it is Coming From/Where it is Now/Where it is Going/What it Will Take to Get There, Original AIDP Proposal, 1974.

Xavier University of Louisiana. Refined Advanced Institutional Development Program Proposal, 1974.

Xavier University of Louisiana. Long-Range Planning Document, 1973 through 1977.

Xavier University of Louisiana. Description of the Planning Process, no date.

Xavier Catalog, 1976-78.

Xavier University Planning Office. Documents and Correspondence.

Xavier University Commission on Governance. Final Report: Recommendations for a New Governance System for Xavier University of Louisiana, 1970.

Xavier completed both survey instruments. In addition, I conducted two telephone interviews with Mary Ellis, who started as Title III coordinator at Xavier in summer 1980; these interviews took place during October 1980.

NORTH CAROLINA A & T STATE UNIVERSITY

I visisted North Carolina A & T on June 21 and 22, 1977. People interviewed were:

Daisy Weaver, assistant AIDP coordinator
Willie Ellis, AIDP coordinator, assistant vice-chancellor for academic affairs
Edwin Bell, director of university planning
Gloria Phoenix, analyst, management information system
Jesse Marshall, vice-chancellor for student affairs
Ruth Gore, director of academic advising

William Parker, associate dean of student affairs
Robert Wilson, director of counseling center
W. I. Morris, director of placement
Joseph Bennet, director of career education
Lewis C. Dowdy, chancellor
G. F. Rankin, vice-chancellor for academic affairs
Mathew King, vice-chancellor for fiscal affairs
W. A. Blount, director of institutional research
R. Artis, director of registration and records
S. J. Shaw, dean, school of education
A. P. Bell, president of university senate; chairman, department of agricultural education
Naomi Wynn, dean, school of nursing
Dorothy Prince, chairperson, department of education
Talmage Brewer, chairperson, department of animal science
Russell Rankin, chairperson of industrial education
Richard Moore, director of public information
William Streat, chairperson department of architectural engineering
Suresh Chandra, dean, school of engineering (interviewed at Harvard University, institute of education management)

References supplied by USOE or North Carolina A & T State University include:

Dowdy, Lewis C. Annual Report of the Chancellor, 1975–76, North Carolina Agricultural and Technical State University.

McManis Associates. First Annual AIDP External Evaluation Report, North Carolina A & T State University, 1976.

McManis Associates. Second Annual Year-End AIDP External Evaluation Report, North Carolina A & T State University, 1977.

North Carolina Agricultural and Technical State University. Grant Application for the Advanced Institutional Development Program, Title III, Higher Education Act of 1965 as Amended, 1975.

North Carolina Agricultural and Technical State University. AIDP Proposal for a Continuation Grant, 1977.

North Carolina Agricultural and Technical State University. The Undergraduate Bulletin–Greensboro, 1976–77.

North Carolina Agricultural and Technical State University. Founders' Day–Parents' Day Exercises, 1977.

North Carolina Agricultural and Technical State University. Planning, Management, and Evaluation Manual, 1976.

University Associates. Reviews of Advanced Institutional Development Program at North Carolina A & T State University, 1976-77.

North Carolina A & T completed both restudy instruments, as well as provided several additional background documents. Of these, the following was cited in the text:

McManis Associates. Report of External Evaluation Visit of AID Program to NCA&T State University, May 14-15, 1979.

VALENCIA COMMUNITY COLLEGE

I visited Valencia Community College on June 7 and 8, 1977. People interviewed were:

Thelma J. Dudley, AIDP coordinator
James F. Gollattscheck, president
Charles W. Sample, provost, Open Campus
Lee Young, vice-president of business affairs
Winona Sorrells, instructor, mathematics, East Campus
Celia Cullom, instructor, English and speech, East Campus
Robert Milke, director, department of governmental services, Open Campus
Kenneth Wagner, director, institutional planning, AIDP
Rubye Beal, dean, East Campus
Donna Nickel, director, curriculum/instructional development center, AIDP
David L. Evans, provost, East Campus
David Fear, instructor, English, West Campus; chairman, board of directors, Valencia Faculty Association
William Prentiss, chairperson, social science department, West Campus
Fannie Butler, instructor, history, West Campus
Annie (Blue) Perry, instructor, reading, West Campus; president, FACC, Valencia chapter
Ruth Senterfitt, instructor, English, West Campus
James R. Richburg, dean of academic affairs, West Campus; chairperson, AIDP coordinating committee
Jerry W. Odom, dean of student affairs, West Campus
Gloria Raines, vice-president, collegewide instructional services
Ruth Salsberry, instructor, English and speech; chairperson, West Campus Faculty Association

Other references used for the case study included:

Gollattscheck, J. F. The Governing Board and Community-Based Education, 1977 (publication pending).

Gollattscheck, J. F. and others. College Leadership for Community Renewal. San Francisco: Jossey-Bass, 1976.

Valencia Community College. Advanced Institutional Development Program Revised Program Plan, 1976.

Valencia Community College, Student Handbook, 1976-77.

Valencia Community College, Catalog, 1977-78.

Valencia Community College District Board of Trustees, Operating Budget for Fiscal Year Beginning July 1, 1977-Ending June 30, 1978.

Valencia Community College completed both questionnaires and supplied several documents for the restudy. The new documents used for the restudy included:

Tadlock Associates. Valencia Community College Advanced Institutional Development Program External Evaluation Report, 1978.

Tadlock Associates. Valencia Community College Advanced Institutional Development Program External Evaluation Report, 1979

Tadlock Associates. Valencia Community College External Evaluation AIDP 1979-80.

REFERENCES

Adkins, D. L. The Great American Degree Machine: An Economic Analysis of the Human Resources Output of Higher Education. Berkeley: Carnegie Commission on Higher Education, 1975.

Arceneaux, W. Higher Education Reauthorization, Compact 1979, 13, 25-35.

Argyris, C. Interpersonal Competence and Organizational Effectiveness. Homewood, Ill. : Dorsey, 1962.

____. Organization and Innovation. Homewood, Ill. : R. D. Irwin, 1965.

____. Intervention Theory and Method: A Behavioral Science View. Reading, Mass. : Addison-Wesley, 1972.

____. Behind the Front Page: Organizational Self-Renewal in a Metropolitan Newspaper. San Francisco: Jossey-Bass, 1974.

____. Educating Administrators and Professionals. In C. Argyris, and R. M. Cyert, Leadership in the 80s: Essays on Higher Education. Cambridge, Mass. : Institute for Educational Management, Harvard University, 1980, pp. 1-38.

Ashby, E. Adapting Universities to a Technological Society. San Francisco: Jossey-Bass, 1974.

Astin, A. W. Preventing Students from Dropping Out. San Francisco: Jossey-Bass, 1975.

Balderston, F. E. Managing Today's University. San Francisco: Jossey-Bass, 1974.

____, and G. B. Weathersby. PPBS in Higher Education Planning and Management: Part IV. Perspectives and Applications of Policy Analysis, Higher Education. 1973, 2, 33-67.

Baldridge, J. V. Power and Conflict in the University. New York: Wiley, 1971.

_____. Organizational Change: The Human Relations Perspective versus the Political Systems Perspective, Educational Researcher. 1972, 1, 4-15.

_____. Organizational Innovations: Individual, Structural, and Environmental Impacts. In J. V. Baldridge and T. E. Deal (Eds.), Managing Change in Educational Organizations. Berkeley: McCutchan, 1975.

_____. Managerial Innovation: Rules for Successful Implementation, Journal of Higher Education. 1980, 51, 117-34.

_____, D. V. Curtis, G. P. Ecker and G. L. Riley. The Impact of Institutional Size and Complexity on Faculty Autonomy, Journal of Higher Education. 1973, 44, 532-47.

_____, and T. E. Deal. Overview of Change Processes in Educational Organizations. In J. V. Baldridge and T. E. Deal (Eds.), Managing Change in Educational Organizations. Berkeley: McCutchan, 1975.

Baldridge, J. V. and Tierney, M. L. New Approaches to Management: Creating Practical Systems of Management Information and Management by Objectives. San Francisco: Jossey-Bass, 1979.

Bassett, R. Postsecondary Education Information at the State Level: Planning Guide. Boulder, Colo.: National Center for Higher Education Management Systems, 1979.

Beach, M. A Bibliographic Guide to American Colleges and Universities: From Colonial Times to the Present. Westport, Conn.: Greenwood Press, 1975.

Ben-David, J. American Higher Education: Directions Old and New. New York: McGraw-Hill, 1972.

Bendix, R. Max Weber: An Intellectual Portrait. New York: Doubleday, 1960.

Bennis, W. G. Changing Organizations. New York: McGraw-Hill, 1966.

_____, and P. E. Slater. The Temporary Society. New York: Harper & Row, 1968.

Benson, C. S. and H. L. Hodgkinson. Implementing the Learning Society. San Francisco: Jossey-Bass, 1974.

Berendzen, R. Population Changes and Higher Education, Journal of Higher Education. 1974, 45, 115-25.

Bergquist, W. H. and S. R. Phillips. Components of an Effective Faculty Development Program, Journal of Higher Education. 1975, 46, 177-211.

____, and W. A. Shoemaker. Facilitating Comprehensive Institutional Development. In W. H. Bergquist and W. A. Shoemaker (Eds.), A Comprehensive Approach to Institutional Development in Higher Education. San Francisco: Jossey-Bass, New Directions for Higher Education. No. 15, 1976, 1-50.

Bowen, H. R. Financing the External Degree, Journal of Higher Education. 1973, 44, 479-91.

____, and G. K. Douglas. Efficiency in Liberal Education. New York: McGraw-Hill, 1975.

Boyer, E. L. and M. Kaplan. Educating for Survival, Change. 1977, 9, 22-30.

Brubacher, J. S. and W. Rudy. Higher Education in Transition: An American History 1936-1956. New York: Harper & Row, 1958.

Carlson, D. E. A Review of Production Function Estimates for Higher Education Institutions. Cambridge, Mass.: Harvard Graduate School of Education, 1977.

Carlson, D. E., J. Farmer, and G. B. Weathersby. A Framework for Analyzing Education Finance Policies. Washington, D. C.: Government Printing Office, 1974.

Carnegie Commission on Higher Education. From Isolation to Mainstream: Problems of the Colleges Founded for Negroes. New York: McGraw-Hill, 1971.

____. Priorities for Action: Final Report of the Carnegie Commission on Higher Education. New York: McGraw-Hill, 1973.

____. The Fourth Revolution: Instructional Media in Higher Education. New York: McGraw-Hill, 1972.

Carnegie Council on Policy Studies in Higher Education. Making Affirmative Action Work in Higher Education: An Analysis of Federal Policies and Recommendations. San Francisco: Jossey-Bass, 1975a.

_____. The Federal Role in Postsecondary Education: Unfinished Business 1975-1980. San Francisco: Jossey-Bass, 1975b.

_____. Three Thousand Futures: The Next Twenty Years. San Francisco: Jossey-Bass, 1980.

Carnegie Foundation for the Advancement of Teaching. More Than Survival: Prospects for Higher Education in a Period of Uncertainty. San Francisco: Jossey-Bass, 1975.

_____. The States and Higher Education: A Proud Past, a Vital Future. San Francisco: Jossey-Bass, 1976.

Cartter, A. An Assessment of Quality in Graduate Education. Washington, D. C.: American Council on Education, 1966.

_____. Ph. D.'s and the Academic Labor Market. New York: McGraw-Hill, 1976.

Cavert, C. E. (Ed.). Designing Diversity '75: Conference Proceedings. Lincoln, Neb.: University of Mid-America, 1975.

Chandler, A. D. Strategy and Structure: Chapters in the History of the Industrial Enterprise. Cambridge, Mass.: MIT Press, 1962.

Cheit, E. F. The New Depression in Higher Education. New York: McGraw-Hill, 1971.

_____. The New Depression in Higher Education—2 Years Later. New York: McGraw-Hill, 1973.

Cherin, E. and M. McCoy. State and Local Financial Support of High Higher Education: A Framework for Interstate Comparisons, 1973-74. Boulder, Colo.: National Center for Higher Education Management Systems at WICHE, 1977.

Cohen, D. K. Loss as a Theme in Social Policy, Harvard Educational Review. 1976, 46, 553-71.

Cohen, M. D. and J. G. March. Leadership and Ambiguity. New York: McGraw-Hill, 1974.

Committee on Economic Development. The Management and Financing of Colleges. New York: CED, 1973.

Cope, R. and W. Hannah. Revolving College Doors: The Causes of Dropping Out, Stopping Out and Transferring. New York: Wiley, 1975.

Corson, J. J. Governance of Colleges and Universities. New York: McGraw-Hill, 1960.

Chickering, A. W. Education and Identity. San Francisco: Jossey-Bass, 1969.

____. Adult Development—Implications for Higher Education. In C. E. Cavert (Ed.), Designing Diversity '75. Lincoln, Neb.: University of Mid-America, 1975.

____. Development as an Outcome of Education. In Keeton and Associates, Experimental Learning: Rationale, Characteristics and Assessment. San Francisco: Jossey-Bass, 1976.

Cross, K. P. Beyond the Open Door. San Francisco: Jossey-Bass, 1976.

____, and J. Valley. Planning Nontraditional Programs. San Francisco: Jossey-Bass, 1974.

Dale, E. The Great Organizers. New York: McGraw-Hill, 1960.

Duberman, M. F. Black Mountain: An Exploration In Community. New York: Dutton, 1972.

DuBois, E. E. and F. A. Ricci. Non-Traditional Study: A Burgeoning Force in Reshaping American Higher Education. In L. C. Vaccaro (Ed.), Reshaping American Higher Education. Irving, Tex.: AMI Press, 1975.

Erickson, E. Life History and Historical Moment. New York: Norton, 1975.

Eulau, H. and H. Quinely. State Officials and Higher Education: A

Survey of the Opinions and Expectations of Policy Makers in Nine States. New York: McGraw-Hill, 1970.

Feldman, K. A. and T. M. Newcomb. The Impact of Colleges on Students. San Francisco: Jossey-Bass, 1969.

Fernko, P. M. Development of a System of Scoring Institutions under Proposed Regulations for Title III Strengthening Developing Institutions Program. Washington, D. C.: USOE, Office of Evaluation and Dissemination (Technical Paper No. 79.), 1979.

Fitzgibbon, R. H. The Academic Senate of the University of California. Berkeley: Office of the President, University of California, 1968.

Freeman, A. B. The Overeducated American. New York: Academic Press, 1976.

French, W. L. and C. H. Bell. Organizational Development: Behavioral Science Interventions for Organization Improvement. Englewood Cliffs, N. J.: Prentice-Hall, 1973.

Fraley, L. E. and C. A. Vargus. Academic Tradition and Instructional Technology, Journal of Higher Education. 1975, 46, 1-15.

Gaff, J. G. Toward Faculty Renewal. San Francisco: Jossey-Bass, 1975.

Garbarino, J. W. Faculty Unionism: From Theory to Practice, Industrial Relations. 1972, 11, 1-17.

_____ Faculty Bargaining: Change and Conflict. New York: McGraw-Hill, 1975.

Garms, W. J. Financing Community Colleges. New York: Teacher's College Press, 1977.

General Accounting Office. Assessing the Federal Program for Strengthening Developing Institutions of Higher Education. Washington, D. C.: Government Printing Office, 1975.

_____ Problems and Outlook of Small Private Liberal Arts Colleges. Washington, D. C.: GPO (HRD-79-91), 1978a.

_____ The Federal Program to Strengthen Developing Institutions of Higher Education. Washington, D. C.: GPO (HRD-78-170), 1978b.

Glenny, L. A. Nine Myths, Nine Realities: The Illusions of Steady State, Change. 1974-75, 6, 24-28.

____, F. M. Bowen, R. J. Meisinger, A. W. Morgan, R. A. Purves, and F. A. Schmidtlein. State Budgeting in Higher Education: Data Digest. Berkeley: CRDHE, 1975.

Glenny, L. A., J. A. Shea, J. H. Ruyle, and K. H. Freschi. Presidents Confront Reality: From Edifice Complex to University Without Walls. San Francisco: Jossey-Bass, 1975.

Gollattscheck, J. F., E. L. Harlacher, E. Roberts, and W. R. Benjamin. College Leadership for Community Renewal. San Francisco: Jossey-Bass, 1976.

Golloday, M. A. (Ed.). The Condition of Education. Washington, D. C.: National Center for Educational Statistics, 1976.

Goodman, P. The Community of Scholars. New York: Random House, 1962.

Groen, G. J. The Theoretical Ideas of Piaget and Educational Process. In P. Suppes (Ed.), Impact of Research on Education: Some Case Studies. Washington, D. C.: National Academy of Science, 1978, 267-318.

Gould, S. B. Diversity by Design. San Francisco: Jossey-Bass, 1973.

Gouler, D. D. Criteria for Determining Success in Open Learning Systems. In C. E. Cavert (Ed.), Designing Diversity '75. Lincoln, Neb.: University of Mid-America, 1975.

Gove, S. K. and C. G. Floyd. Research on Higher Education Administration and Policy: An Uneven Report, Public Administration Review. 1975, Jan.-Feb., 111-18.

Greiner, L. E. Patterns of Organizational Change, Harvard Business Review. 1967, 45, 119-28.

____ Evolution and Revolution as Organizations Grow, Harvard Business Review. 1972, 50, 37-46.

Gulick, L. and L. F. Urwick. Papers on Scientific Management. New York: Columbia University, Institute of Public Administration, 1937.

Halstead, D. K. Statewide Planning in Higher Education. Washington, D. C.: Government Printing Office, 1974.

Haynes, L. L. (Ed.). A Critical Examination of the Adams Case: A Source Book. Washington, D. C.: Institute for Services to Education, 1978.

Hefferlin, J. B. Dynamics of Academic Reform. San Francisco: Jossey-Bass, 1967.

Helsabeck, R. E. The Compound System: A Conceptual Framework for Effective Decision Making in Colleges. University of California, Berkeley: CRDHE, 1975.

Henry, D. D. Challenges Past, Challenges Present. San Francisco: Jossey-Bass, 1975.

Herbst, J. From Religion to Politics: Debates and Confrontations over American College Governance in the Mid-Eighteenth Century, Harvard Educational Review. 1976, 46, 397-424.

Heron, R. P. and D. Friesen. Growth and Development of College Administrative Structures, Research in Higher Education. 1973, 1, 333-47.

Hesburgh, T. M., P. A. Miller, and C. R. Wharton. Patterns of Lifelong Learning. San Francisco: Jossey-Bass, 1974.

Heydinger, R. G., and D. M. Norris. Cooperative Computing: A Process Perspective on Planning and Implementation. Princeton, N. J.: EDUCOM, 1977.

Higher Education Management Institute. Management Development and Training Program for Colleges and Universities, Progress Report #2. Coconut Grove, Fla.: Higher Education Management Institute, 1976.

Hodgkinson, H. L. Institutions in Transition: A Profile of Change in Higher Education. New York: McGraw-Hill, 1971a.

_____ Student Participation in Governance. In W. B. Martin, K. P. Cross, and H. L. Hodgkinson, White House Conference on Youth. Berkeley: CRDHE, 1971b.

_____ The Amazing Thing Is That It Works At All. Berkeley: CRDHE, 1971c.

_____ How Much Change for a Dollar? A Look at Title III. ERIC/ Higher Education Research Report No. 3. Washington, D. C. : AAHE, 1974.

_____ Technology and Education. In D. E. Cavert (Ed.), Designing Diversity '75. Lincoln, Neb. : University of Mid-America, 1975.

_____, and W. Schenkel. A Study of Title III of the Higher Education Act: The Developing Institutions Program. Berkeley: CRDHE, 1974.

Holdaway, E. A. , J. F. Newberry, J. Hickson, and R. P. Heron. Dimensions of Organizations in Complex Societies: The Educa- tional Sector, Administrative Science Quarterly. 1975, 20, 37-58.

Holmes, B. D. Designing the Mission and Role of Institutional Re- search under Difficult Fiscal Constraints: A Case Study. In A. L. Cooke (Ed.), New Directions for Institutional Research: Planning Rational Retrenchment, 24, 1979, 1-10.

Hoos, I. R. The Costs of Efficiency: The Implications of Educational Technology, Journal of Higher Education. 1975, 46, 141-59.

Houle, C. O. The External Degree. San Francisco: Jossey-Bass, 1973.

House, E. R. , G. V. Glass, L. D. McLean, and D. F. Decker. No Simple Answer: Critique of the Follow Through Evaluation, Harvard Educational Review. 1978, 48, 128-60.

Howard, L. C. The Developing Institutions Program: A Study of Title III of the Higher Education Act of 1965. Madison, Wisc. : Institute of Human Relations, University of Wisconsin, 1967.

Jackson, G. A. Financial Aid and Student Enrollment. Cambridge, Mass. : Harvard Graduate School of Education, 1977.

Jacobs, F. and T. Tingley. The Evolution of Eligibility Criteria for Title III of the Higher Education Act of 1965, The Development of Colleges and Universities, Appendix A. Cambridge, Mass. : HGSE, 1977.

Jantsch, E. Design for Evolution: Self-Organization and Planning in the Life of Human Systems. New York: Braziller, 1975.

Jencks, C. and D. Riesman. The Academic Revolution. Garden City, N. Y. : Doubleday, 1968.

Jenks, R. S. An Internal Change Agent's Role in Restructuring University Governance, Journal of Higher Education. 1973, 44, 370-79.

Katz, D. and R. L. Kahn. The Social Psychology of Organizations. New York: Wiley, 1966.

Kaufman, H. The Natural History of Human Organizations, Administration and Society. 1975, 7, 131-49.

Keeton, M. T. Models and Mavericks: A Profile of Private Liberal Arts Colleges. New York: McGraw-Hill, 1971a.

____. Shared Authority on Campus. Washington, D. C.: AAHE, 1971b.

____, and Associates. Experiential Learning: Rationale, Characteristics, and Assessment. San Francisco: Jossey-Bass, 1976.

Kerr, C. The Uses of the University. New York: Harper & Row, 1963.

Kieft, R. N. , F. Armijo, and N. S. Bucklew. A Handbook for Institutional Academic and Program Planning: From Idea to Implementation. Boulder, Colo. : National Center for Educational Management Systems, 1978.

Kilman, R. H. and I. I. Mitroff. Qualitative versus Quantitative Analysis for Management Science: Different Forms for Different Psychological Types, Interfaces. 1976. 6 (2), 17-27.

King, E J. , C. H. Moor, and J. A. Mundy. Post-Secondary Education/2: The Way Ahead. Beverly Hills, Calif. : Sage, 1975.

Kirkpatrick, J. E. The American College and its Rulers. New York: New Republic, 1936.

Kohlberg, L. The Cognitive-Developmental Approach to Moral Education. Kappan. 1975, 56, 670-77.

Kramer, F. A. (Ed.). Perspectives on Public Bureaucracy. Cambridge, Mass. : Winthrop, 1973.

Kuhn, T. S. The Structure of Scientific Revolutions. Chicago: University of Chicago Press, 1962.

Laszlo, E. Introduction to Systems Philosophy: Toward a New Paradigm of Contemporary Thought. New York: Harper, 1972.

Lawrence, P. R. and J. W. Lorsch. Organization and Environment: Managing Differentiation and Integration. Boston: Harvard University Press, 1967.

Lee, E. C. and F. M. Bowen. The Multi-Campus University: A Study of Academic Governance. New York: McGraw-Hill, 1971.

____, and F. M. Bowen. Managing Multicampus Systems: Effective Administration in an Unsteady State. San Francisco: Jossey-Bass, 1975.

Leslie, D. W. Legitimizing University Governance: Theory and Practice, Higher Education. 1975, 4, 223-46.

Likert, R. The Human Organization: Its Management and Value. New York: McGraw-Hill, 1967.

____, and J. G. Likert. New Ways of Managing Conflict. New York: McGraw-Hill, 1976.

Lindquist, J. and J. Noonan. Faculty Development for Open Learning and Non-Traditional Study. In C. E. Cavert (Ed.), Designing Diversity '75. Lincoln, Neb.: University of Mid-America, 1975.

Levine, R. E. The Emerging Technology. New York: McGraw-Hill, 1975.

Lippet, G. L. and W. H. Schmidt. Crises in a Developing Organization, Harvard Business Review. 1967, 45, 102-12.

Lipset, S. M. and D. Riesman. Education and Politics at Harvard. New York: McGraw-Hill, 1975.

Lovinger, J. Measuring Ego Development. San Francisco: Jossey-Bass, 1970.

McConnell, T. R. Faculty Participation in Campus Governance. Berkeley: CRDHE, 1969.

____. The Redistribution of Power in Higher Education, Berkeley: CRDHE, 1971.

_____, and Mortimer, K. P. The Faculty in University Governance. Berkeley: CRDHE, 1970.

McCoy, M. Supplementary Document: Data Values Used in the Development of Analysis Reports for the Study of State and Local Financial Support for Higher Education, 1973-75. Boulder, Colo.: National Center for Higher Education Management Systems, 1977.

McGrath, E. J. Should Students Share the Power? A Study of Their Role in College and University Governance. Philadelphia: Temple University Press, 1970.

McGregor, D. M. The Human Side of the Enterprise. New York: McGraw-Hill, 1960.

McKelvey, B. and R. H. Kilman. Organizational Design: A Participative Approach, Administrative Science Quarterly. 1975, 20, 24-36.

March, J. G. (Ed.). Handbook of Organizations. Chicago: Rand McNally, 1965.

Margulies, R. Z. and P. M. Blau. The Pecking Order of the Elite: America's Leading Professional Schools, Change. 1973, 5, 21-27.

Maslow, A. H. Motivation and Personality. New York: Harper & Row, 1954.

Massie, J. L. Management Theory. In J. G. March (Ed.), Handbook of Organizations. Chicago: Rand McNally, 1965.

Mayhew, L. B. and the Committee On Administration and Policy Analysis. Educational Leadership and Declining Enrollments. Berkeley: McCutchan, 1974.

Medsker, L., S. Edelstein, H. Kreplin, J. Ruyle, and J. Shea. Extending Opportunities for a College Degree: Practices, Problems, and Potentials. Berkeley: CRDHE, 1975.

Miller, J. L., G. Gurin, and M. J. Clark. Uses and Effectiveness of Title III in Selected Developing Institutions. Ann Arbor, Mich.: University of Michigan, 1970.

Millet, J. D. Mergers in Higher Education: An Analysis of Ten Case Studies. Washington, D. C. : Academy for Educational Development, American Council on Education, 1976.

Mills, T. M. The Sociology of Small Groups. Englewood Cliffs, N. J. : Prentice-Hall, 1967.

Missouri Department of Higher Education. Report to the Coordinating Board for Higher Education of the Computer Policy Task Force. Jefferson City, Mo. : MDHE, 1979.

Mitroff, I. I. The Subjective Side of Science. Amsterdam, Netherlands: Elsevier, 1974.

Murphy, J. T. The Craft of Program Review: A Guide for Legislative Staff. Cambridge, Mass. : HGSE, 1976.

Mushkin, S. (Ed.). Recurrent Education. Washington, D. C. : National Institute of Education, U. S. Department of Health, Education and Welfare, 1973.

National Advisory Committee on Black Higher Education and Black Colleges and Universities, Black Colleges and Universities: An Essential Component of a Diverse System of Higher Education. Washington, D. C. : Authors, 1979.

National Commission on the Financing of Postsecondary Education in the United States. Financing Postsecondary Education in the United States. Washington, D. C. : Government Printing Office, 1973.

Newman, F. U. S. Task Force on Higher Education. Washington, D. C. : Government Printing Office, 1971.

Norris, D. M. and E. P. St. John. New Directions in Statewide Computer Planning and Cooperation. Presented at Annual Meeting of Society for College and University Planning, Quebec, Canada, August, 1980.

Nwagbaraocha, J. O. Planning, Management, and Evaluation: In Search of a Viable System for College Improvement, New Directions for Institutional Research: Planning Rational Retrenchment. 1979, 24, 29-43.

Ohio Board of Regents. Management Improvement Program: Planning Universities. Columbus, Ohio: Board of Regents, 1973.

Orlans, H. Private Accreditation and Public Eligibility. Lexington, Mass.: Lexington, 1975.

O'Toole, J. Work in America. Cambridge, Mass.: MIT Press, 1973.

Parsons, T. Structure and Process in Modern Societies. New York: Free Press of Glencoe, 1960.

Perrow, C. Hospitals: Technology, Structure, and Goals. In J. G. March, Handbook of Organization. Chicago: Rand McNally, 1965.

Perry, W. A National Commitment: An International Concept. In C. E. Cavert (Ed.), Designing Diversity '75. Lincoln, Neb.: University of Mid-America, 1975.

_____ The Open University. San Francisco: Jossey-Bass, 1977.

Peterson, R. E. Goals for California Higher Education: A Survey of 116 College Communities. Sacramento, Calif.: Joint Committee on the Master Plan for Higher Education, California Legislature, 1973.

Piaget, J. Biology and Knowledge: An Essay on the Relations between Organic Regulations and Cognition Processes. Chicago: University of Chicago Press, 1971.

_____ Psychology and Epistemology: Towards a Theory of Knowledge. Middlesex, Eng.: Penguin, 1977.

Platt, G. and T. Parsons. Decision Making in the Academic System: Influence and Power Exchange. In C. L. Kruytbosch and S. L. Messinger (Eds.), The State of the University: Authority and Change. Beverly Hills: Sage, 1970.

Potts, D. B. College Enthusiasm as Public Response, 1800–1860, Harvard Educational Review. 1977, 47, 28–42.

Reisman, D. The Academic Procession. In Constraint and Variety in American Education. Lincoln, Neb.: University of Nebraska Press, 1956; Garden City, N. Y.: Anchor Books, 1958.

_____ Meritocracy and its Adversaries. In S. M. Lipset and D. Reisman, Education and Politics at Harvard. New York: McGraw-Hill, 1975.

_____, and V. A. Stadtman. Academic Transformation: Seventeen Colleges under Pressure. New York: McGraw-Hill, 1973.

Riggs, R. Organizational Structures and Contexts, Administration and Society. 1975, 7, 150-70.

Rockart, J. F. Computers and the Learning Process, Sloan WP 802-75, Cambridge, Mass.: MIT Press, 1976.

_____, and M. S. Scott Morton. Computers and the Learning Process in Higher Education. New York: McGraw-Hill, 1975.

Rogers, E. M. Communications in Organizations. New York: Free Press, 1976.

Rostow, W. W. The Stages of Economic Growth: A Non-Communist Manifesto. Cambridge, Eng.: Cambridge University Press, 1960.

Rudolph, F. The American College and University: A History. New York: Knopf, 1962.

St. John, E. P. A MIS Development Framework for Higher Education, CAUSE/EFFECT. 1980a, 3 (4), 24-32.

_____ Computer Policy in Higher Education: Major Statewide Issues, AEDS Proceedings. Washington, D. C.: Association of Educational Data Systems, 1980b, 192-99.

_____ Management System Development: An Intervention Model for Developing Colleges and Universities, Journal of Higher Education. 1980c, 51 (3), 286-300.

St. John, E. P. and M. C. Regan. Students in Campus Governance: Reasoning and Models for Student Involvement. Department of Applied Behavioral Sciences, Research Monograph No. 12. Davis, Calif.: University of California, 1973.

St. John, E. P., T. Tingley, and J. Gallos. Descriptive Analysis of Institutional Change Using HEGIS, CFAE, OCR and Title III

Data Bases. In The Development of Colleges and Universities, Appendix C. Cambridge, Mass.: HGSE, 1977.

St. John, E. P. and G. B. Weathersby. Institutional Development in Higher Education: A Conceptual Framework for Evaluation. In The Development of Colleges and Universities. Cambridge, Mass.: HGSE, 1977.

_____ Management Development in Higher Education: Strategies for Developing Colleges and Universities, International Journal of Institutional Management in Higher Education. 1980, 4 (2), 105-19.

Sarason, E. H. The Creation of Settings and Future Societies. San Francisco: Jossey-Bass, 1972.

Schein, E. H. Process Consultation: Its Role in Organization Development. Reading, Mass.: Addison-Wesley, 1969.

Schumacher, E. F. Small Is Beautiful: Economics As If People Mattered. New York: Harper & Row, 1973.

Scott, B. R. Stages of Corporate Development. Cambridge, Mass.: Harvard Business School, paper 4-371-294, 1971.

Scott, P. Strategies for Postsecondary Education. New York: Wiley, 1975.

Sheehy, G. Passages: Predictable Crises of Adult Life. New York: Dutton, 1974.

Sikes, W. W., L. D. Schlesinger, and C. Seashore. Developing Change Agent Teams on Campus, Journal of Higher Education. 1973, 44, 397-413.

Simpson, M. G. Costs and Benefits of Mass Higher Education, Higher Education. 1973, 2, 203-5.

Smelser, N. J. Growth, Structural Change, and Conflict in California Public Higher Education, 1952-1970. In N. J. Smelser and G. Almond (Eds.), Public Higher Education in California. Berkeley: University of California Press, 1974.

_____ , and G. Almond. Public Higher Education in California. Berkeley: University of California Press, 1974.

Suppes, P. and M. Morningstar. Evaluation of Three CAI Programs. Technical Report No. W142, Stanford, Calif.: Institute for Mass Studies in the Social Sciences, Stanford University, 1969.

Tausky, C. Work Organizations: Major Theoretical Perspectives. Itasca, Ill.: Peacock, 1970.

Taylor, F. W. Scientific Management. New York: Harper & Row, 1911.

Tewksbury, D. C. The Founding of American Colleges and Universities before the Civil War: With Particular Reference to the Religious Influences Bearing upon the College Movement. New York: Teachers' College Press, 1932. Reprint edition, New York: Arno Press and the New York Times, 1969.

Thompson, J. D. Organizations in Action. New York: McGraw-Hill, 1967.

Torbert, W. R. Pre-Bureaucratic and Post-Bureaucratic Stages of Organizational Development, Interpersonal Dynamics. 1974-75, 5, 1-25.

_____ Creating a Community of Inquiry: Conflict, Collaboration, Transformation. New York: Wiley, 1976.

Touraine, A. The Academic System in America. New York: McGraw-Hill, 1974.

Trow, M. Problems in the Transition from Elite to Mass Higher Education. New York: McGraw-Hill, 1973.

Tunstull, J. (Ed.). The Open University Opens. Amherst, Mass.: University of Massachusetts Press, 1974.

U. S. Congress. House Committee on Education and Labor. Higher Education Act of 1965. Hearings before the Special Subcommittee on Education of the Committee on Education and Labor, House of Representatives, on H. R. 3220, 89th Cong., 1st Sess., 1965.

U. S. Congress. Senate. Committee on Labor and Public Welfare. Higher Education Act of 1965. Hearings before the Subcommittee on Education of the Committee on Labor and Public Welfare, Senate, on S. 600, 89th Cong., 1st sess., 1965.

U. S. Congress. House. Committee on Education and Labor. Higher Education Amendments of 1967. Hearings before the Special Subcommittee on Education of the Committee on Education and Labor, House of Representatives on H. R. 6232, 90th Congress, 1st sess. , 1965.

U. S. Congress. House Conference Report. Education Amendments of 1980. Report from the Committee of Conference on HR 5192, Report No. 96-1251, 96th Congress, 2nd session.

Udy, S. H. The Comparative Analysis of Organizations. In J. G. March (Ed.), Handbook of Organizations. Chicago: Rand McNally, 1965.

Vaccaro, L. C. (Ed.). Reshaping American Higher Education. Irving, Tex. : AMI Press, 1975.

Vermilye, D. W. (Ed.). The Extended Campus: Current Issues in Higher Education 1972. San Francisco: Jossey-Bass, 1972.

____. (Ed.). Learner-Centered Reform: Current Issues in Higher Education 1975. San Francisco: Jossey-Bass, 1975.

Veysey, L. R. The Emergence of the American University. Chicago: University Press, 1965.

Weathersby, G. B. Decision Paradigms and Models for Higher Education. Presented at the 48th Meeting of the Institute of Management Sciences and the Operations Research Society of America, 1975.

____. Postsecondary Education, Society. 1976, 13, 52-58.

Weathersby, G. B. and F. E. Balderston. PPBS in Higher Education Planning and Management: Part I, An Overview, Higher Education. 1972, 1, 191-206.

Weathersby, G. B. and A. Henault. Analyzing the Cost-Effectiveness of Experiential Learning Programs. In Keeton and Associates, Experiential Learning: Rationale, Characteristics, and Assessment. San Francisco: Jossey-Bass, 1976.

Weathersby, G. B. , G. A. Jackson, F. Jacobs, E. P. St. John, and T. Tingley. The Development of Institutions of Higher Education: Theory and Assessment of Impact of Four Possible Areas of Federal Intervention, Final Report. In The Development of Colleges and Universities. Cambridge, Mass. : HGSE, 1977.

Weathersby, G. B. and F. Jacobs. Institutional Goals and Student Costs. ERIC/Higher Education Research Monograph No. 2. Washington, D. C. : AAHE, 1977.

Weathersby, G. B. and D. Nash (Eds.). A Context for Policy Research in Financing Postsecondary Education. Washington, D. C. : Government Printing Office, 1974.

Weber, M. The Theory of Social and Economic Organization. Trans. A. M. Henderson and T. Parsons. New York: Oxford University Press, 1948.

Webster, R. S. and B. O. Shorthouse. The State-of-the-Art of Management Development and Training and a Model for These Activities in Colleges and Universities. Coconut Grove, Fla. : Higher Education Management Institute, 1976.

Wilson, L. Changing University Governance, Educational Record. 1969, 4, 388.

Witherspoon, J. P. State of the Art: Current Educational Uses of Public Broadcasting in Higher Education. In C. E. Cavert (Ed.), Designing Diversity '75. Lincoln, Neb. : University of Mid-America, 1975.

Wren, S. C. The College Student and Higher Education Policy. Berkeley: Carnegie Foundation for the Advancement of Teaching, 1975.

INDEX

ABOUT THE AUTHOR

EDWARD P. ST. JOHN is a visiting Fellow at the Institute for Higher Education, University of New England, Australia, where he teaches in an international program for college and university administrators.

He has served as a Postsecondary Education Specialist for the U. S. Department of Education's Office of Planning and Budget, and as Associate Director of Research and Planning for the Missouri Department of Higher Education. Previously he was a researcher at Harvard University Graduate School of Education, where he was co-principal investigator for a federally funded study of the HEA Title III, Strengthening Developing Institutions Program.

Dr. St. John received an Ed. D. from Harvard, and B. S. and M. Ed. degrees from the University of California, Davis.